THE SECRET
Love LETTERS
A FAMILY HISTORY

Published by Melbourne Books
Level 9, 100 Collins Street,
Melbourne, VIC 3000
Australia
www.melbournebooks.com.au
info@melbournebooks.com.au

National Library of Australia
Cataloguing-in-Publication entry
Creator: San Miguel, Dolores.
Title: The Secret Love Letters : A Family History.
ISBN: 9781922129550 (paperback)
Subjects: San Miguel, Dolores--Family.
Johnston, Fay--Correspondence.
Love-letters.
Courtship.
Families.
Immigrants--Australia--Biography.
Melbourne (Vic.)--Social life and customs--
20th century.
Dewey Number: 920.72

www.facebook.com/TheSecretLoveLettersBook

THE SECRET
Love LETTERS
A FAMILY HISTORY

Dolores San Miguel

M

MELBOURNE BOOKS

This book is dedicated to my Mother and Father,
my daughters Hayley and Charlotte, and my Grandparents,
Antonio and Rebecca San Miguel, and
William and Annie Johnston.

Acknowledgments

Once again thanks to my wonderful publisher, David Tenenbaum, for letting me tell yet another true life story. My daughter, Charlotte Callander, for a brilliant job as editor. My loyal assistant, Josephine Simmons, who has been by my side right from the start of researching this book, I would have been lost without her help! Her incredible job putting together the Family Tree on Ancestry.com, a long and arduous task!

My eldest daughter, Hayley Callander, for her support and encouragement, my good friend, Debbie Nankervis, who put me up in Sydney, and was with me as we traipsed around the city on my research there.

I also thank Jennifer Elder, from the Box Hill Historical Society, who put me in touch with my cousin in Queensland, Annette Blight (nee San Miguel). Sue Barnett, of the Surry Hills Historical Society, who has solved a few mysteries for me and been very supportive. Juris and Ilona Briedis, current owners of St. Abbs, they graciously showed Josephine and me through their beautiful home. Ann Simpson, former owner of Hartland, in Elmie St. Hawthorn. Thanks to Peter Rhoden, of Xavier College, and Julianne Barlow, of Genazzano Convent, for their patience and help.

Maudie Palmer, current owner of Green Ivies, for allowing my cousins and me, a tour through her delightful home. My nephew, Greg

San Miguel, and my sister in-law, Jeanette San Miguel for the photos and some amazing ancient letters.

My 'new' cousins on the San Miguel side, Annette Blight, for suppling a bundle of important documents, and her sister, Linda Jane Johnson. David, Chris, and Rodney Allen, for photos and documents of great value and importance. Silvia Vidal Marti, my cousin in Barcelona for her research there.

Thanks to my cousins on the Johnston side, Ron Johnston, for the photos and history he supplied, Phil Johnston, for his support and hospitality over the years, and Jenni Higgins (nee Johnston) for her support. My 'new' Johnston cousins, Mary Ellen Webb (formally Beryl Mitchell) and her daughters, Lynden Thiessen and Alison Webb. Without everyone's help this book would be missing some very important pieces!

FLORENCE (FAY) JOHNSTON JOHNSTON FAMILY TREE (SECTION OF JOHNSTON FAMILY TREE)

Fig i

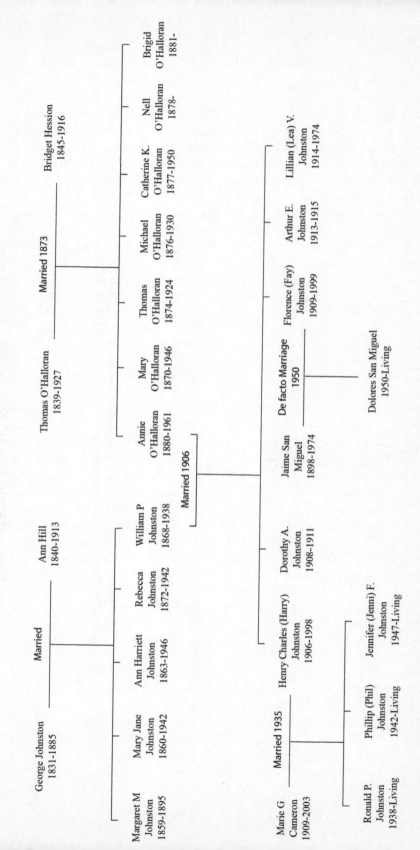

JAIME SAN MIGUEL FAMILY TREE (SECTION OF SAN MIGUEL FAMILY TREE)

Fig ii

Josephine Simmons 2014

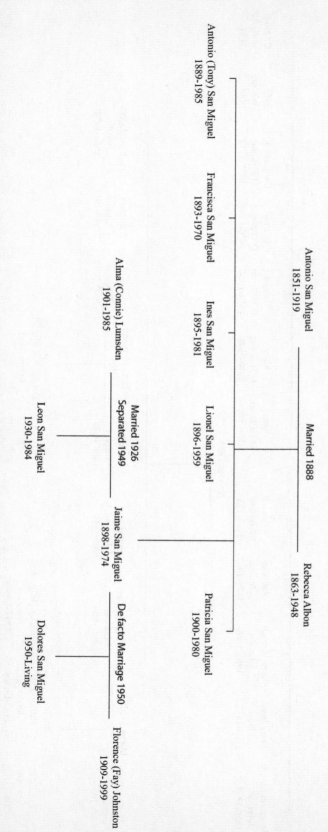

Antonio (Tony) San Miguel
1889-1985

Francisca San Miguel
1893-1970

Ines San Miguel
1895-1981

Lionel San Miguel
1896-1959

Antonio San Miguel
1851-1919

Married 1888

Rebecca Albon
1863-1948

Alma (Connie) Lumsden
1901-1985

Married 1926
Separated 1949

Jaime San Miguel
1898-1974

Patricia San Miguel
1900-1980

Leon San Miguel
1930-1984

De facto Marriage 1950

Dolores San Miguel
1950-Living

Florence (Fay) Johnston
1909-1999

A Death In The Family

I stood looking out of the lounge room window. The rain had finally stopped and small droplets trickled down the glass panes, in rhythm with my tears. Mum and Sister Hill, the kind, elderly nurse who had helped Mum look after my father for the last year or so, waited in the bedroom with Dad. She had been with Mum last Monday when he took another stroke around five-thirty in the afternoon. Dr Wilson was called and recommended Dad be moved to a private nursing home. Mum and Sister Hill tried all night to find one with a vacancy, all to no avail. Finally, a friend of my mother's with a few connections arranged a bed at Heatherleigh Private Hospital nearby in Hawthorn, for today, Wednesday.

The ambulance pulled into the gravel drive, and I watched the two officers emerge. I knew Dad would never return home and I was overwhelmed with sadness. I had no idea how sick he was while I was away in England for the last two years. Mum had kept it quiet, so as not to ruin my trip. I had arrived back late December of 1973, and Dad was totally blind by then. Today was 6 March 1974, so we'd really only had two months together.

I remembered how excited he was when I rang from Barcelona last year on his birthday, 23 July. I had just arrived back from meeting his relatives in Alella, a little village in the hills on the north coast of Barcelona. It had taken some detective work on my part to find them, as Dad's memory and recollections of his family had faded after his first stroke. Mum said he had cried with happiness after the call, and had carried the letter I had sent of the events in the pocket of his pyjamas.

From December of 1971 to December of 1973, I lived in London with my boyfriend, Paul Thompson. In the summer of 1973 we bought an old Bedford van and set off for Europe. During our time in Morocco we met an American girl from California who wanted to share petrol expenses and get a lift to Spain. She spoke and wrote fluent Spanish, so I gave her the details about my father and the San Miguels and she wrote it all down in Spanish. When Paul and I arrived in Barcelona, my main aim was to find my Spanish relatives, and as I had no address or name other than San Miguel (the Spanish equivalent of 'Smith'), it would take a combination of luck and a miracle!

We were staying at a campsite just out of Barcelona. On Monday 23 July, we found our way to the foothills of Alella just as the Bedford van conked out. Paul found a garage nearby but had to wait for the mechanic to arrive, so I set foot along the road to the village of Alella. Two women came out of a house, so I showed them what the American girl had written, gesturing my lack of the language. They read it, spoke to each other, and ushered me into their car where we drove to the village.

We knocked on one door of a family with the name San Miguel, but they were not home. Their neighbours indicated that they would be coming back soon, however, so they gave me a chair to sit on for my wait. I thanked the two women and the neighbours and sat in the sun, admiring the cobbled streets and beautiful old buildings. Very soon the San Miguels returned, but unfortunately they were no relation. The husband had an idea, however, and drove me to another house close by. I was taken up a large, winding staircase where an elderly woman sat, dressed in almost Victoriana attire. She was eighty-eight years old and spoke perfect English, as she had lived in Melbourne fifty years prior. She told me that she had relatives by the name of Carlotta Sands who lived in the Melbourne suburb of Surrey Hills, and who knew the

San Miguels. She spoke in Spanish to my driver and explained that he would be taking me to the home of the Ferrans, a family closely related to the San Miguels and one of the original San Miguel homes.

When we arrived, once again I waited while my story was explained. The family consisted of Agapito Ferran's 86-year-old widow, Josefa (Agapito was my father's first cousin), her three unmarried daughters, Merce, Carolina and Carmen; another daughter, Rosa, her husband, Pere, their teenage daughter, Montserrat and son, Salvador. They asked to see my passport, and then lo and behold brought out a portrait of my father's family, including a photo of Dad's youngest sister, Patricia, on her wedding day. Well, then there was great excitement! They were all babbling away in Spanish, so the teenage son went next door and brought back two young men who spoke English. I explained that my boyfriend was at the garage, so one of them drove me to pick Paul up. We then returned to the two-story white stucco homestead, where the family had laid out home-brewed wine, pineapple brandy, crusty bread drizzled in olive oil, homegrown tomatoes, olives and ham off the bone. They asked us back for lunch on the Wednesday and although I presented 'Mama' with chocolates and flowers, the delicious smorgasbord and tapas delights they had prepared for me outdid my small gifts. It was an extraordinary meeting — almost surreal. Was it luck or a miracle? I pondered over these thoughts as Dad was lifted into the ambulance.

I was allowed to accompany my father and Mum would follow in her car. We said our goodbyes to Sister Hill, knowing her services would no longer be needed. I gently squeezed Dad's hand as the ambulance turned into Princess Street. He was conscious but his speech was very slurred. He seemed frightened and confused, like a small child.

I held back tears as I whispered, 'Everything will be alright, we are just getting you to a lovely hospital.'

I was only twenty-three years old and my father was dying — he was seventy-five.

Mum and I kept vigils at the hospital and on the weekend Mum only returned home late in the evenings. On Monday 11 March, Leon, Dad's 43-year-old son (my half-brother) and his mother spent the afternoon with him. Ten years later, Leon, would also be dying — of prostrate cancer.

When Mum returned from her visit on Tuesday, she was tearful — Dad was getting weaker. When we visited him on Wednesday, he was unconscious. On Thursday I spent an hour with him and Mum wouldn't leave his side. Later that night I was at home with Paul. The telephone rang — it was 8.15pm. Mum's voice came on the line and my heart sank.

'My darling Jaime, your wonderful father passed away at 8pm tonight. He is at last in peace. I'll be home soon.'

I walked back into the sun lounge and burst into tears. I was glad Paul had stayed with me.

After Paul left and Mum had made the necessary immediate phone calls, she made a pot of tea and said she had something very important to tell me. Although she was exhausted, I could tell by the look in her eyes that whatever it was she had to say, it was extremely significant to us both. I sat close to her on the couch as she poured the tea and began her story.

∾

Florence Annie Johnston was born at home on 6 October 1909 at 46 Birkenhead Street, North Fitzroy, Melbourne. She was the second daughter of William Patterson Johnston who came from a staunch, Protestant Irish background and Annie Johnston (née O'Halloran) from a Catholic Irish one. Annie's mother, Brigid O'Halloran (née Hession) was born in Galway, Ireland in 1845. In June 1862, aged seventeen, she left Southampton on board the *Boanerges* bound for Melbourne, although she took residence in the country area of Wangaratta. She married Thomas O'Halloran on 5 September 1873, and they moved to

Beechworth in the north-east of Victoria. Thomas was born in Kilkenny, Ireland in 1839, and at age twenty-five he left Liverpool on board the *Royal Dane,* heading for Melbourne. Brigid and Thomas had seven children between 1874 and 1881: Mary, Thomas Jr, Michael, Catherine (Kate), Nell, Annie, and Brigid.

Annie and William Johnston's family began with the birth of Henry, also known as Harry (1906), followed by Dorothy (1908), then Florence, Arthur (1913), and Lillian (1914). They soon moved to a larger home at 215 Holden Street, Fitzroy.

The family managed to get by on William's mediocre salary as an insurance clerk; however, he had an eye for a pretty face, drank far too much, and loved to gamble. William's father, George Johnston, was born in the County of Fermanagh, (Northern) Ireland, in 1831, and after meeting an English girl, Annie Hill, they migrated to Australia in 1862. George then worked as a warden at Pentridge Gaol; it was here he gained a reputation as a cruel and vicious man. Many a prisoner was beaten during his violent outbursts. A crack shot with a rifle, George won trophies for his expertise and was present at the execution of Ned Kelly. The family had lodgings at Pentridge and it was here that all the children (apart from Margaret Matilda, born in Ireland in 1859) were born. George Johnston died at just forty-seven years old on 19 February 1885, five years after the death of Ned Kelly. It was a relief for 17-year-old William, who also received beatings from his father, the memory of which would lead to him finding solace in whisky.

William's drinking and gambling increased after two major tragedies. On 3 January 1911, little three-year-old Dorothy died of pneumonia after a nasty bout of whooping cough. Then, on 3 December 1915, William's two-year-old son Arthur died after contracting diphtheria. During this time diphtheria killed more Australians than any other disease. Although Florence was only six when her baby brother died, she had vivid memories of visiting him in the hospital. He was under quarantine, so she could only wave to him through the large glass doors. When she learnt that Arthur was not coming home, she cried in her bed every night for a month. Her parents were devastated, and not long afterwards their arguing escalated. The two deaths caused a rift between Annie and William that only increased as the years rolled by.

Regardless of their problems, William became a top salesman with AMP Insurance; however, he eventually blotted his copybook with an unethical transaction and lost his permanency. After this he had to rely on commissions, and it was around this time that he became an illegal S.P. Bookie. Very early on, Annie began to take wads of cash out of his winnings when he was too drunk to realise. She opened a new bank account and watched as the balance rose, along with the interest. She had to plan for the future, especially when she learnt that William had a mistress. She turned a blind eye to the affair — at least she didn't have to succumb to her marital duties as often — so, in a way, it was a relief, and she kept the secret to herself for twenty odd years. She confronted the woman when she turned up at William's funeral, the first week of January 1938. He had died on New Year's Day, and no one in the family enjoyed New Year's Eve after that, especially Florence, who had adored her father.

Florence was a happy child with golden, corn-coloured hair, bright blue eyes and an inquisitive nature. She was born the year that her birth state, Victoria, had finally granted women's suffrage. It was something that made her feel somewhat important, and led her to be always ahead of her time, and very independent. By her early teens, she had asked to be called Fay. Florence, she had stated, was far too old-fashioned and staid. She attended the local Catholic school, although Harry was back and forth between Protestant and Catholic schools. William wanted his eldest son to be bought up just like him, and yet Annie disagreed, hence the juggling of schools. In the end, Harry made the decision to be Protestant, so William won out after all.

Fay daydreamed all through school. She was excellent at English, loved to read, and she would write poetry and school compositions. Mathematics, however, remained her worst subject. Although Lillian was five years younger than Fay, they were always very close. Even though she didn't remember her older sister Dorothy, as she was only two years old when Dorothy died, it did make Fay feel a sense of loyalty to Lillian, the remaining sister. Lillian was extremely shy in comparison to Fay and Harry. Their mother took advantage of this, persuading Lillian to remain at home with her after she left school. Fay, on the other hand, was extremely ambitious and started a course at a secretarial business college. She excelled in Pitmans shorthand and her typing skills were top-rate. Lillian, contrastingly, grew skilled in cookery, sewing, and domestic duties.

By 1926, 17-year-old Fay was anxious to become a Flapper. The Roaring Twenties were her teenage years and she embraced all things and styles modern. Lillian would watch in wonder as Fay experimented with rouge and lipstick, bought from her salary as an office secretary. She also began to make her own straight shift dresses using a Butterwick pattern. Her mother tried in vain to put a stop to Fay's insistence of a short, sleek hairstyle, but managed to confiscate the long cigarette holder (although only used as a prop)! When the family purchased a wireless, Fay would practice the Charleston and Black Bottom to the sounds of Jan Garber singing 'Baby Face', Gene Austin's 'Bye Bye Blackbird' and 'Five Foot Two, Eyes of Blue'. She yearned to epitomise the spirit of a reckless rebel who danced the night away at a smoky Jazz Club.

Just after the Great Depression, Annie pulled out her trump card and bought a generous home at 123 Tooronga Road, Malvern. It was paid with the money she had been taking from William all those years. The house was in her name and the family moved in, enjoying the luxury of a large back and front yard.

Every Sunday morning Fay and Lillian would attend Mass with their mother. Harry, of course, was never expected to attend. They became parishioners of St Joseph's Catholic Church close by. Annie hoped her eldest daughter would meet a nice Catholic boy and settle down. After church one sunny, autumn day in 1932, Fay was introduced to an extremely handsome, dark-haired man with sapphire blue eyes. At thirty-three, Jaime San Miguel was eleven years older than 22-year-old Fay. It was a short but animated conversation, and on the walk back home with her mother and sister, Fay couldn't stop thinking about him. Although Fay had many ardent admirers seeking her attention, she hadn't really met anyone who had touched her heart. She was a born flirt with a dynamic personality, and enjoyed the attention she always gained.

The following Sunday, he was there again, and after the service came straight over to Fay. This time they chatted for a good hour, Lillian and their mother hadn't attended due to both having a nasty cold, so Fay relaxed and listened intently to Jaime's conversation. She learnt that he had attended Xavier College in Kew, and had been Captain of the school for two years running in 1916 and 1917. She also discovered he worked as a sales representative for the Dunlop Rubber company at 108 Flinders Street in the city centre. Meanwhile, Fay had recently landed a job as private secretary to Roy Rostron, of Rostron and Company Solicitors at Chancery House in Little Collins Street. Jaime suggested as they both worked in the city, they should meet for lunch.

'Perhaps this Wednesday at 1pm?' Jaime inquired.

When Fay heartily agreed, he asked if she knew the Teapot Inn, and they made plans to meet there. Jaime offered to drive Fay home, but knowing her mother's sticky-beak nature, she declined. She did, however, skip all the way home!

Fay decided, for now, not to tell anyone about her invitation. She wanted to know more about this charming stranger before all the questions started from her somewhat interfering parents. At work that week she found it hard to concentrate, and by Wednesday morning she was a nervous wreck in anticipation of the looming lunch.

When she walked into the café a minute after one o'clock, she spotted Jaime at a window table, and made her way through the busy lunchtime crowd. He stood and greeted her warmly as he helped her into a chair. Mixed sandwiches and a large pot of tea were ordered from the plump, cheerful waitress. They talked incessantly for an hour — Fay was intrigued to hear that Jaime's father was born in Spain and that his mother was English. He spoke of his time at boarding school in Spain as a little boy, and also his passion for sports, especially golf and tennis. The lunch break flew by, and Jaime wrote down Fay's office phone number, promising to ring her the following morning.

'Perhaps a drink on Friday evening?' Jaime suggested.

Fay shook his warm, firm hand as she made a dash back to the office, grinning from ear to ear. Jaime was also smiling as he hurried up Flinders Street. Fay was such a cheerful and animated young woman, something he'd been missing for several years — the problem was, he would have to explain his situation to her very, very soon.

An Enterprising Young Spaniard

In late August of 1870, 19-year-old Antonio San Miguel, the dark, broad-shouldered, handsome second son of successful Catalan wine grower Cipriano San Miguel and wife Francisca (née Mirambel), of Alella, Spain, set off from his homeland in a spirit of adventure to seek his fortune in Australia. Besides his parents, Antonio left behind his 22-year-old brother, Francisco, and sisters Carmen, twenty-seven, and Maria, twenty-five, who were both married.[1] He carried a 'Passport for Abroad', an identity card which gave him the right to travel to France and overseas as a Spanish citizen. Close friends of the San Miguels, the Parer family, also from Alella, had arrived in Australia in 1858 and had a number of prosperous restaurants, hotels, and catering establishments. So this optimistic and confident young man was determined to succeed.

Antonio arrived in Paris en route to England shortly after the commencement of the Franco-Prussian War.[2] He heard that the Prussian troops were about to cut off each railway line out of the city and realising the danger he was in, made a desperate dash to the Gare du Nord train station where he caught the last train out before the siege of Paris on 19 September. It was a story he often related over the years. He arrived in Calais and boarded a ship bound for Australia, arriving in Sydney late November 1870. He took lodgings at an inner city hotel. With the money he had saved working for his father and the money his family had given him, he would be comfortable for a suitable

Registrado al núm. *213.*

PASAPORTE PARA EL ESTRANJERO.

D. JUAN ANTONIO CORCUERA,

Gobernador de la Provincia de Barcelona.

SEÑAS.

Edad *18 años*
Estatura *alta*
Ojos *pardos*
Nariz *regular*
Cara *oval*
Barba *cerrada*
Color *sano*

Señas particulares.

Firma del portador.

Concedo libre y seguro pasaporte, en virtud de autorizacion del Excelentísimo Señor Ministro de la Gobernacion á D. *Antonio Sanmiguel y Mirambell* natural de *—* provincia *—* de edad empadronado en *Alella* calle de *Guerí* núm. *—* piso *—* segun cédula de vecindad que queda en este Gobierno señalada con el núm. *20* para que pase á *Francia y Ultramar*

Barcelona *22* de *Agosto* de 187*0*

Pagó *una* pesetas.

amount of time. Antonio eventually moved in with a Catalan family, whose son was a good friend of his. He had plans to import his father's wine products, plus other ideas that came to him as he toured around Sydney. An economic boom was just beginning in Australia and young Antonio was extremely optimistic. He soon had interests in a number of billiard parlours, and began importing and selling Alella wine.

Around 1876 Antonio had become very close friends with two brothers, Andres and Joaquin Mauri who had come from the southern province of Andalusia, Spain, a year before. The brothers had experience in the cork industry and by early 1877 had begun a partnership in Sydney called Mauri Brothers. They traded as cork merchants and importers with their headquarters in Seville. On 12 September 1877, Antonio acquired a Publican's license for the Australian Hotel in Druitt Street Sydney, taking over from Antonio Plannis. He continued importing wines and later spirits; soon, his hotel (which also had lodgings available for rent) became a very successful establishment. Antonio also took some risks, however, and on a number of occasions was fined for trading on Sundays and other offences against the Publicans Act. In 1882 he transferred his license to Joseph Gilnot and left Australia to visit his family in early 1883. Although Antonio had plenty of pretty girls seeking his attention, he still hadn't met a potential bride, and wondered whether the girl of his dreams was back home in Alella. He remained in Spain for a number of months before returning to Australia to settle down.

On 20 June 1884, Antonio acquired a large interest and the proprietorship of The Sydney Coffee Palace Hotel Company at 393 George Street, Sydney. His good friend, Martin Arenas became a partner. Martin was a cousin-in-law of the Parers and also a relative of the San Miguels through marriage, and had lent him money back in 1877 to take over the Australian Hotel.[3] The Sydney Coffee Palace Hotel had originally opened on the 2 October 1879 as a temperance hotel. The idea was not to serve alcohol and create a sober environment for

their uppercrust clients. This movement failed and when Antonio took over, he applied for a Publican's licence to continue his importation and selling of wines and spirits.

It was a grand building of eight floors, each 18 by 70 feet with a large ground floor frontage on George Street. There was an entrance for carriages to discharge under and the façade had high Victorian architecture. Antonio made plans to do extensive alterations and improvements and obtained a license to sell postage stamps. The building comprised of a basement that housed a very modern kitchen, with a lift to the numerous dining saloons. The ground floor housed an elaborate bar made of oak wood and marble-topped. Bronze statues and decorative busts were in abundance, and immediately in front of the bar, tables and morocco lounges were provided for the patrons' comfort. On the ground floor was a dining room to accommodate one hundred persons. Each table was marble-topped with ornamental iron stands, and had room for six diners. Large gilt mirrors with one above every table complimented the white and gold surroundings and linoleum floors.

On the first floor were a gentlemen's dining hall and a ladies dining saloon, the latter admitting gentlemen if accompanied by a lady. The men's reading room contained large comfy armchairs and the lavatories all over the establishment were marble-topped. Close to the ladies dining area was a reading room where ladies arranged their toilet, read, wrote or gossiped in large, light and airy conditions.

The second floor contained a billiard room with oak ornamentation and Australian landscape scenery. Vienna billiard seats surrounded the tables. Adjoining the billiards room was a charming and comfortable smoking room where men could relax with a brandy, pipe or cigar. Gas lights and electric service bells were on every floor, and the fifty bedrooms on the remaining floors provided accommodation for both single guests and married couples. The Coffee Palace soon became a booming, busy and profitable establishment, attracting the aristocracy of Sydney.

Antonio regularly dined in the ground floor saloon and one evening in 1885 he noticed a large family enjoying the cuisine. His gaze fell on one of the daughters, 20-year-old Rebecca (Birdie) Albon. Glistening fair hair, azure blue eyes and an English rose complexion, Antonio was mesmerized by her beauty. He made his way over to their table to make his acquaintance and inquire if everything was to their satisfaction. 20-year-old Birdie, as she was affectionately called, blushed when her eyes met the striking Spaniard. At the table that night, Antonio met her parents, James and Rebecca Albon (née Poulter), and her siblings: 22-year-old Grace, teenagers Jesse, Annie, and Maud, and little 9-year-old Geseyne.

Originally from Bedfordshire, England, and having lived at Lambeth and Surrey, the family and their 18-year-old servant girl, Harriet, had arrived from Plymouth, England on the ship the *Pericles*, on 5 December 1877. Birdie's father James Albon was a successful builder, plumber and home decorator, skills he had learned from his own father. Birdie's other brother James Jr, had returned to England after a short stay in Australia.[4] John, the first born son, had died at around nine years of age. The remaining children, Jane (known as Jenny) and Thomas, had both recently married and remained in England.[5] The youngest, Geseyne, was not blood related, and had been adopted as an infant when her birth parents, friends of the Albons, tragically died. They now lived at Glebe Point, Sydney, where James Albon carried on his profitable business.

Birdie's older sister, Jenny, often wrote to the family of her life in England.

29 May 1878
Bushey Heath, Hertfordshire
Beloved Mother and Father,
For these last two months I have anxiously been looking out for letters from you. The last I received was 20 March, and the last I sent out to you was on 12

April. I hope, dear Mother, that you have received all my letters. I feel I want another letter from my precious mother. I find it is very trying to my health when I am expecting news and hear of the mails coming in and then to be bitterly disappointed. But I am trying to learn the lesson of patience, and I bless God I have again experienced the faithfulness of His precious promises to His tried ones has thy day thy strength shall be. I hope, darling Mother, that this will find you with dear Father quite well, also James Jr, Birdie, Jesse, Annie, Big Babe [Maud] and the dear precious Little Baby [Geseyne]. Give my fondest love to them all, kiss each dear one for their sister Jenny [Jane], not forgetting you and my dear Father. How I long to see you all once again, will it ever be? Do you know, loved Mother, now that I am absent from you I often find myself thinking of the many ways in which I could have contributed to your comfort and happiness while I had you with me? I often feel that it is but few returns I have made you for the unearned love and kindness you have ever shown me.

I have very little news to give you this time. Of course, you may have heard about dear Grandfather who is still alive. I think you may be prepared for what I am about to tell you since I wrote this letter a telegram from Shillington on Monday that dear Grandfather has gone home to God. He passed away ten minutes to six that evening. I can't give particulars at present. Do not fret of his great happiness, for some of us will see him again. God bless you and comfort you with His abiding love. I do not forget to pray, so does my dear husband.

I must tell you, we had Daisy Browning here for a week at Easter and she is coming again a week next Friday 7 June and will stay with us another week. She likes to be here at Bushey and she is very fond of my dear husband. Daisy sends much love to you all. We often talk together about you. Poor girl, she is not very strong; she tells me one of her lungs is gone and the other she feels is going but she is under a good doctor and does not want for anything. I try to persuade her to give up school life but she does not seem as though she would. On Easter Tuesday I had Martha and her mother to see me, and also Mrs. Thorogood — she has sold her business and says she would like to live in the country. She wishes she could get a shop near us. She wants to have a week in Bushey and thinks it would do her good, but Uncle Tom hardly knows how to spare her.[6] They have got a very nice shop and I think will do well. A week last Friday I had Sarah Ann for a few days. She returned the following Tuesday.

I have had Miss Hills here — poor girl, she has been very ill and has had to go under a most painful operation. The doctors spent two hours taking a cancer out of her right side. What they took from her weighed 3 lbs! They had to strap her down as they would not give her ether or anything to make her insensible to the pain, poor thing. Her sufferings have been something fearful and she is only twenty years old. She sends love to you, Mother.

And now I must say goodbye. I don't have anything more to say. I hope you get this letter safe with fondest love and kisses.

Ever your loving daughter,

Jenny

PS I forgot to tell you: Jenny Moss sends love to you all. She and Mr Moss send much love to you with kisses to all the dear children and both temporal and spiritual love.[7]

A year later after the birth of her son, Jenny wrote again to her parents in Australia.

22 April 1879

Beloved Mother and Father,

Ere this reaches you, I hope you have received my dear husband's letter telling of the arrival of our little son. I am very thankful to tell you I am getting on very nicely; in fact, I feel there is nothing the matter with me which is all God's goodness and loving kindness towards me. We never thought we should have a living child for it went hard with me — 24-and-a-half hours of hard labour — but my Heavenly Father brought me safely through nature's trial and my beloved Husband did not cease praying for me. My doctor was with me all the time and he was very patient with me and helped me all he could.

I have a good nurse who looks after me so I am sure I ought to do well, don't you think so? And best of all I have a lovely baby. Nurse says she believes he weighs from 12 to 14 pounds so you may know he is a fine boy and he is so healthy. How I should love you to see our jewel. He has got such a lot of hair on his pretty little head, I will enclose you a piece and I know you will prize it.

Oh, Mother, my very heart seems to swell out in love and gratitude to God for giving me such a precious, precious gift. To feel myself a mother seems almost too much and sometimes too good to be really true, Mother, you must still pray for me for I feel I need great wisdom to help train our child for Heaven. Sweet Mother, you know how to pray and the value of prayer, so then unite your prayers with ours that my precious Boy may be one of the Lord's fold.

I feel more than ever the desire to come out to you but we must be patient and it will all come right. I am not going to write much this time but I know you would like me to tell you in my own hand-writing how I am getting on. Yesterday I received a letter from Miss Mascall with kind congratulations and the promise of a pair of shoes for the baby. Last Friday I received a beautiful white robe for him from Polly which she made herself. Sarah Ann is making him a hood like the one little Babe had and I am to be kept supplied with shoes from one and another of them. I had a letter from Thomas last Sunday and he tells me that Mary-Ann was confined with a boy on Easter Monday.

I am so anxious to know how you all are. I hope you are keeping well.

~

33-year-old Antonio was so taken with young Birdie upon first meeting her, that he asked her family to be his guests for dinner on the following Saturday night. When her father accepted the invitation, Antonio ordered a complimentary bottle of Alella sweet wine to accompany their dessert. It didn't take long for Birdie and Antonio to begin courting and soon she was a regular dinner or luncheon guest at the Coffee Palace Hotel.

A year later, on Birdie's twenty-first birthday, her mother wrote her a heartwarming letter.

12 June 1886

My own precious Birdie,

Today is your Twenty-first Birthday. To me, a memorable day. Well, do I remember the hour you first saw daylight! Well, dear, it's little I have to give you on this your Natal Day. I present you with a small token of love — the books of all books. And I trust for my sake, as well as your precious soul's sake, you will read it and learn to love its truths, and in reading it, I sincerely hope and pray you may find Redemption in the Atonement of Christ. My dear, I cannot say just how, but the few words I have said comes from a loving mother who is always thinking of her children and I trust, dear Birdie, it may keep in your heart. With much love, hoping you may live to see many, many Natal Days. Believe me, your affectionate and loving mother.

Rebecca Albon

By 1887, Antonio had become involved in some areas of the Mauri Brothers importing company, and had also become interested in the cork importing side of their business. When he and Birdie married on 20 March 1888 at St Patricks Church, Church Hill, Sydney by the Reverend Father Piquet, Andres Mauri was best man. Birdie had embraced Antonio's religion and became a convert to the Roman Catholic Church prior to the wedding. It was a big day for the Albons, as Birdie's younger sister, 19-year-old Maud, married Edwin A. Purches on the same day at the Mariners Church of England. Fortunately, both churches were close by in The Rocks.

On 2 February, two months before his wedding, Antonio dissolved his partnership with Martin Arenas by mutual consent, and Arenas took over the business of the Sydney Coffee Palace Hotel. Shortly after their wedding, Antonio and Birdie set off on a honeymoon, travelling on the steam ship, *Zealandia* to the US, Europe and England. Life on board the ship was extremely pleasant for the happy couple. They were in first class accommodation, and dined with the ship commander each evening. While in San Francisco mid-April, Antonio contributed along with others to a fine gift for the captain. During their time in London, they heard the news of the serial murders of prostitutes in the Whitechapel area, by a killer dubbed Jack the Ripper. The murders were so horrific it was the talk of the town.

They travelled to Portugal where Antonio met with cork growers; he also visited the headquarters of the Mauri Brothers[8] in Seville and made contacts in San Feliu de Guixols on the Costa Brava in Catalonia, Spain, another rich cork area. He introduced his beautiful new bride to his delighted parents, relatives and friends and they celebrated with many a lavish party. They were away for nineteen months and during this time Birdie fell pregnant. After a sojourn in Paris, they went to Marseilles where they caught the French ship, *Yarra*, heading back to Australia. In Australian waters, Birdie gave birth to their first born, a son, Antonio (Tony) Stanley Joaquin (after good friend Joaquin Mauri) who was also on board; they landed in Sydney on 12 November 1889.

Over the next two years, Antonio made several trips to Melbourne and in 1892, the family moved to Melbourne, Victoria. He then set up the company, A. San Miguel and Company Cork Merchants and Importers in McKillop Street, Melbourne, and they took up residence at 1 Victoria Street, Mont Albert.[9] In 1893, Birdie gave birth to their first daughter, Francisca Margarita Leonore.

A. San Miguel and Co. went from strength to strength. By 1894 they had moved to larger premises at 304 Flinders Street, specialising in the importation of corks, brewers' requisites, and vignerons' supplies.

On 28 February 1895, Antonio appeared in the County Court. He was being sued for damages by Alfred Condor of Abbotsford. In October of 1894, Antonio's horse and cart was being cared for by his servant when it bolted away in Little Collins Street, running into Condor's hansom cab to which it did serious damage. The case was not proved and it was dismissed by the judge.

In 1895, Andres and Joaquin Mauri disposed of their business to Ninian Miller Thomson and Edwin Charles Guttridge, changing the

business name to Mauri Bros. & Thomson. By 1899 Antonio was taken into partnership with Messrs Thomson and Guttridge and they in turn became partners in A. San Miguel and Co. By this stage, each company had an office in Melbourne and Sydney.

On 20 April 1895, a second daughter, Ines Alma Irene was born at home in Mont Albert. Seventeen months later, on 13 September 1896, another son, Lionel Dudley Alfonso came into the world. Throughout 1895–98 Antonio made many trips overseas, setting up an office and headquarters in San Feliu de Guixols, Spain. In 1895, his older brother's son, Antonet, arrived in Australia to attend school at Xavier College. He remained at school for four years, taking up residence with the San Miguel family in Mont Albert. During Antonio's absence, Birdie had the help of nursery housemaids, servants and cooks. With four young children and her husband's nephew to take care of, plus attending social and charity functions, her days were extremely busy.[10] She was now fluent in Spanish, and all the children spoke it as well.

Early in April 1896, Tony San Miguel aged six years old had a nasty fall and badly broke his arm. The Melbourne doctors wrongly diagnosed that his arm would need to be amputated. X-Rays had been discovered a year before in 1895 by the German scientist Wilhelm Conrad Roentgen. Antonio made the decision to take his son to Barcelona to seek medical attention using the new technique. The result was a success and his arm was rectified, however, Tony's handwriting remained shaky throughout his life. Father and son returned to Spain five months later for the doctors to re-examine it, returning to Australia on the French steamer, *Armand Behic* on 8 October.

1898 was an important year for Antonio and the San Miguel family. He obtained his naturalisation certificate on 19 April under the provisions of the parliament of Victoria, making him a British subject and an Australian resident, able to buy property and land with the ability to vote. Then on 23 July 1898, a third son, Jaime Cipriano San Miguel, was born at their home.

∽

The Argus
Situations Vacant
Friday 31 December 1897
Superior girls, general, nursery housemaid, sisters, friends, references, fare paid.

Mrs San Miguel, Mont Albert.

In late 1898, the whole family, plus a servant maid and nursery maid left for Europe. They mainly travelled between Alella, San Feliu Guixols and Seville where Antonio continued with his business dealings. On 23 May 1899 they arrived back in Australia on board the SS *Australian* but returned to Spain later that year. Their youngest child, Patricia Mercedes, was born in Seville on 17 June 1900. The family remained in Spain for three years, returning to Australia on the RMS *Victoria*, 8th December 1903.

Throughout the three-year hiatus, Antonio made trips back to Australia. In early May of 1903, he bought a large amount of land at Milson's Point in Sydney.[11] He set up house at Hartland in Elmie Street, Auburn, Melbourne.[12] A grand, two-story Victorian mansion, Antonio rented the property from Francis Catford, who lived in a home directly at the back of Hartland. He was a successful publisher who ran the Southern Cross newspaper and had arrived from England all by himself, aged just thirteen years old. He eventually brought his whole family to Australia to settle.

The Argus
Situations Vacant
Tuesday 2 February 1904
General good cook and laundress, personal references; housemaid kept.
Mrs San Miguel, Elmie Street, Auburn.

1903 was also the year Antonio took in another major partner, Mr. T.S. Harrison of T.S. Harrison & Company, Melbourne, and changed the business name to Harrison, San Miguel & Co. He had met Harrison through his partnership with Mauri Bros. & Thomson as both were agents for Hayward-Tyler & Co. who specialised in machinery for aerated waters, winning gold medals in London, Paris, Calcutta, Melbourne and Adelaide. Antonio's big picture was to expand his business into many different areas, and Harrison, an astute businessman, seemed to be the answer.

Soon Harrison, San Miguel had added 'Specialties and Requirements for Aerated Water Manufacturers, Bottlers, Confectioners, Machinery and General Merchants and Importers and Bakers' Supplies' to their profile, and moved to Little Collins Street. Business was booming and they now had branches throughout the Australian Colonies and New Zealand, a Spanish house and cork factories in Seville, plus agencies in London, Hamburg and New York and their Sydney House of Mauri Bros. & Thomson, at 36 York Street. At the beginning of February 1905, Harrison, San Miguel became a public company. Listed as partners in the firm dated 3 February 1905 were Antonio San Miguel, Ninian Miller Thomson, Edwin Charles Guttridge and Harold Furley Harvey with no mention of Harrison.[13]

Life Goes On

Little Jaime San Miguel loved his family and was close to all his siblings. It was an exciting life for a young boy, travelling the world on fine ships, visiting exotic ports and capitals and spending time with Grandpapa Cipriano and Grandmamma Francisca, Aunt Carmen and Aunt Maria, plus his cousin, Agapito. In 1906, aged eight years, Jaime was placed in boarding school at the College of Valldemia in Mataro, Barcelona. As the business grew and grew, Antonio and Rebecca travelled extensively. By now, both Tony and Lionel were boarding at Xavier College and Francisca and Ines at Genazzano in Melbourne. Jaime missed his family very much although his parents visited him as often as they could, bringing butter and sweet treats and sending him postcards.

Alella
February 1 1907
Dear Jaime,
We are not able to come to Mataro before February 17, that is next Sunday, two weeks, so I am sending you this little girl and lovely doggie to see if you are quite happy and well. If you want butter tell the Director to buy you a tin. Hope your books are good and have no holes. With fondest love besos y abrazos from Papa, Patricia, and loads from Mother.

Jaime returned to Australia with his father and 12-year-old sister, Ines, on board the *Mongolia* on August 22 1907. This was the first time he had seen the new family home. In 1906, Antonio had purchased a 3.5 acre property, St Abbs[1] in York Street, Mont Albert from Mr John Lothian of Lothian Book Publishing Co[2]. The house, a slate-roofed weatherboard villa was built around 1875 and contained nine rooms. Beginning with a 6 foot wide hall, four generous bedrooms, a large dining room, drawing room, sewing room, bathroom with a porcelain enamelled bath; there was also a large pantry, scullery and kitchen. The out buildings included a laundry, man's room, two-stall stable with loft, and a coach house. Two wells were on the property, as well as an asphalt tennis court. Antonio planted a variety of fruit trees, vegetable plots as well as a cork tree, which he bought over from Spain.

On September 8 1908 at Our Redeemer's Catholic Church in Surrey Hills,[3] Jaime celebrated his First Holy Communion. He began school at Xavier College in 1911, and was a boarder in later years. He had to repeat a year when he started, due to his school years in Spain, resulting in him being a year older than his classmates. It was here he excelled in all sports, eventually becoming Captain of the Running Team and rower for Xavier at the Head of the River. Jaime was also a school prefect and then Captain of the School in 1916 and 1917. His two older sisters, Francisca and Ines, had both been school captains at Genezzano in 1911 and 1912, so Jaime was keeping the family tradition alive. All the San Miguel girls had attended finishing school in Spain after they left Genezzano.

At the end of 1917, Jaime finished school and in 1918, just before the end of World War I he volunteered and enlisted in the AIF (Australian Imperial Force). Although Jaime trained at the Broadmeadows camp for six months, this was a short-lived experience, as he was demobilised once the war ended.

All the San Miguel brothers were sought after by many pretty girls, loads of tennis parties and garden parties were regularly held at

St Abbs. Antonio always encouraged his sons to entertain the pretty, dark-haired Parer girls, as he knew their families so well; however, they all only remained good friends.

Early in 1918 Jaime met his first true love, Alida (Ally). Her family lived nearby, close to Wattle Park, and it was here they often shared a picnic lunch and many stolen kisses. Ally was as pretty as a picture, with light brown hair, a perfect heart-shaped face, rosebud lips and a coquettish personality. They soon became besotted with each other, and Jaime would often also include Ally's mother and her two sisters for jaunts in his newly acquired Ford T motor car. He became a regular guest at their home, and Ally was at first a welcome visitor to St Abbs. The romance soon blossomed and they became inseparable.

An extremely sad day occurred on 25 April 1919. Antonio San Miguel passed away at his beloved, St Abbs, aged sixty-seven, surrounded by his family. Around 1908, not long after Antonio had advertised the Perth business of Harrison, San Miguel for sale,[4] Birdie had noticed a change in her husband. At first his facial expressions differed, he seemed to not blink at all, and she felt he was staring at no one in particular. Then when he was sitting, tremors occurred in his hands and face, and he felt sharp pain when he walked. The doctors diagnosed him with Paralysis Agitans (Parkinson's Disease). The family were told there was no cure. By 1910, Antonio was too sick to take an active part in his company; however, he didn't retire until 1915, when he needed the use of a wheelchair to get around. Eventually dementia set in and the family was devastated. Birdie felt the loss more than anyone. She had loved her successful and romantic Spanish husband desperately, and she missed him daily. Antonio was buried in a large granite crypt, which was built at the Box Hill Cemetery, and was large enough for most of the family when they eventually passed on.[5]

Genazzano Journal, *Christmas, 1919.*
Francie San Miguel and her sisters, Ines and Patricia, are living in

Mont Albert. During the early months of the year their father's health was gradually weakening, until on April 25, after many years of patient suffering, he passed peacefully away. RIP. The devotedness and love which had surrounded him for so many years must have been to him a constant source of comfort and support in those trying days of helplessness and physical pain. All at Genazzano sympathised deeply with Mrs San Miguel and family in this great and irreparable loss, and many were the prayers offered during those sad days. In November we had several visits from Francie, who very kindly offered to teach the Spanish national dance for the entertainment on the twenty-fifth. It was undoubtedly owing to her painstaking efforts and interest that the dancers achieved such a signal success. We remember how, long ago, she and Ines used to practise these pretty, characteristic dances, which they had learned in Spain. Patricia continues her lessons in elocution and singing, for which she shows much natural ability.

At the beginning of 1921, when Jaime was planning a world wide trip, he and Ally promised to write and wait for one another. On March 30 1921, aged twenty-two years, Jaime set sail on the *Makura*, heading to Vancouver. His mother had paid for the first class passage, and given her son the means to travel. It was a delightful voyage, the San Miguel family was highly respected and handsome Jaime was always asked to dine with the very best guests. All the pretty, young, aristocrats on the voyage prayed that they would receive his dance card, and though he waltzed with quite a few, he never stopped thinking of Ally.

After arrival in Vancouver in April, Jaime set off on a trip through the Canadian Rockies, sightseeing the magnificent Bow River Falls in Banff, Alberta. He also stayed a night in the quaint little village of Paradise Valley, and was awestruck by the picturesque Mount Temple at the splendid Banff National Park. Niagara Falls was everything he had anticipated, and his journey through Canada was an absolute delight. Jaime had obtained an Alien Certificate from the US Department of Labour, which enabled him to work in the US. For nearly six months in Flint and Detroit, Michigan, he gained experience at the factories of General Motors, learning a variety of skills, and taking an interest in the manufacture and distribution of tyres. Whilst working at General Motors, he met a man who worked for The Coca-Cola Company,[6] and suggested Jaime import the beverage into Australia. After tasting the drink, Jaime exclaimed, 'It's just another fizzy drink!' and rejected the idea.

Jaime had met a fellow in Detroit, who lived in Chicago, Illinois, so he decided to spend a couple of days with him, enroute to his next destination of New York. Prohibition had begun two years before in 1919, so Jaime, like many others had abstained from alcohol, although occasionally he'd have a tipple if his hosts had their own private supply (usually French champagne or wines stored in the cellar).

Edmund Scott met up with Jaime at the station; he lived in a stylish apartment at the Le Roy, 836–42 West Cornelia, close to Lake Michigan in the Wriggleyville area of Chicago. Jaime was suitably impressed. They dined with friends of Edmund's that evening, although this time there was no alcohol on offer. The following day, after lunching at Ed's Men's Club, Jaime visited the Home Insurance Building, built in 1884, and designed by architect, William Le Baron Jenney.

'Look how tall it is!' Jaime commented to his friend as he gazed up at the twelve-floor building. He also spent time at *Our Lady of Sorrows Basilica*, a Roman Catholic Church, founded in 1874 by the Servite fathers. He admired the grand Italian Renaissance architecture that featured a barrel-vaulted ceiling, wrapped around a high marble altar. It took his breath away. He genuflected and whispered a quick Hail Mary.

That evening Edmund took Jaime to a midtown Jazz Club. It was here they ran into a former school friend of Ed's. This venue was renowned for their bootlegged moonshine whiskies and so-called gin. Bertie suggested they all indulge. Jaime only partook of wines or sherries, so he declined the offer, but Edmund paid for a bottle of gin. After his first glass, Ed complained that the taste was vile, however Bertie eventually polished off the entire bottle. When Jaime and Edmund left the club around 1am, Bertie was extremely inebriated. Jaime suggested they take him home, but Bertie was engaged in a slurred conversation with Margie, who he'd taken a shine to earlier that evening, and so the boys left him to it.

The following morning, as Jaime was finalizing his packing, Edmund received a phone call. Bertie was dead. The gin he had consumed was tainted with metals and other impurities, poisoning him. Such accidents became more frequent as the Prohibition continued and illegally-produced liquor became more widespread. It was a mammoth shock for the two men, and Jaime thanked God he disliked spirits.

On arrival in New York, Jaime checked in to The Plaza Hotel at 768 5th Avenue, close to Central Park. Lionel, his brother, had arranged a room for them both, as he too was staying in New York doing a postgraduate course at the Beaux-Arts Institute of Design, situated at 304 East 44th Street in Turtle Bay, Manhattan. Lionel had graduated from Melbourne University with Honours in Architecture. They would spend a week at the hotel until Lionel found other, less expensive lodgings. One evening Jaime and Lionel were in the elegant foyer of The Plaza, when a party of five came bursting in. Jaime commented about the only girl in the group, observing her beauty and exuberance, and mentioning how much she looked like Ally, with the same hypnotic eyes. They later learnt her name, Zelda Fitzgerald, wife and muse of author F. Scott Fitzgerald, who had come in with her husband and three of their friends.

Jaime and Lionel had received plenty of invitations to dine with a number of families during their stay in New York. Many took them to lavish restaurants, and another young man, whose home was in Maine, gave them a tour of the Speakeasies and Jazz Clubs of 52nd Street. At one club Jaime thoroughly enjoyed the Paul Whiteman Ambassador Orchestra, and hummed the tune of 'Whispering' all the way home. Jaime also took in all the tourist sights, including the Statue of Liberty,

Grant's Tomb, New York Stock Exchange, and both the Metropolitan and Woolworth buildings. He always purchased a number of postcards to send to Ally and his parents. A week later, he was delighted to find a postcard had arrived from Ally. He took out his wallet and gently kissed the photograph he had of her.

In late September, Jaime boarded the ship, *Adriatic*, in New York, bound for Southampton, England, arriving on 13 October 1921. When he saw the date, Jaime felt a trifle nervy; he had a strong superstition about the number thirteen being unlucky. However, he soon forgot about it, as he began a tour of London. Taking in all the historical sights, he visited Buckingham Palace and the Tower of London on the north bank of the River Thames, and thoroughly enjoyed Hampton Court Palace, former home of the flamboyant King Henry VIII. He caught his breath at the Unknown Warrior's Grave, in the beautiful Gothic church of Westminster Abbey. The unidentified British soldier from World War I had only recently been buried there, on 11 November 1920. The Cenotaph, in Whitehall, had recently been built and designated as the United Kingdom's official war memorial, so he bought a few more postcards to send back home.

His next stop was Paris, before heading back to Barcelona, where he would catch up with his cousin, Agapito Ferran and other relatives. Jaime spent a night at the palatial Hotel Ritz, 15 Place Vendôme, Paris, that was founded the year he was born, 1898. His mother, Rebecca, had supplied some extra spending money, urging Jaime to experience at least one night in the grand hotel. She and Antonio had spent several enjoyable nights there on one of their trips. And now that he was gone, her precious memories were all that kept her going.

Jaime was thrilled to return to Barcelona and the old family home in Alella, where Agapito, his wife, and their three children now lived. Agapito's wife was also pregnant with their fourth child, and they welcomed Jaime with open arms. They all discussed the assassination of the Spanish Prime Minister, Eduardo Dato Tradier, who had been shot on 8 March 1921 by three Catalan anarchists as he was exiting the parliament buildings in Madrid. Agapito told Jaime he knew the brother of one of those arrested, adding that his friend was appalled at his brother's involvement.

A sunny afternoon was spent at Montserrat, the multi-peaked mountain located near Barcelona and site of the Benedictine Abbey, *Santa Maria de Montserrat*. He took a few photographs with his Brownie Box camera, and once again purchased postcards of the magnificent vistas.

As the weeks rolled by Jaime was slightly concerned as he'd heard nothing from Ally since the postcard he'd received in New York. He had been sending her postcards and letters constantly, and she knew the address of the Alella home. Early one morning, after returning from a walk, Agapito greeted him waving a letter from Ally. Thrilled to bits, he retreated to his room to read its contents. What it contained completely devastated Jaime, and he couldn't understand what had happened.

14 September 1921

My beloved Angus,

I treasure every moment we spend together and I count the moments till we meet again, for when I am with you, this world is a different place. Everything but you fades away into the background and becomes dim. But with you there is always that vividness of life. I have written to Jaime and have told him about us. I pray he understands. He has been gone such a long time, and you my darling, have captured my heart.

My eternal love forever,

Ally

Jaime read it again, tears pouring down his cheeks. Who was this man, Angus, and why had Jaime received *his* letter? Obviously, Jaime concluded, Angus had received Ally's break up letter to him. How could this happen? Later that evening as Agapito consoled his cousin, he suggested to Jaime that perhaps Ally had mixed the letters up on purpose. At first horrified at the thought, Jaime eventually agreed that it was a strong possibility, and then he remembered the date he had arrived in Europe, the thirteenth.

Alella,

30 November 1921

My Own Darling little Sweetheart of Old,

Oh, Ally darling, if you only knew what I am suffering, you would never have let me go through this. I cannot realise it all yet, dearest, and what it means to me, and to think it is all true. This will be my first of many nights in agonizing torture of mind, without any possible chance of sleep. It is driving me crazy. Any way I might express myself tonight in this letter is only one quarter of what I feel as words won't express my feelings, but I shall make a feeble attempt nonetheless.

Ally my own, I am going to make one last pathetic appeal to you now, and for the sake of my sacred love towards you my own 'little chicken', do please listen to me. First of all, sweetheart, I love you to death itself, and honestly, I would go through hell itself to have one last small chance of winning you back. My cup is full of bitterness to think that it is really my own fault — that I had you, and so to speak, let you slip through my fingers. Yes Ally, I know that you had every right to wonder whether I was really in earnest, but I was, and I realise it fully now. I know I have been away so long, but I will be home soon.

Somehow your precious nature always made me turn to you, and now that is gone, I have only a dead world to face. Perhaps it was the unhappy relations that existed once between you and my people that has influenced your mind most. Our love for each other has been too great to think anything else, but that state (with my family) has passed long ago, although you may not think it. I have unfortunately, and bitterly so, been lax on that point. But sweetheart I promise you that I would become engaged to you tomorrow if you will only let me, and what is more, with the full consent of my people. If it is a case of your lifelong happiness, surely it is not too late. Ally, just think of the happy times we have had together during the last three years. Do you mean to say we could not have any more such as those? So think about that and your promise to me before I left. If you …

The letter was unfinished and never sent; Jaime often wondered whether it would have changed anything, had Ally received it.

∼

It was now December and soon Jaime would be returning to Australia. He bid an emotional farewell to Agapito and his family and headed to Toulon in Southern France to spend a few days on the Côte d'Azur. Just prior to Christmas, he boarded the *Ormonde* in Toulon, bound for Australia. Christmas and New Year were spent on board, and although the voyage and ports of call were extremely interesting and enjoyable, his heart still bled for Ally. Jaime arrived home on 1 February 1922. He had been gone for nearly two years.

It Had To Be You

During Jaime's absence, his older brother, Tony, had been setting up a business and asked Jaime to be involved. Tony had married Muriel Hay Robison in 1916 and they already had one child, Richard John, and on 22 August 1922, Elizabeth (Betty) was born. They lived at a home, Riccarton, in York Street, Mont Albert, a few houses down from St Abbs, and eventually moved to a flat at Bluff Mansions in Barkly Street, St. Kilda. It was here on 22 January, just prior to Jaime's return, that a thief broke in while the family were at lunch, stealing jewellery worth £100.

Although Antonio's estate had been left to his wife, Birdie, she was generous with money for her family, and gave Tony the funds to begin the business. She had hoped one of her sons would be involved in her late husband's companies, but they all chose different fields. Antonio had created a dynasty of businesses, which his associates all benefited from. The Ajax Tyre and Denby Truck Agencies suited Jaime from the experience he'd had in America with General Motors. They represented a number of tyre and truck companies, and were involved in the importation of tyres and parts. In 1923 they set up the Melbourne Suburban Bus Company, which ran Denby buses from the city to Middle Brighton. Later that year Tony took his family on a trip to Europe, and visited the Ferrans in Alella. The bus company became a public company and on Monday 14 July 1924, they put a block advertisement in the Argus newspaper, offering 100,000 shares of one pound each, with a nominal capital of £100,000. The secretary was listed as Charles Fitzherbert-Howson, who married their sister, Francisca, at Our Redeemer's Church in Surrey Hills on 15 August 1922.

Lionel San Miguel designed a two-housed estate, Montalegre, situated on the corner of Mont Albert and Balwyn Roads, Mont Albert, for his mother. St Abbs was sold on 8 August 1922 to Martin George Brown of Studley Avenue, Kew, for £1850. The family, apart from Tony and Francisca, moved into Montalegre shortly afterwards. Lionel had installed a secret panel in the drawing room, where Birdie kept her jewellery, personal papers, cash, and a replica pistol. One morning after hearing a noise she spotted a burglar climbing in through an open window. As he made his way into another room, Birdie closed the window and retrieved the pistol from the panel, and confronted the hapless thief. By this time her housekeeper had appeared and Birdie instructed her to telephone the police, who arrived promptly and arrested the intruder. The house was a beautifully designed Art Deco style, with Spanish-inspired arches, and a glorious large garden with a tennis court. The residence was admired by all who visited.

Many balls and parties were held at the new home in the large ballroom, and Jaime was always a popular figure amongst the pretty, single girls. He had seen Ally only once since his return, and although it was a painful experience, he had moved on with his life when she married Angus. At one of the family garden parties, on a sultry, summer day in 1924, Jaime was introduced to a strikingly beautiful chestnut-haired girl, Alma May Lumsden, known by her nickname of Connie. She had come to the party with a friend of Lionel's, and when they struck up a conversation, she reminded Jaime that they had met once before. Connie was a friend of Ally's. For a moment Jaime froze, just hearing Ally's name still hurt, but Connie's animated conversation and her exquisite looks soon had him under her spell.

Very soon Jaime and Connie were courting. Nights at the

theatre, intimate dinners, and social tennis parties followed. Unlike Jaime, Connie didn't play tennis — she detested sports, much to his disappointment. He'd already taken an interest in golf and had recently begun lessons. He had hoped Connie would join him on the links, but that was never to be. Still, when they waltzed to the sound of Marion Harris singing, 'It Had to Be You', on the Melola phonograph, which Jaime had purchased in 1923, any regrets with her interest in sport just faded away. He was now besotted with the emerald-eyed beauty, who coyly, always had her own way.

~

On Saturday 29 May 1926, Jaime married Alma May Lumsden at Sacred Heart Roman Catholic Church in Kew. He was twenty-seven years old and Connie was twenty-four. Initially, they moved into a residence at 246 Dandenong Road, St. Kilda, and life was very happy for the honeymooners. Jaime had felt quite smug, when he learnt that Ally knew he had married her old friend; despite his love for Connie, Ally still tugged at his heartstrings, and he had never forgiven her for the letter debacle.

Life changed on 5 May 1927 when Connie's 49-year-old mother died. She was devastated. The favourite daughter of four sisters, Connie was her mother's pride and joy, and completely spoilt. She fell into a deep depression, spending days in bed. Jaime would arrive home from work, exhausted, to find his wife sobbing and still in bed with nothing prepared for dinner. He was at his wits end as to how he could help her. Eventually, things returned to normal, but Connie's happy nature had all but disappeared, and their lovemaking was extremely erratic.

The Argus,
Friday, 6 May 1927
LUMSDEN
On the 5th May, Isabelle, dearly loved wife of Alfred George Lumsden, dearly

loved mother of Vera (Mrs Marnell), Myra (Mrs Tompkins), Connie (Mrs San Miguel), and Edna, died at her home in Glenferrie. Dearly loved.

~

In April of 1929, Birdie San Miguel, aged sixty-five years, along with two of her daughters, Ines and Patricia, set sail on the *Oronsay* headed for Europe. They would spend over seven months abroad, a large number spent in Barcelona and Seville. On 23 May, the ship docked at Southampton and the trio began their holiday. Harrison, San Miguel & Mauri Bros. and Thomson had both continued to gain huge profits, and as Birdie had a large number of shares in the companies, she received a very healthy income, which continued for many years to come.

The Register News-Pictorial (Adelaide, S.A.) Tuesday, 31 December 1929
Elizabeth Leigh's Pages For Women
SPAIN NOW MODERNISED
After twenty years absence from Spain, where she once lived, Mrs A San Miguel of Mont Albert recently visited Barcelona and Seville. She returned today by the Ormonde, accompanied by her daughters, Mrs Pat Henwood and Miss Ines San Miguel.

'The progress of Spain has been wonderful,' said Mrs San Miguel. 'In Seville, old houses have given place to beautiful modern hotels like the Alfonso the Thirteenth, where all the smart people go for tea between five and six o'clock, and dance afterwards. Wherever you travel now in Spain you find someone who can speak both French and English. The accommodation is excellent, cheaper than in England, and is cheap as in the rest of Europe. Americans travel there in hundreds. Everything is modernised. The Spanish dance all the modern dances beautifully. If you want to see the old Moorish dances you have to go to special cafes, where they are now a feature. Education is spreading among the poor of Spain. Girls and young women have more freedom than they ever had. Yes, many of them today choose their own husbands.'

~

The Great Depression began with the Wall Street Crash on 29 October 1929, and rapidly spread worldwide. As in other nations, Australia suffered years of high unemployment, low profits, deflation, and lost opportunities for economic growth. One of the casualties was the Ajax Tyre and Denby Motor Truck Agencies, including the Melbourne Suburban Bus Company. It affected Tony San Miguel very badly, causing him to have a complete nervous breakdown, and he was hospitalised for a number of weeks. He had lost everything he'd invested. Although Jaime also lost a portion, he hadn't been a major player in the company, and immediately began looking for alternative employment.

In early December, Jaime was given some wonderful news: he and Connie were expecting a baby, so now he would have a family to take care of. He obtained a job at the Dunlop Rubber Company, covering the sales of Solid and Pneumatic Tyres, including areas of their general lines to the mechanical section. Jaime was a natural salesman and loved his new job.

On Friday 15 August 1930, Leon Jaime San Miguel was born, a beautiful, healthy baby boy. The couple were ecstatic, although throughout the pregnancy, Connie had been aloof and distant. Lovemaking had ceased altogether and six months after the birth, Jaime still hadn't shared intimacy with his wife. He took his frustrations out by playing competitive tennis. He won a large number of trophies, and his golf games became more frequent. Having no interest in his hobbies, Connie would whinge and complain on his arrival home, hurting his feelings when she failed to congratulate him on winning a game. Heated arguments became a regular occurrence, and Connie's depression again reared its ugly head. Despite all their problems, Jaime purchased a large property at 18 Stodart Street, Camberwell. The generous home with tennis court also included a self-contained flat above the garage. Not long after they moved in, Connie requested separate bedrooms.

Jaime kept his marriage problems from his family. His youngest sister, Patricia had married Leslie Felix Henwood in 1926, and already had two children, Brett and Judy. Just before the birth of Leon, Lionel wed his fiancé, Myra Bullivant, while Ines remained a spinster. The one person Jaime did confide in was his old friend from Xavier College, John Cooke. John listened patiently to his good friend, but could not sympathise completely.

'Jaime,' he said shortly. 'You married Connie on the rebound from Ally and you both had nothing in common. But you have a son now, so you must be patient with her.'

Jaime tried, how very hard he tried, however, nothing he could say or do seemed to make Connie happy; indeed, not even their baby son could allay her misery.

Jaime threw himself into his work, and soon became Dunlop's top salesman. His salary increased with the money he was earning from his commission. Saturday afternoons he would spend on the golf course, often with brother Lionel, another keen player. Jaime adored his little boy and played with him often, but life with Connie was becoming unbearable. Shortly after moving into Stodart Street, he began attending Sunday morning mass at St Joseph's in Malvern. Connie had not converted to marry Jaime, and therefore their marriage was performed in a side altar at Sacred Heart.

One autumn Sunday he noticed a very pretty, vivacious girl chatting to a friend of his who belonged to the Malvern Younger Set, a social club for young residents of Malvern. He made his way over to his friend, hoping to gain an introduction.

'Good morning Gerald, are we still on for that tennis match?' Jaime reached out to shake his friend's hand, adding, 'I hope I'm not intruding,' as he shot the young woman a beaming smile.

'Not at all my good man. Let me introduce you. Fay Johnston, meet my tennis opponent and good friend, Jaime San Miguel.'

Jaime extended his hand towards Fay, and their blue eyes met and held each other's gaze. With a knowing smile, Gerald excused himself and left them chatting.

The following Sunday Jaime encountered Fay again, and this time they spoke for an hour. Arrangements were made to meet for lunch in the city on Wednesday. Jaime felt a trace of guilt as he climbed into his A-Model Ford car to drive home to Stodart Street.

The Four Seasons Of 1932

Fay glanced up at the office clock — it was 4pm

'Only another hour to go,' she mused, as she finished typing her last letter. After the enjoyable lunch on Wednesday, Jaime had rung her on Thursday morning as promised, and they were meeting for drinks and dinner that night.

Roy Rostren stepped out of his office and approached Fay's desk. 'Miss Johnston, I have one last letter to be typed up before you leave for the weekend. You'll need to post it as well.'

Normally, Fay would have been irritated but as she wasn't meeting Jaime until 5.30, she had plenty of time to complete her boss's request. She had spent extra time dressing this morning, selecting a crisp, pale blue cotton blouse with cape angel sleeves, a bias cut navy blue skirt and matching jacket of fine wool crepe. At five, Fay packed up her desk. She took out her compact and refreshed her lipstick, rouge and powder, and combed her recently permed hair. She placed the business letter in her handbag, then popped her head into Rostren's office and bid him goodnight.

It was nearing twilight as she headed up Collins Street, stopping to post the business letter. As she waited for a cable tram, Fay wondered what tonight might bring, and she felt a tinge of excitement. A brisk wind whisked the autumn leaves around as she boarded the tram. Jaime had suggested the Hotel Windsor in Spring Street for their rendezvous.

It wasn't quite 5.30 — she was early — but nonetheless made her way to the entrance where she hoped Jaime would already be waiting.

Fay looked around the grand foyer, lit by magnificent crystal chandeliers, and noticed Jaime seated and smoking a cigarette. She approached him, stretching out her hand. He shook it with a smile, and she noticed how his eyes appeared even brighter against the contrast of the dark blue double-breasted suit he was wearing.

'Let's go into the lounge for a drink and we can have a good chat,' he said. 'I want to know all about you.'

They both settled back in the soft, leather club armchairs, and Jaime ordered two sherries. When they arrived he raised his glass.

'A toast Fay, to new beginnings. Cheers!'

'Yes, to new beginnings,' she echoed, and their glasses clinked. She sipped her sherry, enjoying the way it warmed her throat. 'So how good a tennis player *are* you?'

Jaime sat up, reaching for his cigarette case. He offered Fay one but she declined. 'I've won the odd trophy,' he said. 'But my question is, do you play?'

'I play regularly with the Malvern Younger Set,' she replied. 'In fact, I've played doubles with Gerard on a number of occasions.'

'Well, then, we definitely have a few things in common.' He lit his cigarette and flashed another smile.

'So it would seem,' Fay agreed. 'Perhaps we can have a game some time?'

'I'd like that very much,' he said softly, and they held eyes for a moment. 'Are you ready to dine now?' he added and held his hand out to help Fay up.

They entered the dining room where he had booked a table and were seated by the courteous waiter. Fay removed her jacket as Jaime glanced at the menu. They both ordered roast lamb with mint sauce and seasonal vegetables, and marmalade pudding for desert. A white wine was selected, and the conversation flowed easily. Jaime was delighted to hear how keen his companion was on sport. She asked all about golf and where she could obtain lessons. Jaime hadn't enjoyed himself like this in what seemed like years, but he knew he had to tell her everything before the night ended.

~

Fay tossed and turned in bed and hoped she wouldn't wake her sister, Lillian. The night had been wonderful. Jaime was so charming and handsome, but his confession of being in an unhappy marriage with a 2-year-old son had rocked her. He had waited until after dinner to drop the bombshell, explaining that he wanted to lay his cards on the table.

'I'd like to see a lot more of you Fay,' he had said, placing his hand in hers.

Fay was silent for a moment, then in a quiet, steady voice replied, 'This is quite a shock Jaime. We are both Catholic … I need to think it over.'

Yet at 4am Fay still couldn't stop thinking about it. She struggled with her thoughts, and eventually dozed off. She awoke to the clinking of teacups. Lillian placed a cup on Fay's bedside table.

'You were late coming in last night.'

Fay sat up in bed and rubbed her eyes. 'What time is it, Lil?'

'Don't worry, you haven't slept in. It's only 8.30,' she said. 'So who were you out with? I'm bursting with curiosity!'

Fay reached for her dressing gown and stepped out of bed. 'Just someone I met at Mass. I'll tell you all about it tonight but for now I need to get ready, I have a meeting with the Malvern Younger Set at ten.'

She headed hastily for the bathroom, keen to avoid further questioning.

That evening, they ate dinner with their parents, who were more concerned about brother Harry's new lady love, Marie Cameron, who Harry had met while holidaying in Coogee, Sydney. The following morning she decided not to attend Mass, complaining of a sore throat.

Fay was still in despair, and confused about her increasing interest in a married man.

On Monday morning, she found it hard to concentrate. Rostron had plenty of shorthand for her to take and numerous letters to type. At 10am the tea lady wheeled the cart in and Fay stopped typing.

'Good morning, Kitty. Any sweet biscuits? I'm famished!'

Kitty set a cup and saucer on Fay's desk. 'I have some nice Arnott's Arrowroot biscuits today. How many would you like?'

The door flew open and Elsie, the typist from down the hall, burst in clutching a beautiful bouquet of flowers. 'Fay, these were delivered to our office by mistake. They're for you! There's a card attached. Ooh, who are they from?'

Fay reached for the bouquet, and caught her breath as she opened the card.

My dear Fay,
I had such a pleasant evening last Friday. I hoped to see you at Mass yesterday, I am, yours truly, Jaime.
   PS I hope these flowers brighten up your day.

The intoxicating perfume of the pale pink rosebuds and violets permeated the stale office air. Fay asked Kitty to fetch a vase as she re-read the card. Elsie hovered near the desk, still waiting for a reply.

'It's just someone I know from church, Elsie. Shouldn't you get back to work?'

Although disappointed, Elsie left.

Fay didn't dare take the flowers home. She left them on her office desk. She was in two minds now: Jaime's romantic gesture and the memory of their sumptuous and happy dinner made her anxious to see him again. She was dying to discuss it with Lillian — but she couldn't.

At 11am on Tuesday morning the switchboard put through a call to Fay's office phone.

'Good morning, Fay. I hope you received the flowers?'

Her heart was racing. It was Jaime.

'Yes,' she said. 'Thank you, they're exquisite.'

There was a pause. 'Look,' Jaime began. 'I hope my situation hasn't caused you any grief. I meant it when I said I'd like to see more of you. Any chance we could meet for lunch tomorrow?'

In a spur of the moment decision she impetuously replied, 'What about one o'clock at the Teapot Inn?'

'That will be perfect. I look forward to it.'

Fay put the receiver down and chided herself for being so impulsive. However, the pitter-patter of her heart overruled her negative thoughts.

⁓

Jaime was sitting by the window at a table for two, puffing on a cigarette. Fay was ten minutes late. The smile on his face when she reached the table made her chest flutter.

'I'm sorry to be late,' she said in greeting. 'Mr Rostran had an urgent letter that I had to complete before I left.'

She settled into a seat.

'That's quite alright,' Jaime replied. 'Although I did think for a moment you might stand me up!' He gave a nervous laugh. 'Have you heard the news about Phar Lap?[1] He died at a ranch in San Francisco yesterday. I'm no racing man, but what a horse!' Jaime butted his cigarette into the glass ashtray.

'Yes!' Fay exclaimed. 'The tea lady told us this morning. My father will be upset; he won money backing Phar Lap. He likes to have the odd flutter.'

A waitress appeared and handed them a menu. Fay glanced at it and ordered egg and lettuce sandwiches and tea while Jaime opted for ham and cheese.

'Were you unwell on Sunday? I had hoped to see you at Mass.'

Fay wriggled nervously in her chair. 'My throat was a bit sore …

but to be quite honest, I felt I should avoid you.'

He looked directly into her eyes. 'What changed your mind?'

She lowered her gaze. 'I really don't know.'

The waitress arrived with their sandwiches and a large pot of tea, and the conversation paused as they hungrily tucked into their lunch. Fay wanted to ask him all about his marriage, but didn't know how, and her lunch break was nearing an end. When they finished eating Jaime suddenly squeezed her hand, and the flutters in her chest returned.

'I would like to explain everything to you Fay, I really would,' he said. 'I know this has all been a shock, but I can't stop thinking about you. I just wish it wasn't so complicated.'

∽

Autumn turned to winter and the secret lunches and Friday dinners continued. Fay played a few tennis matches with Jaime at the Malvern Younger Set courts, and he was most impressed with her game. They attended tournaments, and she watched him win trophies a number of times. She was falling in love, helplessly, deeply in love. Fay had confided to Lillian about Jaime, and her sister promised to keep her secret safe. 17-year-old Lil thought it was incredibly romantic. She had seen Jaime at Mass and agreed with Fay about his charm and screen star looks. Both girls were equally keen on the silver screen, and Lillian fantasised that Jaime was Gary Cooper and Fay, Carole Lombard, in a Hollywood romance film. Her daydreams helped her through the boring days of being her mother's maid, so to speak. She wished she could escape to an office like Fay.

Neither their parents, nor her brother Harry knew anything about the relationship. Fay was extremely careful, and always made sure Jaime dropped her off a few houses away from home.

Harry was rarely around much these days; he was a qualified technician and worked for the Post Master General, installing telephones. He spent two years, 1928 and 1929 at Sale after a posting there. It was in this Gippsland town he met Edith Mitchell and they began an intimate relationship. When she fell pregnant, he initially asked his mother for money for an abortion. Fay overheard the heated argument between them both, and heard her mother Annie flatly refuse. Harry did ask Edith to marry him, but she declined, and the baby girl, Beryl, born on 15 June 1929, was placed in an orphanage. As Fay heard nothing more about it, she assumed the girl had terminated the pregnancy. Edith married Doug MacDonald not long after the birth, and three years later she collected Beryl from the children's home, and when she was fourteen years old Doug became her adoptive father. Harry had paid child support for fourteen years, so it was a relief when Doug adopted Beryl. No one other than his best mate, Con Norris, knew about the illegitimate baby. fifty-seven years later, 80-year-old Harry finally met his first-born daughter.[2]

~

Fay had begun taking golf lessons from Jaime. She was keen to participate in another of his sports, and it would also give them more time together. His situation still nagged at her, but whenever they were together, her worries just melted away. A film they attended, *Strange Interlude*, starring Norma Shearer and Clarke Gable moved her, especially when Shearer's character, Nina, declared near the end, 'Our lives are strange dark interludes in the electrical display of God the Father!'[3]

Fay attended confession before Mass the following Sunday, yet failed to reveal her secret. If the priest had told her to leave Jaime, she knew it would be impossible, so she didn't receive Holy Communion.

Fay and Jaime met for lunch at their special café nearly every day and she had begun to pass him little letters, or post them to his workplace at Dunlop's. He in turn reciprocated, and kept Fay's letters in a locked box at work. Life at home was still a mess, however, his young son was his pride and joy, and he didn't want to leave him. Fay and Connie had met one Sunday, when out of the blue Connie had told Jaime she and

Leon would be coming to Mass. It was an awkward moment for Fay and Jaime though Connie didn't seem to notice anything. At least, that's what they thought.

The relationship had gone no further than passionate kisses, yet it was becoming harder and harder to resist taking the next step. Spring was in the air, and the blossom trees were exposing glorious bright hues of pink and white blooms all over town.

Jaime had organised a weekend away for the two of them, explaining, 'There's not much point in pretending it hasn't happened; we have both fallen in love.'

It would be a golf weekend. Fay's game was improving and she loved being out in the fresh air on a course with the man she loved. Jaime had booked a room at a small hotel in Woodend; it was mid-September.

Fay told her parents she was spending the weekend with her best friends, Judy Reid and May Wilson, and had worded them both up. Judy had also started seeing a married man, a wealthy engineer, John Telford-Smith. Jaime's excuse to Connie was that he was playing in a weekend golf tournament. Fay had packed a small case which she had taken to work. She was meeting Jaime at 5.15pm and they would drive to Woodend, northwest of Melbourne. Her excitement was mingled with a touch of fear, as tonight she would be losing her virginity, a mortal sin in the eyes of the church.

It wasn't a long drive to Woodend, and they chatted happily about their weekend plans. On arrival Jaime signed them in as Mr and Mrs Miguel while Fay waited in the car. The wind whipped up a cool breeze as they walked up the path to their bungalow. Jaime had purposely booked a room out of the main building, for extra privacy. The room was small yet cosy, with a double bed covered in a pale mauve bedspread. The fireplace had kindling and newspaper prepared, so Jaime lit a fire while Fay unpacked. The flames flickered, lighting and warming their room. Jaime pulled two armchairs in front of the fire, then unpacked a bottle of cream sherry and two glasses he had carefully wrapped in brown paper.

'I thought it would be nice to have a drink by ourselves before we go in for dinner,' he offered.

Fay sat down and stretched her hands towards the warmth of the fire. He poured the wine, and laid the glasses down on the wooden table, then reached for Fay's hand and pulled her gently towards him. She wrapped her arms around his neck, closing her eyes as their lips met.

The dining room contained eight tables of different sizes, and they were shown to a small one near the bay windows. Three other couples were seated nearby, plus a mixed table of five. They all nodded to Fay and Jaime as they passed their tables. It wasn't a large menu so they ordered the roast of the day: pork with crackling, roast potatoes and peas, plus bread and butter pudding for desert. They commented after the meal what a wonderful table the hotel provided. The dinner was delicious, and after three glasses of wine and the earlier sherries, they both felt relaxed and at perfect ease in each others company.

Jaime stoked the fire on their return to the bungalow, while Fay went to the bathroom, situated close to their room. She had bought an apricot silk nightgown at Manton's Department Store in Bourke Street[4] a week before, especially for the occasion. She removed her brassiere and underwear and slipped into the gown, feeling the soft silk caress her skin. She was ready, emotionally and physically ready.

Jaime was sitting by the fire dressed in pyjamas and a dark green woollen dressing gown. He stood up when she entered.

'You are so beautiful, Fay.' He held out his hand towards her. She moved forward, and they both sat down on the bed. He cupped her face with his hands and softly kissed her lips, then her neck and shoulders. Fay took his hand and led it to her breasts, trembling as he touched her. Jaime removed his dressing gown and lay back on the bed, pulling Fay down beside him as he carefully undid her silken gown. She watched as he slowly unbuttoned his top and slipped out of his pyjamas, turning the bedside lamp off. The glow of the embers was the only light in the room.

The following morning they made love again. Fay was deliriously happy; her emotions had reached a new plateau of contentment. They breakfasted on crispy bacon, eggs, and hot, buttery toast, enjoying every last morsel. It was perfect spring weather, azure blue skies, and golden sunshine — ideal for golf. They were playing at the local course, within walking distance of the hotel. It was 10am when they arrived at the golf course. The plan was to play nine holes, break for lunch at the Golf Club, then have another round in the afternoon.

The weekend flew by far too quickly; Saturday night and Sunday morning were spent in each other's arms, and their love-making reached ecstatic heights. They both felt for once, everything was perfectly right in the world. On Sunday at 5pm they left to drive home to reality, their conversation less animated than the journey down. Jaime dropped Fay off a few houses from her own. They held each other tightly, knowing it would be a while before they could share again what they'd experienced this weekend.

'Oh Darling, I *love* you.' Jaime said as he kissed Fay goodbye. 'I'll see you tomorrow at our usual haunt?'

'Yes, until tomorrow, then.' She collected her case and Jaime closed the passenger door.

As they ended their lunch the following day, Jaime slipped a letter into Fay's hand.

Monday, 19 September 1932
My own darling adorable Fay,
I love you, worship you and adore you. I love you because you are fine, beautiful and lovely, in every way. Your character, your nature, your body, your hair and everything you possess is my ideal of the perfect woman, and that is you my own darling Fay. That is why I love you and you alone. I really

should not tell you or admit these things to you, darling, because you might think I am silly, but if being silly is being in love with you, I would love to be a lunatic!

With all my love to my ideal from her man,

Jaime

They had now been seeing each other for six months. The past weekend had been their first intimate encounter, and they both yearned for the second, not knowing when it could possibly be. Fay was turning twenty-three on Thursday 6 October, so Jaime made plans for another weekend away. He booked them into Dava Lodge[5], a guest house on the Mornington Peninsula, which also housed a golf course and tennis courts. Fay also knew the guest house well, as she often spent her summer holidays there. The fashionable Georges department store in Collins Street was where Jaime shopped for a birthday present for Fay, finally settling on a marcasite brooch in the shape of a bow. He also ordered flowers to be delivered to her office on the Thursday morning.

October 6 1932

Darling,

I cannot resist this opportunity of typing these few lines whilst Mr R is out having lunch. I have heaps of work to do but would probably make a bad job of it whilst in my present frame of mind.

I keep glancing at my lovely flowers and even the Painter just made a remark to me about their exquisite fragrance which is permeating the entire office (if only I dared tell them it was filling my whole being with love for you). When you send me such lovely birthday greetings, I almost fear that the secret feelings in my heart might reveal themselves to all these people working about me. The girls along the corridor are still very curious as to who my ardent admirer is — Darling, I would love to tell them that he is the most wonderful person in the whole world and that I love him very dearly. Perhaps I am telling you too many secrets and you are probably laughing at me.

Well, Darling, seeing as you are such a busy person I daren't take up any more of your very valuable time. Look forward to seeing you tomorrow evening, for our very special weekend.

All my love,

Fay

And their weekend away was truly wonderful with tennis, golf and delicious food. Fay treasured her beautiful brooch.

'You know Fay,' Jaime said on the drive home. 'I'm technically married, but that's all. When Leon is older I will ask Connie for a divorce. Can you be patient for me, Darling?'

Fay rested her hand on his leg, and it was all the answer he needed.

~

When Fay arrived home at 7.30pm on Sunday night, Lillian was waiting on the front veranda.

'The Mater is getting suspicious. She spotted Judy Reid in the city on Saturday morning and you told her she was going away with you. You'd better think up something fast!'

Fay put her suitcase in their bedroom then walked anxiously down the hall. William, her father, was in the lounge room reading the newspaper, whisky glass in hand.

'How was your weekend? Did you enjoy yourself?'

'I had a great time, Daddy, but I'm tired so I'll be heading off to bed soon.'

Her mother appeared. 'I want a word with you, Fay.'

She followed her mother into the kitchen, trying to keep her expression neutral.

'So, who did you spend the weekend with?' she asked.

'What do you mean?'

'It wasn't Judy.'

'Judy couldn't come, so May took her place.' She avoided her mother's eyes. 'I forgot to tell you.'

'I hope you're telling me the truth Fay. Your reputation is in your hands.'

'I know, Mother. Please don't worry. You can ask May next time she comes for tea.'

Fay was about to leave when Annie noticed the sparkling brooch on her lapel.

'Where did you get that brooch?'

Fay hesitated then forced a smile. 'The girls at work all chipped in and bought it for my birthday. Weren't they sweet?'

She gave her mother a kiss on the cheek, and returned to her bedroom where Lillian was waiting.

'I want to hear every romantic detail!' she gushed, patting the bed. 'Sit here beside me.'

~

Jaime arrived home at Stodart Street around 8pm As soon as he walked in the door, Connie flew at him.

'It's about damn time!' she spat. 'I've been at my wit's end. Leon has a fever and I had to call the doctor. What's her name so I can tell your family?'

Jaime was aghast; the last thing he needed was Connie talking to his mother.

'I'm sorry I'm late but the tournament went longer than I anticipated,' he responded evenly. 'And stop these ridiculous accusations, it's embarrassing. Is Leon asleep? I want to see him.'

Jaime left the room, ignoring Connie's screams.

'I'll never divorce you, Jaime! I'm a San Miguel now and I plan on keeping it that way.'[6]

Jaime sat on Leon's bed, his little son was asleep and looked so peaceful, his forehead was cool and Jaime wondered whether he'd been sick at all, so he kissed his cheek and went into the kitchen. He poured a sherry and lit a cigarette, and pondered over his future. Connie would, no doubt, go on a spending spree tomorrow. He had accounts at all the major department stores, and whenever they rowed, she would buy up big. Once again, he felt the prickly, nervous itch on his neck, and he scratched away angrily.

~

Spring turned to summer and Fay made plans for her fortnight holiday. She would be returning to Dava Lodge. Jaime was spending it in Sydney, as Connie wanted to see the Sydney Harbour Bridge which had officially opened on 19 March 1932. Fay and Jaime both dreaded being apart; not seeing each other for two weeks would be hard. Fay was beginning to wonder if all the heartache was worth it. Her mother was still suspicious, and constantly lectured her on moral principals. Still, she loved her man desperately and hated the negative thoughts that would occasionally enter her head.

Jaime was leaving a few days prior to Christmas and would be away for New Year's Eve. Fay was leaving on Boxing Day with Judy Reid, and they would share a room.

Dava Lodge, Mornington

30 December 1932

My Darling,

Here I am again and wishing so hard you were here with me that I almost feel that the wish would come true. Well, my Darling, how are you? Missing me as much as I'm missing you? Darling, every hour of the day I'm thinking of you — wondering what you are doing in Sydney and thinking how complete this holiday would be if we were spending it together. How divinely happy we would be walking round the links together, swimming together and playing tennis. We have become so wrapped up in each other's company that it is not until we are separated like this and trying to put up with other people's company that we realise how much we mean to each other.

This morning, Judy caught the 11.15 bus back to Frankston, as her mother has fallen sick. I gave her the card to post to you, and hope she doesn't forget it. I was sorry she was leaving although it could not be helped, and I think she would have liked to stay on, because it really is ideal for a holiday.

This afternoon I played golf with two chaps (don't be alarmed darling, they were both 50ish) and I played frightfully. I suppose I tried too hard because one of them saw me hitting some good drives yesterday with Judy and he said I would 'probably give him a whipping' (his exact words). Well, Darling, I let your expert tuition down badly, but I will show them how I can redeem myself.

After golf we went for a swim — that is — most of the crowd from the house, and I came back with some of the girls and played two sets of tennis before dinner, so you cannot wonder that I am tired out by nine o'clock because after dinner we all go for a stroll down the road and back before dusk. We sit in the lounge for a while (some playing cards) but not being an expert, I don't bother, and they play for money, so am not providing them with cigarette money!

And now, my Darling, I'm scribbling this before I turn in and am feeling a trifle tired, so I bid you good night.

With all my love,

Fay

The following evening was New Year's Eve, and some more guests arrived. One of them was named Frank Birt. Fay had met him at one of the Malvern Younger Set's dances, prior to meeting Jaime. He was a farmer with a large dairy farm at Lietchville, in the Murray Valley District in northern Victoria, and he had danced with Fay most of the night. She had hoped to see him again but he had returned to the farm the following morning.

Tall with dark brown hair, caramel eyes and a fashionable moustache, Frank Birt was an extremely handsome man. As soon as he spotted Fay in the dining room, he approached her table.

'Fay, how lovely to see you again. How long are you here for?'

'My goodness, Frank Birt! How *are* you? Please join us.'

He sat down next to her.

Over dinner, Fay told Frank all about the activities the guesthouse provided; she said she was booked in until 8 January, whereas he was leaving on the 6th.

'Well, at least we have the New Year and five days and nights to share. What have they planned for tonight?' He gave her a wink.

Dava Lodge had hired a local orchestra to play in the adjoining lounge for the countdown to 1933. They had moved some of the tables and armchairs to create a dance floor and provided balloons, party hats, and whistles for the amusement of their guests.

The band played all the hits of 1932, including, 'Dinah', by Bing Crosby, Paul Whiteman's, 'We Just Couldn't Say Goodbye', and 'Smoke Gets in Your Eyes' by Charlie Kutz. Fay and Frank danced throughout most of the night. He was an excellent dance partner with an engaging personality and a wicked sense of humour, and for most of the night, her thoughts of Jaime dimmed. Fay had chosen her favourite evening dress for the celebrations, a rose velvet gown, with a halter necked bodice, and a skirt that flared from the hips to the hem. Frank looked elegant in a white double-breasted tuxedo, with a black tie and black trousers.

As the guests all rallied around and the band leader counted, '3, 2, 1, Happy New Year!' Frank Birt kissed Fay firmly on the lips. Although taken by surprise; after the champagne they had enjoyed and the magic of the night, Fay reciprocated his advance. The last song the band played was Cole Porter's 'Night and Day', a 1932 hit by Fred Astaire.

Night and day, you are the one
Only you beneath the moon or under the sun
Whether near to me, or far
It's no matter darling where you are
I think of you
Day and night, night and day

It was then Jaime re-entered her mind. They had danced to this song when they were at Dava Lodge in October, and had both declared this was their song. Yet he was celebrating New Year's Eve with his wife and son in Sydney, and once again she wondered sadly whether he would ever be a free man.

Stormy Weather

Jaime carefully tucked Leon into bed. They were staying at the magnificent Australia Hotel[1] in Castlereagh Street, Sydney, right in the heart of the city. The hotel was built in 1889. Sarah Berhardt had performed at the opening, and her name was the first in the hotel register. In the 1920s an extension was added, and the highlight was a circular art deco black glass staircase. Connie had insisted on two adjoining rooms, one for her and the other for Jaime and Leon. It had been an expensive holiday; the three of them had spent New Years Eve dining in the spectacular Emerald Room, with its highly decorated ceiling, regal Italian chandeliers, and leafy palm court garden. Luncheons and afternoon teas they enjoyed in the Winter Garden on the first floor of the hotel. It boasted superb food and accommodation with a hefty price.

They both agreed the Sydney Harbour Bridge was impressive, and Leon enjoyed playing in the shallows and building sandcastles on Bondi Beach. Connie spent that day on a shopping spree. Fortunately, they hadn't argued so far, and Jaime noticed how much happier Leon was. When Connie had a temper tantrum, she didn't care if Leon was within hearing range.

Jaime sat down at the writing desk in his hotel room. Leon was fast asleep and he wanted to write a postcard to Fay. He wondered how her New Year's Eve had gone, and how many men she had danced with. He hoped she was missing him as much as he was missing her. He began writing, knowing he could slip down early in the morning and post it at the front desk before Connie woke up.

> *Sydney, 1 January 1933, 1am*
> *My darling Fay,*
> *I am just having my first opportunity of dropping you a line. I hope you had a safe and pleasant trip to Mornington; you were in my thoughts all the time. I tried to visualise what you might be doing every day, and had a mental picture before me. I do miss you and wish I was with you more than anything I know. Though I love holidays, it won't be too bad to be back at work, so as to see you every day. Yes, darling, I am crazy about you. I realise it when we are parted, for even a few days only. Please think a little of me, won't you? Because I am very jealous when you are away from me.*
> *With all my love,*
> *Your Silent Witness xxxx*
>
> *PS I will write you again if possible.*

Jaime had recently started signing his letters and cards without using his name. They had had a few scares when Fay's office staff had read the notes attached to flowers delivered.

Meanwhile, in Mornington, Fay and Frank spent each day and evening together. They swam, played tennis and went for long moonlit walks. He invited her to his property for a holiday in the fresh country air and told Fay they would ride horses around the vast paddocks. He was smitten, and although she liked him very much, her heart still belonged to Jaime. Still, she began to think that maybe she would grow to love Frank. He was a free man, after all, and the dairy farm provided him with a good income. She felt her parents would approve, and the only drawback was that he was a Protestant — she doubted he would ever convert to Catholicism. However, even if she waited for Jaime, they could never marry in a Catholic Church if he was divorced. On the morning he was leaving, Frank gave Fay his Exchange telephone number, and took note of her office number and home address, as the Johnstons didn't have a phone connected.

~

Fay re-read Jaime's letter from Sydney. Her holiday was nearing an end and she would be returning home the following day. She knew he would be phoning her at the office on Monday and she still didn't know what to say. He'd only sent the one letter, so she assumed his family holiday had gone well. She also knew how much he adored his son and wanted to make him happy, so perhaps it would be best to move on with Frank.

When she arrived back at Tooronga Road on Sunday night, Fay told the whole family about Frank Birt. Both parents suggested she invite him for afternoon tea, as soon as could be arranged, whereas Lillian was rather concerned about Jaime's reaction. She had grown fond of her sister's secret beau.

Sure enough, on Monday morning Fay received a call from Jaime suggesting they meet for lunch. She nervously agreed to meet him at the Teapot Inn at 1pm Shortly after his call, the desk phone rang again. This time it was Frank on a trunk call from his property. He was coming to Melbourne for the weekend, staying at the Victoria Hotel[2] in Little Collins Street, and he wanted to see her. Trying to think rationally, she invited him to tea at her home on Saturday afternoon, and he suggested they dine out at his hotel afterwards. Encouraged by her enthusiasm, Frank also asked her to meet him for drinks on Friday evening, and to perhaps catch a movie. Fay agreed though Friday night had always belonged to Jaime. Despite her trepidation, she would have to find a way to explain her new circumstances at lunchtime.

As Jaime hurried down Flinders Street on his way to meet Fay, he couldn't help but feel a little disconcerted. She had sounded different and aloof on the telephone that morning; he prayed her feelings had not changed. He arrived at the café at a minute to one, grabbed a table by the window, and shakily lit a cigarette. When Fay walked in a few minutes later, he knew something was wrong.

'Darling!' he gushed as he helped her remove her jacket. 'I've missed you so much.'

Fay remained silent as she sat down. Their usual waitress arrived with a menu, and Fay ordered the soup while Jaime opted for corned beef sandwiches.

'So, how was your holiday?' Fay said finally.

Jaime leaned forward. 'It was actually quite pleasant. Connie was on her best behaviour and Leon had a terrific time, but I missed you terribly.' At her silence, he added, 'Darling, is something wrong?'

Fay struggled in her reply. 'You know I love you Jaime,' she began, looking down, 'but I loathe being the 'other' woman. It's not who I am.'

Jaime gripped her hand, willing her to look at him. 'You know I'll leave Connie, but it will take time. You promised to be patient. Have you forgotten? Or is this about something else? Or — ' He released her hand. 'Someone else?'

They were interrupted as the waitress served their lunch. Jaime pushed the plate of sandwiches away and lit another cigarette, puffing anxiously.

Fay toyed with her soup. 'Actually, I did meet someone,' she said, trying to sound casual. 'At Dava Lodge. He seems very keen and is coming to Melbourne this weekend. I want to see how it goes.'

Jaime's face betrayed a look of horror, though he fought to stay calm. He butted out his cigarette and glanced out the window.

'Who is he?' he said coldly. 'Is he from interstate?'

When Fay did not respond right away, Jaime turned back to her. 'Did he make love to you?'

Other diners were starting to stare at the couple.

'No,' Fay almost whispered. 'He's a farmer from the Murray Valley. That's all I want to say for now.'

'Will I see you on Friday? What does this mean?'

Fay put her spoon down; she had lost her appetite. 'No, I don't think I should see you anymore. Connie is already suspicious, as is my mother. Perhaps you should stay married; after all, Leon is still so young.' She stood up and retrieved her jacket and handbag. 'I'm leaving now. I have some shopping to do. Goodbye, Jaime.'

Jaime sat in shock as Fay scurried out of the restaurant. The waitress came over.

'Is everything alright, sir? Neither of you have touched your lunch!'

Jaime didn't reply and just requested the bill. He paid in a hurry, feeling totally bewildered on the walk back to work.

Fay walked along Collins Street, overcome with emotion. She still had a half hour before she was due back at the office, so she cut through the Block Arcade and walked up Bourke Street towards Manton's Department Store. She made her way through the art deco store in a daze, stopping to examine some gloves.

The shop assistant came over. 'These only came in this morning, Madam; we have them in many other colours.'

Fay picked up a navy blue pair. 'These will be fine, thankyou.'

Perhaps, she thought, a new purchase would lessen the pain.

The afternoon seemed to drag on and on; Mr Rostren was out of the office and had only left her with a couple of letters to type, and these she had finished as soon as she returned from lunch. She took out a fresh sheet of paper and inserted it in the typewriter and began a letter to Jaime.

9 January 1933

Dear Jaime,

After I left you this afternoon I have been doing a good deal of thinking and, as I told you, I have come to the conclusion that it would be better to stop seeing one another. To be honest, it has nothing to do with my seeing Frank. I know it is going to be terribly hard but I will really have to try and put you out of my life. You will probably wonder why I have made up my mind about this so suddenly, but after some of those remarks you made today concerning C, I have realised that perhaps, indirectly, I am the cause of it all. You see, Darling, you may not be upsetting her intentionally, but if you have me in your thoughts just as often as I have you (and I think you have), well, you would find it very difficult — in fact, impossible — to show very much interest or enthusiasm in another person's affairs. With me out of your thoughts, things might be different. I have been putting myself in her place and know just how I would feel if someone I liked very much seemed just casual or indifferent.

Darling, do not think I am lecturing or blaming you because I know just how good and generous you are, but I do know this: that if we stopped seeing one another it might make your home affairs very much happier. I should hate to think that I am standing in the way of another person's happiness when that person has a perfect right to that happiness and I have not (where you are concerned). Do not think this has just been an impulse, or the spur of the moment — I have known it for a long time and have never had the courage to face it. I can see where it is leading and it would be very unfair of me not to try and do something towards making it right for the one referred to above.

Time will not permit me to say anymore but try and understand how I feel about it — and if you don't help me, I am helpless to help myself because I know how weak I am when it comes to you. We must both be strong, especially for little Leon's sake.

Goodbye, Darling,

Fay

She read it through, addressed an envelope to his Dunlop office and put a stamp on it, then popped downstairs to post it. She wanted to get rid of it before she lost her nerve.

～

Jaime felt like his whole world had crumbled when he returned to the office; he couldn't believe what had just occurred. Perhaps Fay would have second thoughts — this shred of hope was all that kept him going through the rest of the day.

When he arrived home that evening, Connie was in a hysterical state. She had found an old statement from their Georges account, and noticed the purchase of the brooch that he bought for Fay in October.

'Who did you buy it for?' she yelled, her face red. 'One of your lovers?'

Jaime didn't have time to reply; the telephone rang, and Jaime picked up the receiver. It was his mother, Rebecca.

'I had a very distressful call from Connie today,' was her greeting. 'Whatever is going on?'

Jaime wondered if his day could get any worse. 'Oh Mother, it was a complete misunderstanding. I do hope you were caused no grief.' He glared at Connie. 'I've just explained it all to Connie and I assure you that she is fine now.'

Connie threw a disgusted look at him and left the room.

'Jaime, she seems to think that you're seeing other women' his mother continued sternly. 'I can only hope it isn't so. The San Miguel family will not tolerate any scandals!'

By the time he got off the phone, Connie had retired to her bedroom. As per usual there was nothing for dinner. Leon was already asleep when he looked in on his son, so he poured a sherry and sat down in the drawing room, and wondered why his life was in such disarray. Jaime put a phonograph on his Melola player, a 1930 recording of Cole Porter's 'What Is This Thing Called Love', by Leo Reisman and His Orchestra, one of his favourite big bands.

When the song ended he looked at his diary, he'd lightly pencilled in each Friday with a small 'f' to represent his nights with Fay. He wouldn't be seeing her this Friday 13 January 1933, and he thought to himself, everything that broke his heart seemed to occur around the thirteenth.

When Fay arrived home from work, she told her mother about Frank's phone call and the afternoon tea she had planned. Over dinner, Annie said she would make fresh scones, and Lillian would bake a sponge cake for the occasion. Both Annie and William were already impressed with the size of Frank's property; they had heard his family were also very well respected in the Murray Valley District.

In bed that night Fay wondered how she would ever cope with not seeing Jaime; at least she had the weekend to look forward to. She prayed to Saint Anthony to help her find love with Frank — it would be the only way she could get over Jaime. Still, her dreams that night featured both men, and she woke in a panic after dreaming they had a fist fight.

On Tuesday afternoon, Jaime received Fay's letter and realised she was serious about not seeing him any more. He noticed she had written the farmer's name, Frank, and he was both jealous and curious as to whom this man was, and whether he had really stolen Fay's heart. He decided to wait until Sunday, when he hoped to see her at Mass.

It was a long week, but finally Friday arrived. Frank had phoned Fay on Thursday, and asked her to meet him in the foyer of the Victoria Hotel at 5.30pm He suggested they have drinks and dine at the hotel, before catching a film he had heard was extremely entertaining. The weather had been very humid all week, so Fay had chosen a wrap-around candy-stripe cotton dress with a heart-shaped décolletage, white heels, and a matching white handbag and gloves. Fay had a real flair for fashion, and as she received an excellent pay package, was able to afford the latest designs. Lillian, on the other hand, made her own clothes, and waited for Fay's hand-me-downs.

Just before 5.30, she entered the foyer and spotted Frank straight away, dressed casually in a twill weave shirt and cream trousers, chatting to a desk clerk. He hadn't noticed her so she tapped him on the shoulder.

'How about buying me a drink!'

He swung round and immediately kissed her on the cheek.

'How delightful to see you again, Fay. Yes, let's have that drink!'

He ushered her into the lounge. The evening was extremely pleasant; they both chatted effortlessly and the dinner was first-class. Frank said he had booked seats for the 1932 film, *Forbidden,* directed by Frank Capra, and starring Barbara Stanwyk and Adolphe Menjou. It had only just been released in Australia. They walked to the Capitol Theatre[3] close by on Swanston Street. It was still very warm and the sky was ablaze with stars. He held her hand as they crossed from the Melbourne Town Hall and walked the short distance to the theatre. Frank purchased a box of chocolate-coated scorched almonds for Fay from the kiosk, and then they took their seats. The film told the story of a librarian who falls in love with a married man, with tragic consequences. Fay shed a few tears, hoping Frank wouldn't notice.

'Just goes to show,' Frank commented when the lights came on, 'no one should get involved with a married man.'

They had a light supper at the Victoria Hotel then Frank asked the porter to arrange a cab for Fay's journey home, giving her the fare money for the ride. As she climbed into the car she said, 'Thank you again for a lovely night, I'll see you tomorrow at three o'clock for afternoon tea.'

~

Fay's mother took out the Noritake china tea set and her best linen; she wanted to make a good impression on the farmer. For quite a while she had been concerned about Fay in regards to who she might be secretly seeing. The weekends Fay had claimed were spent with Judy or May seemed a trifle suspicious. When she had questioned May Wilson on one occasion, the girl appeared nervous and red-faced. Annie wondered if perhaps her eldest daughter was getting involved in an indiscreet affair.

A few minutes after three, Frank knocked on the front door.

Fay's father answered it and led him into the lounge room. He had bought flowers and chocolates as a token gift, which thrilled Annie, disregarding the fact that one of the gifts was for Fay. The afternoon tea was a great success; the whole family liked Frank Birt very much, even Harry, who only stayed a short while, as he had to meet his girl, Marie Cameron, who both Annie and William disliked. Only Lillian was dismayed, although she thought Frank a very pleasant chap. She knew that Fay could never love him as she did Jaime and she couldn't imagine Fay coping with farm life.

Frank had arranged for a cab to pick himself and Fay up at 5pm, so he bid goodbye to the Johnston family and thanked Annie profusely. They would have drinks and dine early, as he had to rise at 6am on Sunday to return to the farm. They arrived at the Victoria Hotel and entered the lounge where he ordered them both drinks.

'I've booked a table at the Windsor Hotel tonight; we can catch a tram there, or take a leisurely walk.'

Not the Windsor, Fay thought to herself, another reminder of Jaime. Regardless, she did enjoy herself thoroughly, and when Frank asked her to come to the farm for the weekend after next, she accepted. He softly kissed her goodnight. Nevertheless, she wondered what he would expect of her when she stayed with him as sleeping with Frank was out of the question.

Sunday was blue-skied and hot and Annie felt the heat too much for her to attend Mass, so Fay and Lillian went without her. Jaime was late and took a seat in a back pew, craning his neck to spot Fay. After Mass he approached her and Lillian and Lillian tactfully excused herself.

'I received your letter,' he said. 'So you are truly adamant about all of this?'

She looked around nervously, hoping nobody could hear them. When she didn't respond, Jaime pressed on.

'Are you happy?'

Fay understood the pain in his eyes, and felt equally saddened, but she was determined.

'Oh Jaime, this is so hard for me. Please don't make it even worse.'

He ignored her. 'How is Frank?'

'It's early days yet and I'm still very confused,' she said. 'But one thing I know is that I can never see you again.'

She found her sister and they returned home.

~

Fay didn't hear anymore from Jaime and made plans for her weekend in Leitchville with Frank. She was catching a train on Saturday morning, 28 January, and Frank was meeting her at Pyramid Hill Station, nearby. Her mother, of course, had given her another lecture about moral behaviour.

'By the time you're married, you'll have to put up with letting your husband have his way and believe me, it isn't pleasant!'

Fay rolled her eyes. She didn't dare point out that her mother had been pregnant with Fay's older brother Harry *before* she had married their father.

Summer was at its hottest, although when Fay arrived at Spencer Street Station early on Saturday morning, she read in the newspaper that a few showers were forecast for the day. She hoped they would ease and not spoil her weekend away. She arrived mid morning at her destination, and Frank was waiting on the platform. He looked very different, dressed in an open neck white cotton shirt, work overalls, and a Stetson type hat. They drove to the large dairy farm in Frank's 1922 Mack pick-up truck, just as the rain began to fall. As they entered the homestead, Fay saw what a vast property he owned. Frank pointed out the old barn with its ramshackle roof and rickety wooden building. He insisted the rain would be gone by lunchtime and they would spend the afternoon riding around the paddocks, where they could view his stock of cows.

When they came into the house, Frank's mother and youngest

sister were in the kitchen making tea and they both made a fuss of Fay when he introduced them. Frank showed Fay the guest room where she could freshen up, and she was relieved to have a room to herself. Frank's father had died a couple of years before, and his eldest sister was married and living in Gunbower, a town nearby. Another son had died in infancy. At the large kitchen table they drank tea and nibbled on hot buttered scones, fresh cream from their own produce, and homemade strawberry jam. As Frank had forecasted, the rain soon eased, so he gave her a tour of part of the property, explaining the rest would be done on horseback. Although Fay had never ridden before, Frank said he would give her a quick lesson, assuring her that the horse was extremely docile.

After lunch they saddled up and Fay soon felt relaxed on her mount — she was a quick learner. Frank took her into the dairy sheds, and showed her the latest milking techniques, and also introduced her to two of his workers. She was having the time of her life! The clouds had all but disappeared and the sun blazed down on them as they rode around the farm.

'I hope you brought a pretty dress,' Frank said. 'We're off to a dance tonight at the local hall. I want you to meet my friends. We'll have a gay old time!'

Fay had packed lightly, but included a lilac cotton sundress, which would be perfect for the dance. Country life was turning out to be more enjoyable than she had anticipated.

They ate a luscious roast dinner with all the trimmings, followed by homemade apple pie and cream, and then drove into the small township to attend the dance. Frank was very popular, and everyone gathered around to meet his new beau. A local band had been hired, and a small bar set up selling an assortment of alcoholic beverages. Frank had a beer, while Fay settled on a glass of bubbly, and they danced the night away.

The nearest Catholic Church was too far to walk to, and as Frank had early morning chores he couldn't drive Fay, so she had to miss her Sunday morning Mass. The train was leaving in the early afternoon, so she made the most of her time left, taking in the clear country air and glorious sunshine with another ride on the chestnut, Peggy. When Frank was free he joined her, and this time they took a longer ride, with Fay even experiencing a trot.

'I'll be back in Melbourne in a couple of weeks, so we must spend it together,' he said as they stopped for a rest under a large gum tree.

Already, Fay knew she wanted to spend more time with him; it certainly was helping to soothe her broken heart.

Mrs Birt told Fay she was welcome to stay with them at any time, and emphasised that she hoped to have her as a guest again very soon. Fay bid them goodbye and Frank drove her to the station. He kissed her farewell, promising to phone her at the office this week.

'You certainly have made a good impression on Mother!' he exclaimed. 'You're welcome here any time.'

They waved as the train pulled out of the station, then Fay settled into a carriage for the journey to Melbourne.

~

Jaime had discreetly interrogated 18-year-old Lillian after Mass on Sunday about Frank and Fay's courtship. He was at his wits end to learn she was at the farm for the weekend. He missed her desperately and yearned for their daily lunches and Friday nights together. To take his mind off her, he had been bringing Leon to Montalegre on Friday evenings to spend time with his mother, Rebecca, and Aunt Ines. Occasionally, Connie would join them for dinner. In the past he had always told her Fridays were spent at his Men's Club in the city with John Cook, but of course, Connie was still suspicious.

His mother didn't realise how disruptive their marriage was, and Connie's 'sickness', her depression, was never discussed. Her looks were starting to fade and her weight had ballooned due to her constant time in bed and the lithium medication she was taking. Regardless, the depression and paranoid episodes continued.

Jaime spent most weekends on the golf links or tennis court, and he also regularly attended football matches at Xavier College. He'd played in his school days, and was regarded as a champion. Many of the students took his advice about their game. Jaime often took Leon with him to a match and hot days they would spend at the beach. Nonetheless he still held hopes that Fay would return to him. He'd recently purchased a new record, 'Stormy Weather', written by Harold Arlen and Ted Koehler, and recorded by Leo Reisman and His Orchestra.

> *Don't know why there's no sun up in the sky*
> *Stormy weather*
> *Since my gal and I ain't together*
> *Keeps rainin' all the time*
> *Life is bare*
> *Gloom and misery everywhere*
> *Stormy weather*

The words seemed all too true about his life at present.

A Marriage Proposal

The months rolled by and Fay and Frank spent more and more time together. He came to Melbourne each fortnight, and she regularly stayed at the farm. She attended country race meetings with him, and they often had a picnic at some picturesque location. He had made attempts for their relationship to become more intimate, but Fay wasn't at all ready. Jaime was still in her thoughts, and she wondered if she'd ever really get over him.

Easter was approaching and Fay was spending it at the farm. She had asked Mr Rostren to allow her Thursday 13 April off so she could have the whole holiday at Leitchville. The train pulled into the station at noon. It was perfect Easter weather; although the nights were cool, the days were filled with sunny skies.

Saturday was spent riding; Fay had become rather attached to Peggy, and by now felt totally at home in the saddle. Frank's family adored her, and so did his friends. On the surface, things seemed perfect.

After dinner that evening, he suggested they take a stroll in the moonlight, the stars were at their brightest, and they seemed so much bigger in the vast country sky. Frank seemed a little nervous as they walked along the dirt track. He stopped when they reached the barn, stubbed out his cigarette, then cleared his throat.

'Fay,' he began, 'I've been thinking a lot about how much I enjoy spending time with you. My family thinks you're wonderful, and farm life seems to agree with you.' He paused and took her hands. 'Would you consider marrying me?'

Before she could answer, he rushed on: 'Look, I haven't had time to buy a ring yet, but if you accept, we can shop for it together. I love you Fay and you love me, don't you?'

He leaned back on the rustic fence, clearly relieved to have revealed his true feelings.

Fay was flabbergasted. She knew he was keen on her, but had no idea he was this serious.

'Oh Frank,' she said after a moment. 'I'm very flattered, and I care for you very much, but I don't think I'm ready to commit myself to marriage just yet. We have an issue with our religious differences, and there's so much to consider before I could accept your proposal. Give me some time to think about it?'

Frank took her hand and gave it a gentle squeeze. 'Of course I'll give you time. I do realise it would be a tremendous change in your life, moving up here and not working, but I'm sure you'll take to it like a duck to water!'

~

The following morning, Frank gave Fay a lift to Mass and picked up from where they left off.

'I know your faith is very important to you,' he stated, 'but I'm not at all religious. All the same, I'd prefer if we do marry. Our children would be brought up as Church of England, like my family. I hope you understand.'

When Fay left Leitchville on Monday afternoon she had much to think about. Should she accept Frank's proposal? She was fond of him, and was sure that he would be a good husband, still, the passion and love she'd shared with Jaime made her question her decision.

~

Jaime had stopped attending Mass at Saint Joseph's and now went to Our Lady of Victories on Burke Road, Camberwell. He had often been tempted to phone Fay at the office, but whenever he began to dial the number, he lost his nerve and hung up the receiver. His pride couldn't take another rejection.

A couple of weeks after Easter, Fay was walking along Swanston Street during her lunch hour when she saw Jaime coming towards her. He was on his way back to Dunlop's after having a bite to eat. Her heart began to race, and she was almost tempted to run in the opposite direction. However, she stayed calm, and when he put out his hand to shake hers, she returned the gesture.

'Hello,' he said kindly. 'It's been a long time. How are you?'

How had she almost forgotten his beautiful smile?

'I'm very well, and you?'

All the old memories came flooding back, and she wondered why he still made her feel this way.

'I'm quite well,' he replied, though not very convincingly. 'Do you have time for a quick cup of tea? There's a cafeteria across the road.'

He took her arm as they crossed the road and entered the café. They found a vacant table, and then Jaime bought two cups of tea and sat down opposite her.

'I've missed you terribly,' he said quietly.

Fay stirred some sugar into her cup before replying. 'Things have changed, Jaime. Frank has asked me to marry him.'

'Do you love him?'

Fay shifted uneasily in her seat. 'I haven't accepted yet.'

'You didn't answer my question, Do you love him?'

'That will come in time.'

Jaime took out his cigarette case and held Fay's hand. 'I am very much in love with you and that will never change. I do hope you think very seriously about this.'

Wednesday, 3 May 1933

Darling,

I am writing this note as a friend and advisor only. I have thought very seriously over your perplexities, and am going to endeavour to write what I think.

Don't under any circumstances entirely give up your religion. You would live to regret it. It would not be now but the passing years that would tell the tale. Marry the man by all means if you feel that way, but don't let him interfere with your religion. For after all, the next life is the most important thing. If he really loves you, he would have no objections to not interfering in your religious ideals.

Secondly, don't marry in haste. Think carefully first whether you are both in love, as you will be a long time married. After all, you never get to know a person properly until you live with them. Become engaged, or have some understanding by all means, but get to know one another first. See lots of each other, and see if you are suited. If he loves you and you him, you will both be willing to wait, and then you will know your own mind and have no regrets.

The third thing and a very important one, is your future life and living. You will be going to a very, very different life to what you are used to, that lonely and forsaken place. See and know what might be in store for you. If you are in love, well, you will be prepared to accept those responsibilities as part of your life. But don't go up married in the flush of excitement and think romance will always be there. For eventually romance somewhat dies, and then you have to face cold, hard facts.

I am not saying these things to take away a wonderful chance, but just trying to give you sound advice. My only wish is that you do the right thing for your happiness, and remember this — if it is a love affair, love will find a way. But if it isn't, beware, as it is better to be single and happy, even poor, than married and unhappy.

Your Silent Witness, again.

〜

Fay walked up William Street in the city. It was dusk, and starting to turn a little chilly. She was on her way to the Menzies Hotel.[1] Frank had asked her to meet him for a drink, and she had decided it was time to give him an answer to his marriage proposal. It had been weighing on her mind for a couple of weeks, and Jaime's letter had made it even harder to reach a sensible decision. Still, he had made some interesting points.

She wandered through the majestic foyer, with the classic cream and gold columns, admiring the Persian rugs spread on the wooden parquetry floor. The lounge area was beginning to fill up, with everyone gathering for a Friday night drink with their friends. She spotted Frank at a table near the bar and approached him.

'Good evening,' she said, kissing him on the cheek. 'How was the train trip?'

'Actually, I just made it to the station. Daisy delivered her calf at dawn.' They continued the chit-chat for the next half an hour.

Fay sat forward. 'Frank,' she said quietly, 'I've made a decision about your proposal'.

'Oh?'

'I can't accept. I'm extremely fond of you Frank, but there are our religious differences, and I love my job, my family and friends. I just don't think I could stick out life on a farm permanently.'

Frank lit a cigarette and sat back in his chair, he inhaled deeply before replying. 'I see, well I have to say I'm frightfully disappointed, I really thought we could be happy together. I'll certainly miss you, Fay.'

∾

Lillian was up waiting for Fay when she arrived home.

'Did you tell him?'

'Yes. It's over.'

Lillian handed Fay her nightgown. 'So when are you going to see Jaime?'

Fay sat down at the dressing table and picked up her brush. She toyed with it for a moment, eyeing herself in the mirror, before letting it fall to the ground. Lillian rushed over and put her arms around her sister, who silently wept into her shoulder long into the night.

∽

As Jaime didn't attend Saint Joseph's anymore, Fay wondered if he had done as she'd asked, and made a go of his marriage with Connie. Fay had tried so hard to fall in love with Frank but her feelings for Jaime were more tangible than ever. She missed everything they shared. the daily lunches, their Friday nights, the tennis matches and golf games, but most of all those precious, loving escapades. Anxious as she was to telephone Jaime, Fay kept putting it off. Then one afternoon Judy Reid showed up at her office.

'Fay, I just had to tell you, I ran into Jaime at lunchtime and told him you had turned Frank down. Expect to hear from him very soon. You should have seen the relieved look on his face. Poor dear.'

When Fay finished work that afternoon, Jaime was waiting outside Chancery House. Nothing was said at first; they walked to a nearby arcade, and then he took her into his arms.

'My Darling,' he murmured into her hair. 'Never leave me again.'

Our Love Was Meant To Be

It was a strange relationship Jaime had with Connie. His friend John Cooke had hit the nail on the head when he stated Jaime had married Connie on the rebound from Ally — he had been mesmerised by Connie's beauty, and hadn't looked much further. It was a colourless marriage, yet he felt sorry for Connie and knew she had emotional problems; at the time, however, that was something no doctor could cure.

Now that Fay was back in his life, the traumas at home affected him less. He had come to accept the regular outbursts, and always tried to avoid Leon being a witness. By now, Fay had met the little boy, who she thought was adorable. She yearned to bear a child with Jaime herself one day. They were always extremely careful during lovemaking — a pregnancy would cause far too many problems for them both. Fay continued to dream of the time Jaime would be free and they could marry.

Christmas of 1934 and the New Year, Fay spent in Sydney. Judy now had a car and they'd decided to drive there. Jaime was at Mornington with Connie and Leon as keeping up appearances was all too important.

Mornington

Sunday, 30 December 1934

My darling Fay,

I am writing this note at the same beautiful spot as I wrote that little note to you last year. It is a cosy little spot overlooking the bay, and the day is beautiful. Everything reminds me of you. But, alas, you are missing. Fancy twelve months since I wrote you that last letter, and I am still writing such another after all this time, darling.

Well, Sweetheart, thanks awfully for that lovely letter from Sydney. It was sweet of you to write me that nice long note. I was just dying to know how you had got on on the trip across. My old heart gave a great leap when I got it, as I wasn't sure if you would have time to write it. You made one mistake — you forgot to put Victoria on the address and the letter travelled around New South Wales a bit before I finally got it yesterday. However, better late than never.

I posted you a letter card last Thursday to Coogee. I do hope you got it before you left on your return home. I know you would be terribly disappointed if you didn't receive it, and so would I.

Fay, Darling, I must congratulate you and Judy on the splendid time you made to Sydney, it was pretty quick going with an old car. I never dreamed you would get there much before Xmas day. That is why your little Xmas present (your letter) was such an adorable surprise. My thoughts were with you on the whole of your journey, and I tried to picture myself with you on the trip. In fact, I am thinking of you all day and every day.

Do you know, Dear, three years ago, I myself yearned for your company while I was in Sydney, then here last year I wanted you, and now again I still want you. It's terrible, isn't it?

Fancy you striking the kangaroos! I heard they were very bad on the Sydney highway, and as for the heat around Gundagai, don't I remember it. I think you will enjoy the return trip around the coast much better, and I am glad you are giving yourself a little more time in which to do it. I shall be thinking of you, trusting you are enjoying the beautiful scenery.

Well Fay, one does get that first impression of yours of Sydney, if you travel around the city and suburbs, but if you get on the harbour often, and visit their beauty spots, then you will begin to appreciate the beauty of that city. Darling, how I wish and wish that I was with you, to show you everything nice over there. I wonder whether I will ever have that privilege.

If you feel inclined, you could drop me a line, as before, to Mornington, so as I could get it about Thursday next. We will be returning home on Saturday, and I shall be looking forward to seeing you.

I am having a very nice time down here, and on the whole, the weather has been excellent. There is a fairly nice crowd here, and of course, the beach and swimming is beautiful. We have had the usual golf and tennis tournaments, and yours truly pulled off the tennis trophy, winning the final with my partner.

Well, Darling, it is getting late and I must hurry away from you, otherwise they will wonder where I am. I do hope you have a safe and pleasant trip, and that this will give you a surprise when you get home.

I am just dying to see you at lunch at the Sonora on Tuesday the 8th. Though it seems wicked, I must see and have your company lots and lots in 1935, as I cannot help not meeting you till so late in life. And now I have met you, I just want you and cannot do without you.

With all my love from your Silent Witness

PS Don't forget to destroy this.

Although Jaime thought it a risk to send the letter to Tooronga Road, he also knew Lillian collected the mail, and would keep the letter hidden from her parents.

Fay was excited when Lillian handed her the envelope, and she cherished every word.

Monday, 7 January 1935
Midnight
My Darling,

By the above you will see it is well past my bedtime. I have just arrived home from the pictures, and before turning in, I thought I would say goodnight to you.

Darling, it seems too good to be true that I am going to see you tomorrow after this long, long time. It has seemed ages. I went to the pictures tonight to make tomorrow come more quickly. I hope you had a safe trip back, and sorry to hear the car has been giving you so much trouble. Perhaps it has been playing up because it misses my company, or our company together. I don't think I will be able to eat any breakfast tomorrow morning, I shall be so excited about seeing you.

Well, to make tomorrow come all the quicker, I will now say goodnight, Darling, and will dream of tomorrow.

All my love,
Fay

~

Annie and William were disappointed that Fay had turned Frank down. Both thought the farmer was a good catch, and now Annie's suspicions had returned; she was sure her eldest daughter was seeing someone else and that concerned her. Harry had become engaged to Marie Cameron Blackwell,[1] much to Annie's dismay. The girl came from a very poor background, and she didn't think her good enough for her only son; what's more, she wasn't a Catholic.

Regardless, Harry and Marie married in a side chapel of Saint Patricks Cathedral,[2] Melbourne, on 17 August 1935. In attendance were Fay and Lillian, Con Norris and his wife, Brenda, plus nine other guests. After the ceremony they adjourned to the New Treasury Hotel to celebrate the occasion, winding up with dinner at the London Inn in Market Street. Annie and William refused to attend both the ceremony and the reception which upset Harry greatly.

Lillian had turned twenty-one in January, and taken a job as a sales assistant at Foy and Gibson Limited[3], a department store in the city. She could no longer tolerate being stuck at home all day with her mother, and she wanted to earn her own money and make a better life for herself. Lillian had been at home since she had left school at age fourteen. She was now a member of the Malvern Younger Set, and had taken up tennis and attended a number of dances, although she still hadn't met a young man who had asked her out. She envied Fay's torrid romance, regardless of the trying circumstances.

Fay and Jaime loved the summer holidays, yet both knew it was the time they would spend apart. They still managed to escape for occasional weekends away, and these were treasured like priceless pearls. During Christmas of 1935, Jaime was in Sydney, and Fay was at Mornington.

Mornington,
28 December 1935
Hello Darling,

Once again I am with you in the spirit, and wish it was in the flesh. How are you enjoying yourself? To the utmost, I hope, but not flirting too much, are you? Perhaps you have fallen madly in love with some Sydney blonde or brunette? Well, if you have I will still keep on loving you and hating her.

On Boxing Day we were just coming back from a swim (early in the afternoon, as we had had a late breakfast, missed lunch and were feeling like some afternoon tea) and who should we meet on their way for a game of tennis, none other than Alex and a friend of his named Laurie, who also toils at your worthy establishment. So they came back with us and we introduced them to a tennis court, which is right opposite our house. Beautiful courts too, just been freshly coated. They invited us over for a game, and we had some excellent tennis. They came round in the evening but it was a very quiet one, as there was a fairly big crowd at the house the night before, and Alex and

Laurie had to entertain eight of us (all girls). We played cards and then had supper. Alex and Laurie insisted on becoming very domesticated and washed and dried up. I had a quiet little chat with Alex and he wanted to know, why didn't I go to Sydney with you? I think he must have noticed the love light in my eyes when he mentioned your name, and told me I should have gone with you and what a marvellous time I was missing.

Darling, every day I wonder what you are doing and where you are going and wish I was with you. I received a letter from the Mater today, and she was saying that she heard a report over the wireless that they were having plenty of rain in Sydney. I also had a look at today's Sun and was surprised to read of more floods down the Gippsland area. I hope you were well on the way before it started.

It is rather distracting trying to write a letter on holidays, especially with a crowd of gossiping girls, so I will have to save the rest of the news until I see you. I am writing this down on the sand, so you will excuse the writing and pencil. Hoping you are having an enjoyable holiday, and perhaps think of me occasionally?

All my love,

Fay

PS My bathing suit is the snappiest thing in Mornington — an absolute riot!

PPS I suppose you have received my last letter written on Xmas day? I am still waiting anxiously for a letter from you.

It was nearly a week before Fay received a letter card in return.

Sydney, 31 December 1935

My dear Fay,

No doubt you will be disappointed at not having heard from me before, but really it has been almost impossible for me to write. Everywhere I have been, I have had to share bedrooms, and the chaps in the rooms have not given me much of an opportunity to write. However, I have already started a long letter to you, which is unfinished. In it I am giving you a description of my travels and doings in this State. By the way, I too was disappointed because I only got your letter today.

C is arriving by boat tomorrow, so after you get this note you had better reply to Dunlop, Melbourne, or wait till I get back. We, C and myself will probably leave for Melbourne on Sunday. I will post the other letter tonight.

Fondest Love

Fay read the card from Jaime a couple of times, then put it away in a safe place. Once again their plans had been ruined, they had organised to spend this holiday together, but Annie Johnston had intervened, insisting Fay take Lillian on holiday with her, and everything had to be cancelled. A few days after the New Year, Fay received a long letter from Jaime.

1 January 1936

My darling Fay,

Well, here goes. A Happy New Year to you. I am with you on the first day of the year as you can see. Well, Darling I have torn up the other letter I had half written, and am starting all over again, because I have a little extra news to put in, and I shall endeavour to tell you everything.

It is New Year's Day and I am going to give up my bathe in the surf this morning to write to you. By the way, I too was disappointed because I had not heard from my sweetheart, you see I made enquiries for a letter from you, both on Friday and Saturday of last week, without luck, and it wasn't until I called at the GPO on Tuesday that I got your note. I then immediately sent you a wire. I hope you got it.

Yes, Darling, the more I see of it, and the more I think of what a marvellous opportunity we missed this Xmas. Our plan would have been plain sailing all the way, and as easy and safe as it could possibly have been. We could have had a lovely holiday together, and you would have had a lovely time. There are dozens of flats at every beach resort, and nobody seems to worry about anybody else over here. We were fools, Darling, not to have grabbed our only chance. I would have loved to have had you with me to show you the things I have seen, and to do the things I have done. Much as I have enjoyed it, it would have been threefold with you. Even the journey across by car with you alone would have been easy and safe. But alas, I will just have to sigh, and think of what might have been. However, I hope you are having a lovely time at Mornington, and thoroughly enjoying yourself. But I hope not falling in love, and not too much lovemaking, as I would be terribly jealous. Don't forget you promised to tear this letter up as soon as you get it or have digested it, because it might cause unnecessary embarrassment.

I am going to make this note fairly lengthy as this might be my last chance to write because C arrives by the Nestor *tomorrow. You remember after our plans fell through, I then went ahead and made arrangements for C to come to Sydney by boat? Then the shipping strike⁴ broke out, and that also was off. Well, before I left Melbourne I told the booking agents that if by any chance a boat was available about this time, to ring up and inform C. Well, that is exactly what has occurred, and C wired to ask if she could come. She is leaving the boy at home, though I am disappointed re: him. I think possibly it will be best, as the journey back might be too tiring. The boat available is the overseas liner,* Nestor, *which is available to interstate passengers while our own local steamers are held up, owing to the strike.*

When I arrived in Sydney, I made for Bondi and booked in at the Hotel Astra (that accounts for the note paper). I liked the look of Bondi and was looking forward to a few days here, when the next morning I was told I would have to share my room. Having had to share my rooms so much previously, I was sick to death of this, so I packed up and buzzed off. I tried several places for accommodation, but they all wanted me to share rooms, so finally in the afternoon, landed here at Coogee, and booked in here at the Coogee Bay Hotel.⁵ It is a swanky place and fairly expensive, but after all the poor places I had been in, it was nice to get a single room and comfortable service. However, I soon found out I was paying for the swankiness. When I booked in they told me that being New Year's Eve there was to be a dance for the guests only, and their invited friends. Having nothing else to do, I thought I would go to the dance instead of going elsewhere.

The manageress found me a partner (only so so) and put us in with a party. The dance started and everything was going along smoothly. All this time I thought the dance was on the house, for the benefit of the resident guests. Imagine my surprise when about 11pm the waiter came around and asked for 15 shillings from each man (7/6 for self and partner) for the supper. This added to another 7/3 as my share of the drinks, made the total for the night, 22/3. I was terribly annoyed as I thought it was free for the guests, and had I known, would not have come to the dance, especially when I had to pay for someone I did not know, and wasn't even interested in. It wasn't a bad show, except that it became the usual orgy of drinking. When I finally did get to bed, I was nearly eaten alive with mosquitoes. At twelve o'clock, I did not forget my Own Fay back in Melbourne, including the 'blonde' at Mornington.

I will be leaving this hotel in the morning, and will probably book up in the city after I meet C. It is now after lunch, and as I intend to have a surf, I must hurry off. I believe the coastal road is again flooded, so I suppose I shall have to come back home the same direct route, through Albury. As I know now, we will probably leave Sunday or Monday at the latest, arriving home Tuesday night or Wednesday. Shall I see you at lunch on Thursday?

I trust you have captured all of Mornington with your rubber suit? I suppose you have. Have a good time, and please be careful with this letter. Goodbye for the present and fondest love from your Sydney tourist, who sighs at the thought of what might have been here with you.

Your Silent Witness

Fay was unconcerned with Connie spending holidays with Jaime. The marriage was in name only, and for now she was patient to wait. They had both been so excited about their plans to travel to Sydney and spend Christmas and New Year together, but alas, it wasn't to be. Fay had told her mother she was, once again, driving to Sydney with

Judy, and Annie, highly suspicious, insisted Lillian should join them. Although Lillian said she didn't want to go (aware of Fay's romantic plan), their mother had made up her mind, so the girls booked in at Mornington together.

Once again, Fay took pen to paper to reply to Jaime.

Melbourne,

6 January 1936

Hello, my Darling,

It was heavenly of you to write me that lovely long letter. I certainly could not have had any further proof of how much you were thinking of me, after perusing all those pages of your sojourn in NSW with a wish on every page that I had been with you. I wonder do you realise just how much I have been wishing the same. On New Year's Eve I felt terribly morbid. It is strange how it affects one — somehow one wants to be very near to the ones they love best in the world on this particular day of the year. I suppose it is because we know we will never see 1935 again and when I think of some very precious hours we spent together not so very long ago, it makes me wish that 1936 will be even happier.

Darling, I felt terribly jealous when I read in parts of your letter that you met this girl and that girl on New Year's Eve and probably kissed them (although you said you did not make love to them). We both know you should have been kissing me alone.

And now, Darling, I am off out to lunch and I hate the thought of not meeting you at our old haunt but I shall hold my breath until Thursday at 12.15pm

I have got fairly sunburnt and hope it does not disappear before Thursday. I have also lost weight — now down to nine stone. But you can't play strenuous tennis, swim, go yachting, and attend fairly late parties without it taking some effect. It is certainly not through dieting. We had marvellous meals, and you know how hungry one feels down at the seaside.

Cheerio, my Love,

Fay

PS Tear this up, please.

~

Most of the Trust Fund Jaime and his siblings received after the sale of *St Abbs* he had spent on buying the Stodart Street property. His wage at Dunlop's and some interest from Mauri Bros & Thomson shares were now his sole income, and with Connie's spending sprees he had to watch every penny.

Meanwhile, his brother Lionel San Miguel's career was booming. He was now a Fellow of the Royal Institute of Architects. In the early thirties he designed and built a modern home in Balwyn for his growing family. He also designed a hall for Genazzano College in 1936, plus an art deco showroom at 111–125 A'Beckett Street[6] in the city. The motor showroom and offices were built for the Catholic Church, as were many other buildings Lionel went on to design, including the Sacred Heart Hospital of Coburg, the Sacred Heart Monastery at Croydon, and Our Lady of Good Counsel Catholic Church in Deepdene. Jaime rarely saw his brother, and with his increasing escapades with Fay, nor did he see much of his mother or other siblings.

By 1937, Jaime and Fay were finding it harder to keep their affair a complete secret. The numerous bouquets of flowers that Jaime sent to Fay's office had all her co-workers gossiping. The frequent weekends, and occasional holidays away made Annie interrogate her daughter constantly, and they had some terrible rows. Jaime had also begun doing some sales travel for Dunlop's, and he was often on the road.

25 January 1937

Darling,

The flowers were exquisite, and these few lines are written to convey my thanks until I see you and can thank you in person. I had to sign for them and my hands just trembled with excitement. You can't imagine the lovely surprise I received when upon opening the box, I found a spray of superb Red Roses and Lilly of the Valley. Darling, I am wearing them now and their fragrance fills me with love and desire for you. I wish you were here right now. No, Darling, not here with the family around, but some remote corner of this folly old planet, where I could have you all to myself.

My only consoling thought is of our weekend together very soon — but not soon enough. I feel terribly impatient. At the present moment I could fill up a tablet telling you how much I love you and want you. But I will save it all up until the weekend after next.

The Mater keeps on reading articles out of the Herald and what with the other distractions in the room; it is rather difficult to write any further. So, Mon Beloved, I will very reluctantly have to love and leave you until tomorrow at 2.30?

> *All my love,*
> *Fay*

PS I hope your cold has vanished and that you are feeling much better. You should have had an early night tonight Darling, you will certainly have to catch up on some sleep before our weekend starts (now tear this up).

Jaime did tear up a number of letters, but preferred to keep most of them in his locked box at Dunlop's.

～

2 February 1937
My darling Fay,
Am just on my way home, so thought I'd drop you this note. Well, Darling I got home alright after the drive, but it was a struggle. It was a tremendous fight against sleep — gee, I was tired. We had a big day and I only had about

one hour's sleep the night before after the row with C. The car ran very well, and I must have rectified the trouble I had earlier.

Any rate, I got home about 10.30pm and the house was in darkness, so I crept in and went to sleep. This morning C bounced in and asked me how I enjoyed my 'secret day'. She was very hostile because in the first place, she didn't know where I had been — she had completely forgotten I was working in the country for the day. I know there will be trouble when I tell them I am going away, but I can't be worried about that. I took my laundry to town, and will get it Friday. I took the precaution as I thought C may refuse to do it, and I didn't want to be stranded.

Well, it's 6.25pm now, so I had better hurry, as there will be the usual storm if I am late. They will think I am with you (worst luck that I am not). Am taking some work home tonight, so I will be busy.

For the present, all my love,

From your Jaime

Connie knew in her heart that she had pushed Jaime away. She loved him dearly, yet couldn't bear to be close to him. Her depression was constant, and she was often unable to get out of bed. The anger outbursts were increasing, yet she had no control over them. One thing she was determined about, and that was she would never divorce Jaime. She was proud to be a member of the respected San Miguel family, and had no intention of severing that tie.

Jaime and Fay returned to Woodend for their holiday, the same guest house where they were first intimate. Once again they spent it with lovemaking, tennis, golf and fine food. When they were together, it felt as if paradise and heaven had combined just for the two of them.

10 February 1937
Darling,
Once again I take up the pen to write and thank you for yet another

beautiful gift. Sometimes I have to pinch myself to realise that it isn't all part of a lovely dream but the real thing — and thank you again, Darling, it was a heavenly surprise. I have tucked myself away in my bedroom on the pretext that I am retiring early, but it is only to have you all to myself. If we can't have one another in the flesh when we are apart, we can at least have each other in the spirit, and even now I can feel you very close. I am looking forward to our next evening together — are you?

Even tomorrow will not come soon enough just to hear your voice over the telephone. By the way, I might be able to have morning tea with you. I have several calls to make at various offices and could perhaps wangle it. Well, Darling, I have just glanced at your precious little gift on my dressing table, and it says nine o'clock, so I will have to love and leave you, and dash up and post this (an office letter) so as you will get it in the morning.

Until tomorrow, goodnight,

Fay

PS Tear this up immediately.

Jaime continued to travel for Dunlop's as the year progressed. It suited his married life, although he missed Fay whenever he was on the road. In September he travelled to Sydney, taking his brother, Tony.

Sydney

20 September 1937

My dear Fay,

Just a hurried note to let you know we arrived in Sydney safely. This is the first opportunity I have had of even writing you anything, as my brother has been with me until now, every minute. He has just left me for a few minutes only, so I thought I would grab the time to drop you this short note. I very much doubt if I shall get the chance to buy you that present, but if I don't here, I shall on my return. Sydney is fine and a wonderful city. I wouldn't mind coming over here for twelve months or so. I am leaving here Tuesday

night, so I will be back Wednesday morning, as I probably will go home for
lunch. I will ring you in the afternoon. I hope you are well and missing me.
It would be great if you were here with me. I have been terribly busy as my
time here is short.

In haste, and with fondest love,

Jaime

Fay hated the business trips Jaime made, and always looked forward to
his cards or letters. She always replied immediately.

Melbourne
21 September 1937
Darling,

I was wondering if you would get an opportunity to write, knowing most
of your time would be spent in the company of the second party, and when
the postman handed me your letter card, all but a few minutes ago, I received
a very pleasant surprise.

I simply devoured the contents, and perhaps it was just as well I was in
the office on my own, as I felt like having a little weep. I missed you so terribly.
You scarcely left my thoughts after Friday evening, and I seemed to be with
you each hour of the clock, wondering how you were faring and hoping you
would reach your destination safe and sound. These last few days have simply
dragged and they seem so uneventful and uninteresting when they do not
include you. Darling, if you take on any more of these trips, I am coming with
you. The thought of you being so far away from me is certainly not good for
my nerves; they have been on edge since Saturday. Do not worry about that
other little matter, Darling; I know you won't get any time to go shop-seeing.
You are more important to me than anything else in this world, so don't go
spending twelve months over there.

Hoping I will hear your voice on the phone tomorrow afternoon.

All my love,

Fay

Fay had taken up smoking to calm her nerves; it seemed to work for the stars of the silver screen in the films she saw regularly, and the cigarettes kept Jaime more at ease. Pretty soon Lillian followed suit, much to their mother's dismay. She felt she had lost control of both daughters.

The complex love affair Fay was in sometimes caused her to panic, and her fear of losing Jaime was overwhelming at times.

5 November 1937

Darling,

I have about two minutes to rattle off a few lines whilst the two bosses are conferring in the other room, and any minute I will be called in to take notes. I have just finished speaking to you on the phone and hated having to drag myself away from it. It was so lovely hearing your voice again. I missed you terribly and thought you were really serious about not seeing me again when you did not turn up at lunchtime.

I think I will be able to make it for morning tea tomorrow. Mr Rostren will be away and if you ring me about 10 or 10.30 I would have some idea as to what time I could slip out. Perhaps I can still remind you that I love you more than anything else on this earth, and if ever you stopped loving me, I should be guilty of doing something really desperate, so do love me forever.

In haste,

Fay

In October, Fay's father, William, fell ill and the family was very concerned. He was diagnosed with bowel cancer, and told it was a terminal disease. As Christmas approached, Fay hoped there might be a chance that she and Jaime could spend it together, as last year had failed.

2 December 1937

My Sweetheart,

I just hated dragging myself away from you in the lunch hour, and have been thinking of you ever since. Such heavenly thoughts, Darling. Mr Rostren has left me with plenty of work whilst he is out at lunch but I could not possibly concentrate on the latter before fulfilling my promise to write you this note.

I think by this time we have both made a perfect study of the language of lovers, so if I continue to write in this strain, I hope you will forgive me, because I love telling you (in case you are not sure) just how much I love and want you more each day. Sometimes I have been guilty of lying awake at night thinking of all the lovely places we could go to over the Xmas holidays (if only we dared) such as Lorne with tennis in the mornings, swimming in the afternoons, and dancing in the evenings, and then Darling, home to our little cottage by the sea. It is the most beautiful secret I know of.

Darling, your exquisite flowers have just arrived and I feel positively mad with joy at the very sight of them — in fact, my hands are still trembling with excitement to say the least of my palpitating heart. I have just been along the corridor to put them in water, and as several of the girls stepped out of the lift when they arrived, they have been firing me with questions as to the identity of my ardent admirer, and if he is the one who sent all the previous bouquets. Darling, I would love to tell them he is my darling lover, and the dearest person in all the world. Your lovely flowers almost seemed to nod their stately heads to this remark. They have made me deliriously happy and make me feel as if your very presence was in the room. They are an exquisite combination of Sweet Peas, Delphiniums, Lupins, Cecil Brunner roses, and Stocks, with maidenhead fern intermingled. As for the shades, they blend from pale blue to deep blue and pale pink to deep pink with mauve lupins. They are the envy of the entire corridor, everyone who passes or comes into the office remark on their loveliness.

And now, Darling I must do some work. If I do not see you this evening I will be on the very tick tomorrow for lunch and hope you will have some good news concerning tomorrow evening, because if I do not have you to myself for at least three hours very soon I will not content myself with just lunch hours for the rest of the week, you will have to arrange to have a 'meeting' on Monday night.

Cheerio my Darling,

Fay

Fay and Jaime didn't get to spend Christmas together. William was seriously ill and the family was gathered by his bedside.

Thanks For The Memory

On Friday 31 December 1937, the Johnston family rallied together as William's condition gravely deteriorated. Harry and Marie had come down from Stawell. Marie was five months pregnant.[1]

New Year's Day, Saturday 1 January 1938, 69-year-old William Patterson Johnston passed away, surrounded by his family. Fay and Lillian were deeply upset, while Harry comforted their mother. The New Year would, from then on, always have a shadow over it.

The Argus
Monday 3 January 1938
Johnston — *The Friends of the late William Patterson Johnston are informed that his remains will be interred in the Coburg Cemetery. The funeral will leave his residence, 123 Tooronga Road, Malvern THIS DAY at two o'clock.*

The funeral turned into an ordeal for the family, when Annie came face to face with William's long time mistress. She strode up to the woman, and in a loud and angry voice declared,

'You are not welcome here. Leave immediately!'

Fay and Lillian were shocked when they learnt about the affair, whereas Harry had always had his suspicions. The day was also a reminder of the family's previous losses, as William was buried alongside little Dorothy and Arthur, who had died tragically long ago.

Fay became all the more anxious to be with Jaime permanently, and she made that clear in a letter written ten days after the death of her father.

11 January 1938

My Darling Beloved Sweetheart,

Is it any wonder that I should want to sit down and type these lines just as soon as I arrived back from lunch, when I had you with me all the way back to the office, loving and adoring you for your unselfishness in the little matter we were discussing at lunch time. I enjoyed our little chat together, but it hurts me to think that perhaps I have made you a little jealous and unhappy over something that will probably amount to nothing.

Sometimes, I too get a little jealous when I think of you living with and sharing the same roof with someone else, when I am wanting to be in your company every hour of the day and night. It is mostly the weekends when I get these little attacks of moodiness, especially when I see everyone else going off to the theatre and such with their boyfriends, and the very one I love best in all the world is going somewhere with someone else. So you see, it is mostly a weekly event with me, whereas you have a very occasional attack when some un-pretentious male comes along and takes Yours Truly out of a fit of the miserables.

I once looked forward to seeing you every Sunday morning but now I only see you in the lunch hours, and occasionally in the evenings. Unless you see me more often in 1938, I will be quite guilty of having you kidnapped and transferred to another portion of the globe, where I can have you entirely to myself. Darling, I am getting terribly desperate and love and want you more and more each year.

I know I should try and forget you, and stop seeing you. I would too if I thought it would make someone else happier, but you have already convinced me that it would make no difference, so I am going to still keep seeing and loving you, no matter what happens.

Darling, I will be looking forward to seeing you on Thursday, at the same time and place, so be sure to say, 'Present', otherwise I will be perfectly miserable for the rest of the day.

Always your beloved,

Fay

Jaime had a risky yet tempting idea, which he shared with Fay at lunchtime. He, Connie, and Leon, were going to Lorne for a holiday, and taking a nurse-maid to help look after seven-year-old Leon. What if Fay came too, and stayed at the Cumberland, while they were booked in to Erskine House.[2] The two guesthouses were close to each other and both near the beach. Jaime explained that the only time Leon had met Fay was a few times at Mass, and at a tennis tournament. They could happen to run into each other, and Fay would explain she was on holiday, getting over the death of her father. They would be able to play tennis and golf, as Connie detested all sports. He was positive that it was a foolproof idea.

At first, Fay protested, saying it was all too dangerous, but the sheer risk excited her, so she agreed to make bookings at Cumberland House, and received her boss's approval for time off. The holiday would begin on 20 January for ten days.

It was impossible for Jaime to consider leaving Connie at this point in time. Leon was already attending Xavier College, and it was important the boy had both parents at home, and he couldn't risk upsetting his mother and the family name. Perhaps, when Leon was much older, he could make his escape.

The summer holiday went to plan. Fay had been lucky and obtained a room due to a cancellation. On the afternoon of arrival, she went down to the beach, as she knew Jaime and his family would be there. Connie was sitting on the sand, fully clothed, while Leon was in shorts and a shirt. The nursemaid, Miriam, was in a swimsuit, as were Jaime and Fay.

The excuse of her arrival went over well, and she spent the afternoon with them. Jaime even took holiday snaps, and had Miriam take some of the four of them. It was quite extraordinary, as Fay and Connie seemed to enjoy each other's company. Connie shared her condolences over Fay's sad loss, and explained how devastated she was after the death of her mother. So when Jaime made plans for tennis and golf with Fay, Connie appeared unperturbed. Besides, she always had an afternoon nap; Miriam could take Leon to the beach, while Jaime would partake in his sports. One thing Fay commented to Jaime about was how beautiful Connie was. She had lost her figure, but her face remained as exquisite as ever.

Fay and Jaime found they had plenty of opportunities to slip away together, and many fervent kisses were stolen in the sand dunes. In the evenings, however, Jaime spent time with his family. Still, Fay pondered, at least she saw him nearly everyday. It was certainly better than nothing.

The holiday soon came to an end, and Fay and Jaime returned to work and their daily lunch hours, and occasional nights. The love letters continued, especially Fay's, which became more passionate and poetic as her love for Jaime soared.

22 February 1938

My Darling Beloved,

I just hated letting you go today, and when I realise just how much we mean to each other it makes my happiness supreme. Sweetheart, I could never give you up now, our bond is too strong, and as Kingsley says, 'The friends thou has and their adoption tried, grapple them to thy soul with hoops of steel.' But Darling our souls are united with something stronger than mere 'hoops of steel'. To me our love is like some exquisite flower that has to be cherished and preserved — the only difference being that flowers usually die and our love, I hope, will live forever. Sweetheart, I love you with such an intensity that it sometimes frightens me.

I often sit and dream of the time when I can have you entirely to myself, without prying eyes or gossiping tongues, to criticise where we go and how we spend our time together. At this very moment, if I could stretch my imagination, I would be spending the day with you at some quiet little wayside inn, sipping luscious coffee, consuming homemade cakes, and then a heavenly drive into the hills with only 'Love' as the third party. So you see Darling, you must never think of yourself as being selfish because (although I suppose I should give you up) I could never live without you now. We love each other too dearly.

By the way, many thanks for the lovely little gifts this afternoon. They are lovely, like all your gifts, but as you already know, the best gift of all is yourself and I cherish that with my very life.

Semper Fidelis,

Fay

~

In July, Fay started a new job as private secretary to the Honourable Frank Brennan, MP.[3] He had a legal firm at 20 Queens Street, Melbourne. Brennan had been a Labor Member for Batman, and he was Attorney General for Victoria in 1929 until 1931. Fay's appointment meant a huge rise in salary and far more responsibilities, but she loved a challenge, and soon became a major asset to the company.

Although their affair was kept secret, sometimes Jaime felt the need to come clean to Fay's mother. He wanted to be able to visit her at Tooronga Road and therefore spend more time together.

3 August 1938

12.45pm

My darling Fay,

I only have ten minutes to write to you before meeting your sister at lunch, and as I want to give her this note for you, I shall have to hurry. Well,

Darling, I had a feeling in my bones today that all was not well with you. I rang the office at ten, and you did not answer so I hung up. I then rang again about 10.30 and Miss Brennan answered, so I again did not speak. By this time, I was getting anxious so when I rang again at 11am and young Sullivan spoke, I knew then something was wrong, so I spoke to him and he told me you were not coming in. I then rushed around to see your sister at Foy's and she gave me your lovely note. She said she was going to come around to the Victoria, so I suggested that she should still do so, so that we could have a chat.

Yes, Darling, I said to you last night in the car that I did not think you were well. Do you remember? Darling, I don't think I will be able to stay away from you. I just will have to come out; do you think your mother would mind? Let me know, as you are wiser than me, and I don't want to do anything to spoil things so I will wait for your good counsel. I suppose if I do come out, I shall be quite nervous when I meet the Mater. I shall feel like a naughty schoolboy.

Get well soon Darling, as I hate town without you.

Of course, Jaime never did come over to Tooronga Road. Fay couldn't possibly risk it. She knew her mother would be enraged, and life at home would be unbearable, so their secrets continued.

～

Towards the end of November, Fay was confronted by her mother. A neighbour had spotted Jaime dropping Fay home, and knowing he was married, told Annie all about it. The quarrel quickly turned ugly. Fay told her mother she had no intention of ever leaving Jaime and tried to express how much she loved him. Annie told her daughter she was an adulteress who was committing mortal sins every day, and would end up in hell. She chastised Fay about her morals, saying she was disgusted and disappointed in her eldest daughter. Fay stuck up for the relationship, but cried an ocean of tears that evening.

26 November 1938

Darling Fay,

I nearly sent you stockings, and it was nearly sweets, but once again I chose flowers, as they convey to you far more plainly what I am thinking. Well, this little surprise is to let you know how greatly I admire you for your 'great pluck', and to help you along should you not be feeling so well after your recent ordeals.

Again expressing my admiration for your courage.,

With all my love.

Jaime

26 November 1938, 11.30am

Jaime,

Have just received your exquisite box of flowers, and they seem to fit in with the glorious day. Mr Brennan is not back yet so am scribbling this note in the interim.

Darling, they convey to the writer all your best love and have made me forget all my aches and pains and sorrow. I have been thinking of you all morning, and your message of cheer came along right in the midst of all my lovely thoughts of you.

Miss B and Mr S were quite convinced that wedding bells were very close at hand and Mr S even suggested that I might be taking a sudden flight to Reno.

Well, Darling, I must love and leave you till lunchtime on Monday, which is a terrible long time to wait.

Until then, with all my love,

Fay

~

Once again, Fay and Jaime spent Christmas and New Year apart. Fay had booked in to Dava Lodge for late January, whereas Jaime was playing in a tennis tournament at Colac, and then going to Lorne. Sometimes the desperation they felt for seeing each other became almost obsessive, as was the case when Fay had been away from work sick for a couple of days.

11 January 1939

My darling Fay,

I am up at the corner of Tooronga and Wattletree Roads, writing this little note to you and watching and waiting, hoping that perhaps I might just get a glimpse of you, or better still, hoping your mother would come up the street to do some shopping. It is now 3.30pm and I have been here since three o'clock. I came out from town acting on an impulse that possibly I might see you, but my luck seems out. I have driven past, twice, slowly, hoping you might come out on to the veranda, but I daren't toot. I am just dying to call in and see you, yet so near, but yet so far. I suppose I must be patient, dash it all.

A car has just pulled into my line of vision, and I can't see your front gate. I must move as I must watch in case you come to your gate. Darling, it is just terrible this longing and aching to be with you. Nothing seems to matter but you. I should right now be in town working, but the call of you is too strong, and I just had to come, even to be in the same vicinity as you.

By the way, I must order the snaps for you. I think those of you in the gown are delightful. Your body is a dream, and I have been looking at them all day, adoring you as I never thought possible. Darling, I thought I had reached the peak of my love for you, but since last summer at Lorne, when I saw you so often, I realise that to see you more often is only making me more crazy than ever. Darling, I love you; yes, it is getting desperate and unquenching. I do hope and yearn that our heart's desire will come to pass very soon.

I hope you will soon be better, as I am longing to see you more than ever. The taste I've had of you has made me hunger for more.

Goodbye, I love you.

Jaime stayed watching Fay's house until 4.30pm before returning for a short time to his office, and later to Camberwell, where Connie and his son were waiting. Whenever Jaime mentioned 'their heart's desire', Fay's hopes rose that they would soon be able to marry. Jaime, on the other hand, knew it would take time, but felt by mentioning it, Fay would remain patient. Little did he realise the bomb that was about to explode.

The week had begun with a heat wave, and each day was hotter than the last. Fay remained at home for the week, and wrote to Jaime most days.

12 January 1939

My darling Beloved,

When your letter arrived this morning about 9.30, I wondered if I would be perusing it at precisely the same time you would be perusing my letter to you. It seems that a great deal of telepathy must have taken place yesterday afternoon. I was having a sleep about three when you were waiting for me, and strangely enough (or is it strange?), I was dreaming of you. As soon as I awakened I started that letter to you, but if I had known you were so close in the flesh, I would have got to you somehow, although I was only in my dressing gown.

Darling, your avowals of love did much to soothe an aching heart, because my heart is aching and longing for you always. I am sorry I missed you yesterday afternoon, Darling. I got dressed purposely about 5.30, thinking you might pass on your way home, but I had very little hope, as I thought C might be in town with you, as she missed Monday and Tuesday.

Darling, I want to make love to you. The wireless is playing all the love songs, and each song seems to remind me of you. Darling, they are just playing Thanks for the Memory: 'Thanks for the memory, of lunch from twelve to four, sunburn at the shore, that pair of gay pyjamas that you bought and never wore'.[4] Remember Darling when we saw the film, The Big Broadcast of 1938, and Bob Hope sang it with Shirley Ross? What a perfect night that was.

Sorry we cannot spend tomorrow evening together Darling, but we will make up for it somehow. If by any chance the Mater should go out tomorrow, I shall ring you between 2 and 2.30, failing that, I will have to be patient and wait till Monday lunchtime.

The nosy neighbour, who had informed Annie about Jaime being married, was also snooping around on Wednesday afternoon, and spotted Jaime parked in his car. Once again she took great pleasure in telling Annie all about it, even the length of the time he was there. Annie was furious, and disregarding Fay's ill health, stormed into her bedroom when she found out on Thursday afternoon.

'What in the Lord's name was that married philanderer doing parked near our house all day yesterday afternoon? How dare he!'

Fay had only just finished writing the letter to Jaime, and quickly hid it under her book.

'Mother, he was worried about me. He loves me.'

Annie almost bristled as she exclaimed, 'If you don't leave this man, I will banish you from the house. I will not have an adulteress living under *my* roof.'

Fay was beside herself with worry. Would her mother really throw her out of the house? She'd never seen her so angry except when Harry had asked for the money for the pregnancy termination. Fay didn't dare risk going down the street, so she added a postscript to the letter, and had Lillian post it for her.

Thursday, 5pm

PS Darling, the Mater has gone berserk. That awful Mrs Davis saw you parked yesterday and she's told me to leave you or leave the house. I don't know what to do. I will have to tell her I will give you up; I think it's the only solution. Please help me, I'll try and ring you tomorrow. In haste, Fay.

On Friday 13 January 1939, Melbourne's weather soared to 45.6°C and was the hottest day recorded at that time. A large number of bushfires erupted and the day was dubbed Black Friday. It was one of the worst natural bushfires in the world: seventy-one people died, and several towns were entirely destroyed. In central Victoria fires raged in a large number of towns including Dromana on the Mornington Peninsula, Marysville, Kinglake and many others.

When Jaime arrived at work on Friday morning, he was thrilled to receive Fay's letter, until he read the PS.

Friday, City.
Unlucky number 13 Janurary 1939

My darling Fay,
Tell your mater that as you have asked me I shall try to help you in your promise to her. I shall try if you think it will make you happier, but I shall try because you have asked me. Not for anyone else would I do it. Perhaps your mother is right, perhaps she is wrong, but though I am a rotter (what your mother thinks of me), I don't think I am quite as bad as she thinks I am. But still, she has the right to think the worst of me.

I trust, however, that this big decision we are going to endeavour to carry out will add to your happiness. If it does, it will be worth it, if it doesn't, well life is very short, and the future so uncertain, that one could not be blamed for snatching a few hours of happiness. For myself darling, the less said the better. I shall have lost my only real happiness, but these words are wasted as your mater would not believe me.

Well, one thing is certain in my mind now. That is, if ever that day arrives for which we have hoped for so long (that is provided you have not been pushed into something which you have not wanted) I shall take you and you only. We shall want neither friends nor relatives. We always said that if we were lucky enough to ever get married, we would have none of our relatives, and Darling, I mean that. We shall remember the friends who are our friends now, not then.

Talking of marriage, Darling, I shall give you a little advice. When the boys enlisted in the AIF during the war, some did it of their own free will; others did it because of what people would say. People waved flags and said it was the right thing to do. But what happened to these boys after the war? Did people care what happened to them now? Did they help them to get jobs and make them happy? No, they had to fish for themselves. These boys had found out to their sorrow that public opinion wasn't worth a damn. So it is the same more or less with some girls about marriage. It is easy to say yes, but mighty hard to get out of it. Marriage is not a magic carpet ride; it can be a splendid dream, or a frightful nightmare. With you darling, it would be a delicious dream. Should our day really arrive, we will know that we have not loved in vain.

Darling, I love you and will always love you. If ever you want any advice, help, money, or anything I can possibly do for you, I will always be at your beck and call.

Ever yours, with always all my love,

Jaime.

13 January 1939, 2.30pm

Well, my Darling,

Things quietened down but I ate in my room and have been walking on eggshells all day. How are you surviving all this heat? The wireless announced before lunch time today that the temperature had reached 44°C. I do hope you are taking things easy and not working too hard. The mater absolutely refused to let me go up the street, saying it was too hot, and what was I up to? So I was not able to ring you at 2.15. If I had my way I would have done so, but for peace and quietness I just had to look at the darned clock pass from 2 to 2.30 with an ache in my heart that you might have been looking forward to my call. I hate to think this is our Friday night going to waste, but I will be thinking of you the whole time.

The wireless has just announced that it is 45.5°C and that the bush fires are even worse. What a tragedy for some poor country folk. The drought was bad enough for them, and then to have all this. The office will think I must have known something, escaping all this heat. I do hope you are not out in it too much, Darling. Always believe me and never doubt me when I say I love you, and will go on loving you forever. I cannot see anyway of meeting each other before Monday, so I will see you at our usual place, and hopefully all will be well. I cannot give you up, no matter what the mater says.

At the Teapot Inn on Monday, Fay told Jaime she had no intention of giving him up, and was prepared to risk defying her mother. They decided to be as careful as possible from then on.

Fay's holiday nearly had to be cancelled. She had developed boils all over her body, and they had to be dressed daily by her mother. Jaime was preparing for his golf tournament at Colac and had been missing Fay while she recuperated at home. Fay also missed Jaime, and wrote him a quick note before retiring to bed on 25 January.

26 January 1939
7.30pm

Darling,

I have about three minutes in which to scribble this note. Lilly handed me your lovely letter, which I very eagerly perused and told me about the nice long chat she had with you at lunch time. I had better be very careful of that young sister of mine She is also falling in love with you, and she even went so far as to say this in front of the mater, who said she would 'have to meet this wonderful man,' and see if she couldn't cut us both out. But of course this latter remark was made rather sarcastically, with a stern remark to follow. As regards your calling, Darling, I think we had better keep the peace as much as possible.

I will see you on Friday up at the corner at 11.20am. Darling, I nearly forgot to thank you for the delicious fruit and lovely magazines, when Lilly gave them to me I felt rather teary, as I miss you so.

Lilly is getting a little impatient, so I will have to conclude, and write you again tomorrow.

Once again, all my love,

Fay

Lillian loved being a messenger for Jaime and Fay; she did have a small crush on him, and wished that she too could meet someone as handsome and romantic. She had hoped to join Fay down at Mornington, but was not due for annual holidays. At the end of January, Fay left for Dava Lodge. Jaime had spent the weekend playing in the tournament at Colac and had spent Sunday afternoon at Lorne with his tennis partner, Doug. He had planned a longer holiday with Connie and Leon, but she refused to go to the tournament and the discussion ended in another row, so the family holiday was cancelled. In a way, Jaime was relieved, but it was a disappointment for Leon.

At Colac on Sunday 29 January, Jaime wrote a letter to Fay before retiring for the night.

Colac, 11pm

29 January 1939

My dearest Fay,

I am sitting on my bed in my pyjamas, writing to my darling before I turn in to go to sleep, and wishing you were here with me. It isn't long since we returned from Lorne, yes lovely Lorne, but oh how empty without my Darling. The bush country between Colac and Lorne was completely burnt, and how terrible the fires must have been. All the lovely vegetation that used to beautify the road was gone. We were very interested to see how Lorne had fared in the fires, but considering how black the forests were, I think the township was very lucky to escape so lightly. As we drove down the hill into

Lorne, my heart missed a beat as I saw the lovely Cumberland Guest House, and as we passed it, I could almost see you looking out of the window and waving to me. As Doug had not been to Lorne before, I drove around past the Pacific Hotel along the coast road, as far as our favourite spot to show him the scenery. What do you think? Our little nook was no more. The bushfires at this point had come right down to the beach, and burnt everything. I was quite depressed that our memory should have been wiped out.

On our return as we passed the Pacific, we noticed a great crowd on the pier, so we drove down to be sticky, and heard the sad news that a surfer had drowned. It appears he was a long way out, with a board, and could not swim. When he lost the board he simply sank. This little incident dampened our ardour a little, but not for long. We soon got down on the beach, hired a board, and into the sea, it was glorious in. After a while Mal and some of the others from Colac arrived and they joined us in the water. The beach was terribly crowded, and, would you believe it, dirty and covered with seaweed. Apparently adverse winds had caused this. Later on Doug and I had tea at Tully's Café after which we quietly drove back to Colac. Tomorrow at noon, we are in the doubles finals, and after that we shall drive home.

Forever yours,

Jaime

When Jaime returned home on Monday evening, he was verbally attacked by Connie. She had spent the weekend seething about the cancelled holiday, and by the time Jaime walked in the door, she was ripe and ready to explode. He made the decision that night to move into the flat above the garage. At least that way, he could have some peace and quiet. When Fay found out about his move, she was tickled pink. Could this mean that their 'heart's desire' would be coming true?

A couple of weeks later, just when things were running smoothly, another drama unfolded. Fay had been out on Sunday with Jaime, and when she arrived home, Annie was in one of her moods and took it out on Fay.

12 February 1939
6pm

My dear Jaime,

For the first time this is the one occasion which I have hated writing to you, because when you have finished reading it you will realise why. When I arrived home this afternoon, you will remember it was fairly late (I did not realise it was so, time doesn't seem to mean a thing when I am in your company) The mater went for me well and truly, and the lecture and threats I received have really frightened me in to thinking seriously of trying to stop from seeing you.

What actually transpired would take too long to mention here, but I promised her I would not continue seeing you. I have been terribly upset ever since, and I am writing this note whilst the mater is entertaining my aunt on the front veranda (I pleaded a headache).

I am going to ask you, Darling, not to see me for a while, and see if I can be brave enough to give you up. Perhaps I am all what I have been told this afternoon, and it might make things better for everyone concerned. If I cannot stand things by the end of the week or so, I might go to Sydney — anywhere — to forget.

Please do not ring tomorrow or try and see me, because if I hear your voice, or see you, all my promises and efforts will be of no avail and something might happen which could cause a lot of trouble. I know you will get a shock to receive this, but in my present state I have had to write it and perhaps it is better to part like this, as it is impossible to do so in person.

But always remember, Darling that no matter what happens, I shall go on loving you till the day I die. Without seeing you in the future, I shall probably hope it will be soon. Perhaps if my mater knew just how much I loved you, she would not be so dictatorial. Excuse the scribble, Darling, but my heart is breaking.

Fay

On Monday morning 13 February when Jaime was at work, the postman delivered him Fay's letter. Initially he thought it a lovely surprise on his unlucky day. Very soon he realised that was not the case. He read the letter three times. It was only a month ago, on 13 January that he had received the same type of letter. This had to stop; her mother had no right to keep them apart. Fay was turning thirty this October and should be able to live her own life. He believed with all his heart that they eventually would be together permanently, and knew he had to make Fay understand and believe it. The first thing he did was write a very short note to her.

13 February 1939

No matter what happens, or if anything ever does, which I sincerely hope never will (except what we are praying for), I shall always love my lovely fair-haired darling.

This he delivered to Fay's office post box, knowing she would get it around noon. The next stop was the florist, where he ordered a bouquet of flowers to be delivered to her office in the afternoon.

When Fay collected the mail she was rather stunned to see a letter from Jaime, when she read the brief note, she shed a few tears, realising he had received her letter. Already she regretted writing it, but her mother had been so adamant, and Fay was really very frightened, she felt she'd had no choice.

Just as Fay stopped typing for her afternoon tea break, the bouquet of flowers arrived. He really was making this hard on her, she thought, as she put the flowers in a vase, and wondered whether or not she could respect her mother's demands. At 5pm Fay packed up her things and left the office. As she exited the building Jaime appeared at her side.

'Darling, I just had to see you and have a chat. Let's go and have a drink at Menzies.'

Jaime's ardent plan worked and by the end of the evening, Fay had agreed she could never leave him. The following morning she wrote him a letter.

14 February 1939

Darling,

The reason for this little note being written is because I have been thinking so much about the little heart to heart we had last evening, that I thought I would write and tell you just how much I enjoyed it. I could not sleep last night thinking about it. I kept turning over in my mind everything we had discussed with each other, and it made me realise just how impossible it would be to give up seeing you.

A few years ago I used to have a fight with the old conscience, as to whether I was doing right by allowing our friendship to continue, and that perhaps I was not being fair to someone else. But we fell in love, so desperately in love. I go back over all the pleasant hours we have spent in each other's company, all our little escapades and adventures, and even read your lovely letters written to me in the past. I am sure, Darling, no poet could pen such genuine words of love. I should one day like to have them in book form, and I would call them 'My Book of Poems' by my beloved J.S.M. What would you call mine? Perhaps we could have them all in one big book, and then everyone would know how much we love each other.

Only Forever

By now the San Miguels were aware that Jaime's marriage had major problems. As yet, they had no idea about Fay. Connie led them to believe he saw a bevy of women. Whenever he went over to Montalegre for a family get together, he felt uncomfortable as he received a frosty reception. He felt sad that they didn't seem to understand his plight, and how unhappy his married life was.

Easter of 1939 Fay had booked into Keating's Hotel[1] in Woodend, country Victoria. Judy Reid was going with her, as well as her mother and sister. Coincidentally, they had booked into the same guesthouse where Jaime and Fay had spent their first night together.

7 April 1939, Good Friday
9.50am

My darling Jaime,
We had quite a pleasant journey, Judy and I put our heads together and had a good old yarn, and it seemed no time before we reached Woodend (OUR Woodend). Some boisterous lads who were sitting at the back of our carriage were eating pickled onions (the odour permeated right through the corridor), and drinking beer or some such alcoholic beverage. They came to our rescue with the cases and golf clubs, and carried them out for us. Fortunately for us, a friend of Lillian's motored us all to our respective quarters. We were shown

to our room, I think it must be the bridal suite; it is the largest room I have ever slept in. There is a big double bed, a single bed, a balcony out onto the main street and two or three duchesses (dressing tables, I should say), and a nice big roomy wardrobe.

It was lovely of you coming out to the station last night, and I appreciated it to no end. I really thought you had gone in the interim of my taking the luggage onto the train, and I said to Judy that you had gone, but then to my (pleasant) surprise I saw you coming along onto the platform. How I wish I could have kept you all the way to Woodend.

Saturday, 11am

Well my Darling, I don't suppose you will be able to get much tennis, what with all this wet weather. We haven't been able to play golf yet, and have spent all our time indoors. The crowd here are quite nice; there is a young solicitor here from Colac. He and a much older chap have been chatting to us, and have asked us to play golf with them, but don't worry sweetheart, I would rather have one minute of your company, than six weeks of theirs. Darling, I love you too desperately now to ever think of us parting, and you need have no fears that I will ever marry anyone as long as I have you to love me.

Sunday, 11am

By the way, the solicitor from Colac is an old Xaverian; he knew Mr. Prendergast (being a solicitor) and also knew all the San Miguels, mentioning all your names. How your name was mentioned: he was saying that Colac had a tennis tournament every Easter etc. etc. I asked him if he knew Grace McKnockiter, which he did, and when I mentioned your name, casually, with a few others he told me all about the San Miguel family. Darling, you will laugh when I relate the conversation. It would take too long here to tell you about the San Miguel millions. I asked him, 'Doesn't Jaime work at Dunlop's?' and he replied, 'God, no! He might just have an interest there and a hobby or *sideline, but Jaime and his brother own Harrison, San Miguel.'*

By the way, I had better tell you his name: Arthur Welshman (nephew of Kerr, of Doyle and Kerr, solicitors) who is reputed to be enormously wealthy, but so are you, my dear, according to the latter. So other people know more about yourself than you do. He is a terrific skite in my opinion, and talks the leg off an iron post.

I have just found out the train service and I will be coming back on Tuesday on the five o'clock from Woodend, and should get into Spencer Street about 6.30pm but will ring you beforehand. Judy just told me to give you her love, and also said that I have been a very good girl, so put that in your cigarette and smoke it!

All my love,

Fay

Now that Jaime was living in the flat at Stodart Street, he and Fay spent more evenings together, as well as weekends. They regularly played golf and tennis, and met for their daily lunch during the week. Annie never did go through with her threat to throw Fay out of the house. She still gave her a hard time, but by now Fay was standing up for herself. As Jaime had said, she was nearly thirty and had to live her own life regardless of her mother's wishes.

Jaime continued to shower Fay with presents, and sometimes even clothing if he spotted something in a shop window. As he passed the windows of the Myer Emporium one afternoon he noticed a classic two-piece jade green, gabardine suit, and thought it would complement Fay's blue eyes and flaxen hair. As he knew her dress size, he purchased the suit at once.

2 May 1939

Darling Jaime,

Since receiving your lovely gifts last evening, I have not been able to concentrate on work, and as we are not very busy, I am scribbling these few lines.

Oh, Darling, it is the loveliest suit I have ever been fortunate enough to have, and fits me perfectly. It is not often that the Mater raves over anything (I) buy, but she certainly thought it a beauty and knows good material and workmanship when she sees it.

And now my Darling, how are you? I was quite worried about you yesterday. You must not let all these people worry you so much, otherwise they will be giving you 'nerves'. I was thinking, on my next Saturday off I think we should make a full day of it, even if we don't go on a links but just have a practice hit. Then we could lunch at some nice little café off the main road.

I am looking forward to seeing you at lunchtime, but in the meantime I will be thinking of you, loving you, wanting you and aching for you. But is that unusual?

Au Revoir till lunchtime, Sweetheart,

Fay

One Friday evening when they met for their usual night out, Jaime told Fay he was taking her to somewhere very different for dinner as he had planned a surprise for her. They drove to the top end of the city, where Jaime had booked a table for two at the Café d'Italia.[2] One of Jaime's co-workers had dined there recently, and raved about the food, especially the spaghetti bolognese. The Italian waiter sat them at a table by the window, and Jaime ordered a bottle of champagne. Fay admired the wonderful European atmosphere of the café, including the romantic lit candle on the red checked tablecloth. They ordered the spaghetti, and then toasted each other with their wine.

'My darling Fay,' said Jaime. 'I love you very much, and you've been so patient. I want you to have this little gift, so you know that we will marry some day.'

And with that, he took out a little leather box which contained a blue solitaire aquamarine set on a band of white gold. He took it out of the box and placed it on Fay's wedding finger, then kissed her hand fondly.

'Oh Darling, it's exquisite,' she said softly. 'I hardly know what to say.'

Fay was both surprised and deeply moved; she was sure this was the happiest night of her life.

When she arrived home that night, she immediately wrote a note to Jaime.

23 June 1939, 1am

Darling,

I just had to thank you for the lovely ring you gave me tonight. I will treasure it, Darling, like all the other treasures you have given me, and trust it will be symbolic of what we are hoping for.

I am afraid our efforts to refrain from seeing each other over the last seven years have been rather futile on both our parts, and the only solution must be that 'Love Conquereth All Things'. Whoever quoted that little proverb knew what he was talking about because it is a losing battle when two people are genuinely in love, as we are, and try to fight against it.

Darling, how much more complete it would be if only we could share all our pleasures together. We could combine dancing and golfing in winter, tennis and swimming in the summer, to say the least of a thousand other things that we seem to be mutually inclined to do (especially our lovemaking). How I would love to go to Sydney with you. My first impression of that state was very dull and uninteresting, but how different it would be with you to show me the sights. It would be transformed into a veritable fairyland, and the Blue Mountains a paradise. Darling, I hope our patience will be rewarded some day and we can do all those things together.

And so My Beloved, I shall bring this little missive to a conclusion, hoping that my thoughts and desires, which are only of you, are forgiven for the very plain and sane reason that I love you.

Fay

Fay decided it probably best to wear the ring on her dress finger; the office staff were far too nosy. One thing she did do was introduce Jaime to her mother. He was at Mass one Sunday, and after the service she took Annie over to meet him. Jaime was at his most charming, and shook Annie's hand warmly, saying how delighted he was to finally meet her. She was suitably impressed, for now.

Although Fay had a token of their love to wear, the waiting around for Jaime's freedom frequently got the better of her, and she would lose patience. This happened one Monday evening in August after they had been out for a meal. A friend of Jaime and Connie's, Ida Brady, had invited the married couple to a ball at the Palais in St. Kilda,[3] and Connie insisted they should go. This caused Fay concern and a hot surge of jealousy.

8 August 1939

Darling,

I am terribly sorry I spoilt a perfectly lovely evening last night. I cannot imagine what possessed me to hurt you so much. I know I left you with doubts in your heart, but Darling, I do love you, and please forgive me. I don't know whether to blame myself for being jealous, or whether my patience sometimes feels exhausted and makes me despondent and a little tired of waiting. I don't know what put me in the mood last night, but I think when you mentioned the play over the wireless, it made me feel that I was 'the interloper' and that I had no right to be seeing you when the other party was making such an effort to win back your affection.

Darling, I could tell you a thousand reasons why I am so much in love with you, but it is quite impossible to write them all down. Have I ever told you I love watching you talk, love watching you smile, love the way you twist your collar when it seems too tight for you. I love your little moods, when you pretend to get jealous, yet in your heart of hearts you know you reign supreme in my heart. I hope that someday all my heartaches for you will be cured, every beat of my heart is for you, and when the great day arrives that we can really be together, my heart will be too full for words. I may grow a little tired waiting, but your love will help me in the meantime, so hold on to me Darling, and never let me go.

Always, all my love,

Fay

Another little tiff occurred a few weeks later, Fay had arrived at the Teapot Inn to meet Jaime for lunch when an old Xaverian, Kevin Anderson, came in to the restaurant with a friend. Fay knew him vaguely, and also knew he would know Jaime and the San Miguel family, so she rushed out of the café, standing Jaime up. After he'd waited in vain for Fay, he rang her at the office in a rage. However, when he heard the real reason as to why she had left, he was most apologetic. The two men had left by the time he had arrived, so he didn't run into them after all. Fay too was full of apologies, but as she pointed out, she was only trying to save him from any embarrassment.

In late September they started making plans to spend Christmas and the New Year in Sydney. They would drive there in Jaime's car, staying at various places on the way.

Jaime spoilt Fay on her thirtieth birthday, taking her out to dinner at the Windsor with French champagne, a box of red roses, and a dainty marcasite wrist watch as tokens of his love. They spent the whole evening discussing their up and coming holiday.

6 October 1939

My darling Fay,

Well, first of all let me wish you a very happy birthday. My thoughts were with you from the moment I opened my eyes this morning. I trust that you will have many more happy birthdays, but perhaps in even more happy circumstances. I must rush to the florist now, so please excuse the hurried

scrawl. Just dying to see you tonight.
    For the present,
    All my love to my Darling,
    from J

~

On 3 September 1939, Britain and France declared war on Germany following the German invasion of Poland. Everyone was on tenterhooks with the anticipation of another World War.

Meanwhile, Fay was busy knitting Jaime scarves, jumpers, and cardigans in her spare time. She was an excellent knitter, and enjoyed the hobby for the relaxation it gave her. It also stopped her from worrying about world events, especially the upcoming war.

A perfect plan needed to be worked out for their summer holiday, and again Fay enlisted her dear friend, Judy Reid. As Judy had a post box address in the city, Jaime made the bookings for their accommodation giving them her address. Judy and a girlfriend planned to catch a train to Sydney, but would stay at a different flat to Jaime and Fay. Judy's romance was on hold as John Telford-Smith's wife was ill. The story given to Fay's mother was that Jaime, Fay and Judy were driving up and staying together at a flat, and Judy would act as their chaperone. Fortunately, Annie accepted the explanation but had a stern word to Judy all the same.

On 24 December 1939, at 8.50am Jaime picked Fay up from Malvern, and they started their much longed for holiday together. At Pranyip Creek, not far from Euroa, the car, a 1937 Pontiac, had a puncture and Jaime had to change the tyre. They drove on and stopped for lunch in Euroa, where Jaime purchased another tyre. Arriving in Gundagai in the early evening, they ate dinner at the Niagara Restaurant[4] then drove on to Goulbourn, in the Southern Tablelands of New South Wales, where they spent the night at a quaint hotel. Although there had been a storm, the night was very hot, so they both had a restless night. They set off in the morning around six, arriving in Picton at 7.20, where they had breakfast at the Royal George Inn, the oldest hotel in NSW that had been standing proud since 1819.

On Christmas Day, they drove in to Sydney, stopping to pick up the key from the agent's office, as well as dropping in to see Judy, who was staying in a nearby flat. Both flats were in Bondi, overlooking the beach, and the view was spectacular. After unpacking, they went for a stroll, stopping for a light lunch. That afternoon they made love, then both fell asleep, exhausted. For the very first time they shared Christmas dinner, celebrating the festive meal with four scrumptious courses at the historical Wentworth Hotel.[5] Judy joined them for the meal, later leaving to meet up with some Sydney friends.

After dinner Jaime and Fay made a wish at St Patrick's Catholic Church, diagonally opposite the hotel. Both of course, wished for the same outcome. Little did they realise this was the same church Jaime's parents were married at in 1888. After a pleasant drive to Neutral Bay, they returned to their room and retired for the night.

Boxing Day was hot and sunny, so the morning was spent at the beach. A leisurely lunch at Manly, then a look at Rose Bay where they had a sherry. That evening they joined Judy and her friend, Margaret, for dinner at a café near the flat, and all agreed Sydney was marvellous. Fay and Jaime were on top of the world; their holiday was everything they had wished for.

They took ferry rides, caught the Underground Railway to Milson's Point and went shopping. Jaime bought Fay a blue and white cotton sun dress at David Jones, where they indulged in afternoon tea. That night they dined at the Monterey and then saw the film, *The Rains Came*, starring Tyrone Power and Myrna Loy at the Regent Theatre.[6] One of Jaime's co-workers, Alec Cathcart, was staying in Sydney with his wife, Betty. She was an actress, singer and dancer, and was currently cast as principal boy in the pantomime *Mother Goose*. On the Saturday, 30 December, they attended a matinee session of the show at the New

Tivoli Theatre.[7] In the evening they attended a dance at the Palladium, only to find it was old time dancing, so had one dance and left. Jaime took Fay to The Australia Hotel for a drink in the magnificent Emerald Room, where he had spent New Year's Eve with his wife and son in 1932.

On the morning of Sunday 31 December, Jaime and Fay intended to go to Mass, however, the car would not start, so they had to leave it in the garage for two days. In the afternoon they went to the golf course and got drenched to the skin when the weather turned sour. After a leisurely dinner, they caught a taxi to King's Cross where they saw in the New Year and looked forward to a happy 1940, kissing on the stroke of midnight.

On New Year's Day, they didn't wake up until 11am, so skipped breakfast and went straight to Taronga Park Zoo and bought sandwiches and coffee at the kiosk. Later they visited the Aquarium, and then had a light dinner before collapsing in bed for an early night. The following morning was spent on the Harbour in a ferry, lunch at the Clifton Gardens Hotel in Mosman,[8] and they took snaps on the Coongarna Show Boat. Fay had her hair set late in the afternoon, as they planned to see the adventure film, *The Four Feathers*, starring John Clements, Ralph Richardson, and June Duprez that night.

They had three more precious days to go, before they would be returning to Melbourne, and they planned to make the most of it. On Wednesday, 3 January, they got up at 6am, had breakfast, and then left Sydney to head to the Jenolan Caves in the Blue Mountains. They stopped and had refreshments at the Lapstone Hotel and arrived at Katoomba mid-morning. More snaps were taken at Echo Point, and a delicious lunch was had at the Caves House before they explored the spectacular Lucas Cave, among others. After leaving the Caves at 5pm, they had a quick bite to eat at The Paragon[9] in Katoomba, and then headed back to Sydney.

The following morning they swam at Coogee, and in the afternoon visited Alec and Betty at their hotel in the city. That night they dined at Cahill's Restaurant[10] in Castlereagh Street, before returning home to change for a dance being held at the Princes, where they ran into two Melbourne friends.

Their last day was spent shopping, eating a lavish lunch with Alec and Betty at David Jones, and enjoying a drive to Watson's Bay. They had a quick swim before dinner, then packed a few things before catching a ferry to Luna Park, where they had much fun on the dodgem cars. Their last night in Sydney was mainly spent in each other's arms: they ate at a local restaurant then returned to the flat and jumped into bed and listened to the wireless — Bing Crosby was singing his hit 'Only Forever'.[11]

> *Do I want to be with you, as the years come and go?*
> *Only forever, if you care to know.*

They decided to spend the night in Albury on their way home, and booked in at the historical Soden's Hotel, built in 1855. This would be their last whole night together for a while, so they made every minute count. After breakfast on Sunday morning, they headed off, feeling rather sad that the holiday was over.

As Fay had annual leave of four weeks, she headed down to Clifton Springs, on the Bellarine Peninsula near Geelong for two weeks. She had booked in to the majestic Clifton Springs Hotel; the original had burnt down in 1921 and was rebuilt in 1926. The weekend Fay arrived, Jaime was in Sorrento. He had relented and arranged a brief holiday with Connie and Leon.

Sunday, 14 January 1940

My darling Jaime,
I arrived safe and sound and hope you did the same. Darling, how I wish you were here now, it is such a heavenly day, the sky as blue as your eyes, and just a lovely cool breeze to caress my suntan. How complete it would be with

you, I know this sounds terribly greedy, but having had you for breakfast, lunch, and dinner in Sydney makes me hungry for more, and I could never get enough of your company (or love).

I hope you enjoy the few days in Sorrento, but how I wish I was with you, not C. Darling, why do the happy days go so swiftly? I seem to have had you, only to lose you, but just thinking of you helps, and the happy thought of seeing you in a week's time is something to look forward to.

A couple of old boys have been trying to do a line just before dinner; one in particular will probably be a bit of a bore, as he is here until Easter. Seems to have plenty of money, and plenty of talk. He says he generally goes to India (or as he pronounces it, 'IndiAH') this time of year, but with the war etc. etc. He is one of the ugliest men I have seen in years, like Joe E. Brown of the films. It is very quiet here, most of the guests left after the New Year. A Dr Raphael, and his wife, and another family who are with them, are at my table. He is a big fat man and looks more like a plumber than a doctor. His wife is a salesgirl 'mannequin' at Myers, and struts round like a peacock.

Well Darling, I am longing for next weekend, so 'til then, I love you.

Fay

PS I was not successful in giving you the impression of my lips, but there's luck in odd numbers, and three is my lucky number.

Jaime managed to play some golf while he was at Sorrento with Connie and Leon. They were staying in a guesthouse, and Connie had already complained that it wasn't adequate; nevertheless, he managed to slip away and have a game. When he received Fay's letter at work on Tuesday afternoon, he replied immediately.

16 January 1940

Fay, Darling,
I am so glad you are having such a nice time. How I wish I was with you, and not back in town on my own.

The weekend was so-so. I managed to have a few rounds of golf with a couple of chaps I met at the club. C complained that our accommodation was insufficient and that the table was appalling. It seems nothing suits her. Leon enjoyed the beach and I took him into the surf one day.

I will definitely be down for the weekend, either Friday night, or first thing Saturday morning, but probably Friday. I will keep this brief as I want to catch the post. Just remember, I LOVE YOU, and only YOU.

Love from your Jaime

When Jaime arrived home that night, he and Connie ended up having an enormous argument.

17 January 1940

My darling Beautiful,

You know what? I love you, I love you, I love you. I am on my way home.

Thanks for your letters, I will treasure them. Things were rather hectic when I got home last night, and a few home truths were told. I have not mentioned this weekend as yet, but I will definitely be down on Friday night. By Jove, I am looking forward to seeing you, and am excited already. At any rate, Darling, I will be down for your last weekend to take my lovely back to town.

Have lots to tell you about the hectic storms that took place. Who knows? It may be just around the corner (you know what I mean). Well, Beautiful, all my love and adoration forever. Dying to see you and hear your voice.

From your Jaime

The magnitude of Jaime and Fay's affair meant that he was spending much less time with his son, Leon, who was turning ten in August. Jaime decided to buy him a puppy, and purchased a Kelpie that Leon named Blackie. At least his little boy would have company while he was away with Fay. Jaime's eldest brother, Tony, seemed the only sympathetic member of the family to understand his side of the story; however, Tony's wife Muriel was abhorred with the situation. In 1935, Tony had purchased a beautiful seven-roomed house and property, Green Ivies[12] in Box Hill, originally built around 1893. The property was huge and spanned more than twenty acres, with a tennis court, garage, stables, orchard and fowl pens. Occasionally, Jaime would visit his brother if he knew Muriel was out. After the failure of Melbourne Suburban Buses during the Depression, Tony had returned to his old profession as an accountant. Not long after buying Green Ivies, he became a poultry farmer, which he thoroughly enjoyed.

At the beginning of January 1940, Annie Johnston had a telephone installed at their home on Tooronga Road. Fay and Lil were thrilled, however Fay knew it would be a taboo for Jaime to ring as her mother was still against the relationship.

14 March 1940

Darling,

I was going to write you this letter in any case, but since receiving your very special surprise today, I felt I must write immediately and thank you. It was a lovely surprise, Sweetheart, and many thanks. But life is one long, heavenly surprise with you. Our love for one another is immortal — it will never die. As the days and years pass, they only strengthen and nurture it.

Sometimes when I do not feel particularly sleepy, I lie awake at night and re-live some of our very pleasant hours, especially some very precious ones we spent together in Sydney. That lovely day we had on the Harbour, going to the pictures together, swimming at Bondi — shopping together, dancing at Princes in lovely surroundings, and perfectly content with only each other's company. The trip to the Caves, our ride in the Underground Railway, Tooronga Park, teeming with animal life. Our games of golf, and getting soaked to the skin, it was a perfect holiday.

Darling, when I first met you eight years ago, little did I think that some unknown entity was weaving a web around us, from which neither of us could escape. Many times we have both tried to fight it, but have been weaponless because our love for each other has surmounted everything, and try as we may, our resolutions melt into thin air. I suppose if the world knew our secret, I would be the criminal, but they could not stop me from loving you, Darling.

If there is anyone who loves as sincerely and deeply as we do, they would be the only ones who would understand. My consoling thought is that I have not stolen your love, because you have reassured me of this many times. Perhaps it is not so criminal to wait indefinitely for someone you love without wishing anyone harm, and that is proof of our love for each other. I suppose it is natural for me to wish that a certain party would fall in love with someone else. But these things only seem to happen in books and pictures. If my mood has seemed introspective, or vice versa, forgive me, but believe me to be,

Always Yours,

Fay

Jaime had given Fay a bedside lamp — a crystal hobnail made of milk glass, as he knew she both read and wrote in bed. As the nights were getting colder with winter approaching, he felt it would be convenient and save Fay from having to get out of bed to switch off the main light. The look on Fay's face when he presented her with a gift made Jaime all the more intent to shower her with presents.

In August, Jaime came down with the flu, and was off work for a whole week. Fay missed him terribly and wrote to him constantly.

13 August 1940

Well, my Darling,

How are you after this long time? It seems like a thousand years, the time has dragged so since I saw you last. Darling, do you realise it has been nearly a week? I have missed you terrifically; the lunch hours have been monotonously boring without your cheery countenance to brighten me. When five o'clock comes, the thought of not having you to meet makes the

*day seem not worthwhile. I do hope you are quite well again, and that you
have been looking after yourself. After an attack of flu it leaves you terribly
weak, and you have to avoid getting any chills.*

*The Mater arrived home this evening (we did not expect her 'til tomorrow
evening) and she was full of news. My brother is much better, so she was able
to return sooner than she thought. I sat up until 10.15 then got into bed to
finish this letter, as I was half way through it before the Mater arrived home.*

*It was a very pleasant surprise hearing your voice on the phone this
morning. Each time you rang I wanted to tell you how much I love and miss
you, but did not like to say this on the phone. I missed you most of all on
Friday evening. I wandered round town from five o'clock until about 6.30 (I
did not really have any shopping to do) then had some dinner and went to the
Gazettes.*[13] *Most of the news stories were about the war, so I felt thoroughly
depressed. I got home about nine and had a cup of tea ready for Lilly, who
arrived shortly afterwards.*

*What a shocking air of tragedy today. It seemed too fantastic to be true
at first, and was thought to be only a rumour. The news came to the office
about 12.30, but no one seemed certain about it until lunchtime. The blinkers
are feeling rather heavy, Darling, so I will say goodnight and Thursday will
seem much nearer. You do not have to be nearer because you are right here
in my heart.*

All my love,

Fay

~

On 13 August 1940, an RAAF Lockheed Hudson crashed near
Canberra, killing three members of Cabinet, and the Chief of the
General Staff, General Cyril Brudenell White. Also killed were the four
crew members aboard. The Ministers, General White and their staff
were being flown from Melbourne to Canberra for a Cabinet meeting.
Fay's boss, Frank Brennan, being a former Member of Parliament, knew
all of those killed.

Fay's brother, Harry, had to be taken to hospital in August as he had pneumonia, so Annie travelled to Warragul to see him. Once a month, Harry would receive written confirmation that his child support payment had been received. This was sent to a post office box, and collected by his friend, Con Norris, who would deliver it to Harry. One day while still in hospital, Con had just left, and Harry had the written confirmation still in his hand. All of a sudden, he heard his wife's voice coming down the corridor, and terrified she would learn the truth of his illegitimate child, he ate the piece of paper, swallowing it just as she walked in to the room!

~

Not long after Lillian began working at Foy's she decided to call herself 'Lea', as she felt that it was a much more modern name. She loved her job and her new life, but had still not met a suitable beau.

A Federal Election was taking place on 21 September 1940. The current Prime Minister, Robert Menzies,[14] had commenced his first term in 1939 after the death of United Australia Party leader, Joseph Lyons. Annie Johnston was a staunch Labor voter and wanted John Curtin to win. Jaime, however, like his family, hoped that Menzies would remain Prime Minister. Fay sided with Jaime. Robert Menzies narrowly won the election.

Spring was in full bloom again and Fay looked forward to a summer holiday with Jaime. On her birthday, 6 October, he again lavished her with gifts and flowers, and everything seemed wonderful. In November she wrote a short letter, proclaiming her excitement of summer.

12 November 1940

Darling,
I am yours forever, nothing or nobody can alter that now. We are one, and I am proud of it. I am just longing for the holidays to come, which will

mean we can be together 'Night and Day'. Darling, I think I am your slave for life — enslaved to love — but it is an exquisite bondage, and I would not have it any other way. You are my whole world, and it is a beautiful world with you, nothing but sunshine. Darling, even if a few little clouds come along, we can weather them together. I must go now, Darling, hope to see you in the morning and have morning tea with you.

 Always all my love,

 Fay

Little did Fay know, as she wrote of her love, of the storm that would erupt and the betrayal by a so-called friend.

So Near And Yet So Far

Plans had been made for Fay and Jaime to return to Lorne for the New Year. They had booked in to the Cumberland for a fortnight and were extremely excited; this would be the longest holiday they had spent together. Both celebrated Christmas with their respective families and then on Christmas night, Connie received an anonymous phone call from a woman who told her about Jaime and Fay's plans. She also spilt the beans about their recent trip to Sydney. Although Jaime denied some of it, all hell broke lose at Stodart Street. The trip was cancelled.

26 December 1940

My darling Fay,

This will be very short as I have only a few minutes to write this note. Things have happened here since Friday. I cannot say much, but I or you have a very dangerous enemy at large. Some dirty scoundrel rang here anonymously last night, and said things that certainly shocked me and will probably surprise you. It certainly has made things a bit difficult for me, but I took your advice and denied everything.

I am sticking to you and have advised the other person accordingly. However, Darling, I don't want you to worry and for the time being I have smoothed things over. I suspect two persons, and two only. First of all Betty

(Alec's bitch) or Audrey, but I suspect the former. The full details will have to wait till I see you (I hope that will be Monday, although possibly it might not be until Wednesday). I will try and ring you tomorrow.

All my love to you, Fay,

Jaime

Alec, Jaime's co-worker at Dunlop's, and his wife, Betty, had entertained Fay and Jaime during their Sydney holiday the year before. Jaime always confided in and trusted Alec, yet his wife had made some derogatory comments to Jaime about his relationship with Fay.[1] This ruined her husband's friendship with Jaime for many years. It was eventually discovered that a nosy female co-worker at Dunlop's had overheard a conversation between Alec and Jaime and she had taken it upon herself to cause havoc by ringing Connie. Fay was so frightened that she didn't write to Jaime throughout most of January. She booked in at Clifton Springs again for the summer, and Jaime took Leon to Sorrento. Connie refused to go, and remained in Camberwell. It was a rotten blow to their plans, but as Fay told Lea, 'This is the price I pay for loving a married man.'

Jaime had denied that he and Fay were going away together, although he admitted spending the holiday in Sydney with her as the facts made it impossible to contradict. Connie always thought that Jaime had a string of ladies. When she finally learned that there was only one love, she realised the marriage was over. She had no intention of letting him go, however, or giving him the freedom to remarry. Now she remembered how much time Jaime had spent with Fay at Lorne the year before, and she was angry at her own naivety for not suspecting something was going on.

While Jaime was at Sorrento he wrote to Fay in Clifton Springs lamenting their lost holiday.

Sorrento Hotel, 8 January 1941

My very own adorable Fay,

I have just a few minutes to drop you this short note. The room we have is right overlooking the bay, and I spend a lot of time gazing over at your direction. How I wish you were here with me. I shall never forgive the person who put our show away. Just imagine, Darling, if it were not for that insidious person, we would have been together all these last few heavenly days. Leon and I are going home this afternoon, and I am glad as I am dying to hear from you. A holiday without you is no holiday at all. I'm afraid, Darling, that all the joy of seeing and being with Leon is no compensation for the happiness of being with you.

I will ring you Thursday about 1.30. Things are only fair, and I think there will be a big crisis soon, but I am with you, Darling, and she knows it now. I will try and get down to Geelong on Saturday to pick you up.

All my love to you,

Your own Jaime

Now that Connie knew about Fay, Jaime felt a little more relaxed when making plans to see her. From now on, if they planned to holiday together, Connie would just have to accept it. Fay and Jaime met every lunch hour and most evenings. If they didn't dine out or see a film, he would drive her home.

25 February 1941

Darling,

I just couldn't resist writing you this little note. Perhaps you can give a little thanks to Richard Tauber because he was the inspiration. He has just been singing Night and Day on the wireless and it reminded me so much of you that I just had to tell you at this very moment how much I missed not seeing you today. Darling, it was bad enough not seeing you all day, and the yearning in my heart for you was sufficient, but to sit and listen to that song made me miss you a thousand times more. I hope you ring me this evening — just to hear your voice over the phone will heal the aching in my heart. Darling, look out — when we get together next, I will want to gobble you up.

All my love, Fay

~

From 24 January 1941, Prime Minister Menzies spent four months in Britain discussing war strategy with Winston Churchill and other Empire leaders, while his position in Australia deteriorated. During his absence the Siege of Tobruk began in Libya on 31 March. Tobruk was attacked by an Italo-German force, led by Lieutenant General Erwin Rommel. The Nazi propaganda called the tenacious defenders 'rats', a term that the Australian soldiers embraced as an ironic compliment. On 30 June, HMAS *Waterhen* was heavily damaged by Axis aircraft in Libya, and attempts to tow the ship to port were unsuccessful. She sank. It was the first Australian naval vessel lost in the war.

As the war news continued to saturate the wireless airwaves and the film Gazettes, all of Australia wondered how it would affect their lives. Jaime was turning forty-three on 23 July, and as he'd only had limited experience with the AIF in 1918, he didn't enlist, much to Fay's relief. The year went by and there was still no sign of Jaime obtaining a divorce, and Fay's patience was wearing thin.

3 July 1941

Sorry, Darling,

I was in such a miserable mood when I left you this evening. No matter how much I weigh the pros and cons of our problem, I can only strive at one decision (not a solution, as only kismet knows the answer to that) and that is with the passing of the years, my love for you will have to strengthen my patience. I suppose when I look around and see my (so-

called) girlfriends settling down to wedded bliss, I get a bit down in the dumps, when I think how happy we could be living together. When I leave you of an evening, it tugs at the old heartstrings quite a bit.

Darling, forgive me once again, and the next time I get into one of these insufferable moods, take no notice. I will see you at Chapel Street at 6.15 tomorrow evening, unless you want to make it otherwise, and I will show you just how much I adore you.

All my love, Fay

When Jaime received Fay's apology letter the following morning, he immediately ordered flowers to be delivered to her office. The one thing Jaime wanted to avoid was Connie and Fay running into each other. As he was working out of town for the day, he added a warning in the note he sent along with the bouquet.

4 July 1941

Darling,

Thanks a million for your lovely letter. I am reciprocating with flowers as that is the nicest way I know how. The flowers say all I want to say, and I know you understand their language. Patience is a virtue and we both have to try our best in that way. Keep away from Manton's in the lunch hour, as C may be going there. I will see you at Chapel Street this evening.

All my love, Jaime

Occasionally, Jaime and Fay would have drinks and dinner at a quaint hotel Jaime had found in Argo Street, South Yarra. Sheppard's Hotel[2] was originally built around 1866, and as it was tucked away in a side street, they both felt relaxed and away from prying eyes. The hotel also had rooms for accommodation, and on Jaime's birthday he booked them a room for the night. At lunchtime Fay gave Jaime a note to celebrate his birthday.

23 July 1941

Darling,

Once again many happy returns of the day, and may today be the happiest and luckiest day of your life. Darling, there is one thing I am certain of, our birthdays may come and go but our love goes on forever. If we keep on loving each other as we do, our love will keep us in stride with youth, and as we reach or pass each milestone in life they are only more beautiful to reflect upon — and 'looking back and looking forward' to something heavenly makes life worthwhile. We will celebrate this evening Darling, and I cannot wait to see our little room as then I can really show you how much I love you and ache for you. I know one day we will have our own 'little room,' where we can be together for ever. 'Til this evening Darling,

Fay

On 29 August Robert Menzies resigned as Prime Minister of Australia, and Arthur Fadden, head of the Country Party became the new leader of the land. Although Jaime and Fay had no real interest in politics, both were shocked and disappointed that Menzies had gone.

9 September 1941

Darling Jaime,

I am sorry I get a bit tense at times, but it is only because I love you so much, and I get so possessively jealous that I cannot even bear to share your company. I want to be with you all the time morning, noon, and night especially the latter). I wish every night was Friday night. If we didn't have Fridays and golf to look forward to, I would get terribly impatient, but it does help and I look forward to those hours more than the whole week put together.

Darling, I am so sorry I had to be brief on the phone this morning, but Mr B came out and needed an urgent letter typed up. With all this change in leadership he has been rather busy, and has had a few meetings with his

Labor cronies. I daren't mention I support Menzies, I think I'd lose my job. Well, enough office talk, Darling. We must have another weekend together soon, with all the glorious spring weather in the foreground, just imagine how inviting the links at Torquay would look — and afterwards a dive in the surf to cool off, and then just you and I all to ourselves. Just to let you know again that I love you intensely and more terrifically as each year passes, and hope we will always love together, live together, and be together for the rest of our days.

All my love, Darling, Fay

On Tuesday night 23 September, industrial centres throughout southern Victoria and the whole of metropolitan Melbourne were completely blacked out for one hour between 9 and 10pm More than 1700 police and wardens observed the effect of the blackout, and emergency services were on standby. Failure to extinguish lights meant heavy fines, and no motor cars or cyclists were permitted to travel in the blackout areas during the test. All lights, including torches, cigarettes and the striking of matches was forbidden. This test proved to the public that Australia really was at war, and many tuned into the wireless that night to listen to news broadcasts, wondering what the future might bring.

23 September 1941

Darling,

I want to thank you for the lovely gift you handed me on Saturday. Almost everything I possess now seems to be part of you, even myself. I wish we were spending this evening together. Remember our last blackout, when the rest of the world ceased to exist?

I wish we could both retire to some remote part of the country, for at least a few months of the year, just playing golf and having early nights. Perhaps we will some day; it would be the ideal existence. I always thought I would hate the quietness of country life, but so long as we were together, I would not mind where we lived.

Well Darling, I will say adieu and hope to see you tomorrow,
Fay

Arthur Fadden resigned as Prime Minister on 3 October, following the rejection of his budget by two independent MPs and on the 7 October, Labor Member, John Curtain, was sworn in as Prime Minister.

News came through on 19 November that a sea battle in the Indian Ocean, near Shark Bay, between HMAS *Sydney* and the German auxiliary cruiser *Kormoran*, had caused both ships to sink. All 645 on board the *Sydney* were killed, along with 82 personnel from the *Kormoran*.

On 9 December, Australia declared war on Japan and the Axis powers of Finland, Hungary and Romania. Now Australians were realising that the war was closer to their shores than they thought.

26 December 1941
Darling,
The last two days have seemed endless what with the heat and being caged in the house for the last 48 hours and the yearning to be with you. My heart has cried out for you a thousand times, but in vain. I am just living for Saturday to see you again. With the exception of going up for the morning and evening papers, I have scarcely been outside the door, and the thought of these hot days passing without as much as a lounge on the beach makes me see red. I wish in a way now, I had gone to Torquay without Judy; if it hadn't been for the blackouts here and the mater on her own, I most certainly would have. But enough of my moans, Darling — I have missed you like HELL. It has been the latter too, in more ways than one. Each day I have tried to imagine myself back in Sydney, and last night as I sat on my lonesome on the back veranda, I relived our Xmas day in Sydney. What seemed to stand out uppermost in my mind was the church we visited and had a wish under its mortals. It helped quite a lot reliving those hours over again, and made me feel that perhaps this waiting was worthwhile.

Every time the phone rang today, I hoped it might be you, but each time it happened to be for Lea — she is certainly having ideal weather for her sojourn down at Chelsea. The mater is hosing the garden at the moment, so I am rattling this off on the typewriter before she finishes.

The Prime Minister is to deliver his speech in about another ten minutes, so she will be coming in to listen, and this letter will have to be finished before then. Forgive me if I sound forlorn, but I am longing to see you and I am going to bed early tonight to hasten tomorrow. I wish all the tomorrows could be spent with you Darling and then every day would be a lovely day.

All my love, Fay

On the evening of the 26 December, John Curtain addressed the nation in a radio address that made it quite clear that Australia was in grave danger from the Japanese, and reflected Curtin's disillusionment with Winston Churchill's assurances that Britain would furnish powerful support if Australia was threatened with a Japanese invasion.

'Without any inhibitions of any kind, I make it quite clear that Australia looks to America free of any pangs as to our traditional links or kinship with the United Kingdom.'

Jaime had spent Christmas with his family, which saddened Fay, though he found the time to meet up with her on Saturday 27 and they spent the day at Mornington soaking up the sunshine on the beach, swimming, and enjoying every minute together. On Wednesday 31 December while in town shopping, Fay wrote him a letter while at Georges department store in their writing room. As Connie was spending the New Year with her sister Vera, Jaime made plans to meet up with Fay.

31 December 1941

Hello Darling,

Have just been addressing a few New Year cards and thought I would send you this little greeting. Seeing it is the last day of 1941, I thought the hour very appropriate to wish you happiness and prosperity in the coming year.

I do hope 1942 will bring you loads of good luck, and that this darned old war will come to an end soon. I hope too that we are going to see lots of each other in the years to come, and that the war will not make any difference to us but instead draw us closer together. Well, Darling, I must now resume my shopping expedition and am looking forward to seeing you in the next hour.

   Fay

Being able to celebrate the New Year together was something they both cherished. As they kissed each other at midnight, they wondered what 1942 might bring. The war hovered over all their thoughts, and for now the future was not looking so bright.

   Jaime was taking Leon and Connie to Mornington for a holiday in late January. Fay understood that he had to spend time with his son, but missed him desperately each time they were apart. They decided it would be best if Fay addressed her letters to J. C. Farrell c/o the Mornington Post Office. Even though Connie knew about her rival, Jaime wanted to avoid any conflict during the family holiday.

   2 February 1942

   My Jaime,

   Have just read your letter and am glad to hear you are having a good holiday. Darling, I can't ever remember missing you as much as I have this holiday. I seem to be going about my work in a detached sort of way, as if my other self is down there with you. At night I just ache for you. Last night was a glorious night with a full moon, and I wondered if you were longing for me just as much as I was for you. I know you were, Darling, and I felt like hugging Old Man Moon and telling him we would soon be making his acquaintance again.

   I did not go out on Saturday, just sunbaked on the back lawn. On Sunday, we (Judy, Mollie and Hilda) went to Edithvale. Hilda bought the car, feeling pretty guilty about petrol, but she had her pleasure rationing amount. We all took our tea and had a great spread after our swim.

Georges Limited
162 COLLINS STREET, MELBOURNE C1
Writing Room

31.12.41
3.45 p.m.

Hello Darling,

Have just been addressing a few New Year cards and thought I would send you this little Greeting for the New Year.

Seeing as it is the last day of 1941 I thought the hour very appropriate to wish you Happiness & Prosperity in the coming Year.

I do hope 1942 will bring you loads of Good Luck and that this darned old war will come to an end soon.

I hope too Darling that we are going to see lots of each other in the years to come & that the War will not make any difference to us, but draw us closer together.

Distinctive Fashionwear!

Well Darling I must now resume my Shopping expedition & am looking forward to seeing you in the next hour.

Until then My Darling.
all my love,
Fay

Darling, I am missing you terrifically in the lunch hours and after 5.
I realise now that I could never give you up. I have been dreaming of you
almost every night, and when I wake I sometimes wish so hard that I could
reach over and clasp your hand. I almost feel you are there in the flesh. You
have taken complete charge of this old heart of mine, and without you to
regulate its beating, I think it would play all sorts of tricks on me, because
it aches for you night and day and it is only happy when it is beating
against yours.

Goodnight, My Beloved,

Fay

Dava Lodge, Mornington, 2 February 1942

My Own Darling Fay,

Leon and his little friend have gone down to have a ride on the horses,
and Connie has gone down with them, so I have grasped the opportunity to
drop you a line. Another chap wanted me to play golf but I turned him down
to drop you this note. So you see, Darling, I am still thinking of you first and
always.

How are you? I miss you terribly and am just dying to get back to see
you. Loving you isn't so good now as it spoils my holidays. If I wasn't missing
you so much, I would love it down here. But the desire for you is greater than
the pleasure of a holiday. We MUST have another weekend together soon.

With the big military camp being so near, you see a lot of soldiers, but
they don't come to Dava. Military cars and wagons pass continuously along
the road and the boys get very excited. Yesterday afternoon about 100 gun
carriers drove past — they were AIF from Puckapunyal on manoeuvres.

Well, Darling, I must hurry away as I have promised to go down and
meet the folks.

Jaime

Almost one million American service personnel passed through Australia during World War II. American troops started arriving in Australia in December 1941. At first they were welcomed as saviours, but as time went on the glamour of their presence wore off. Australians became a little more critical of American ways even though the importance of the American alliance was never in question.

4 February 1942

Well, my darling Jaime,

I have just finished dinner and made myself comfortable by the wireless, complete with book as a pretext for writing this note, and I have also just read your second letter several times (I read your first one a dozen times). It reassures me that you are missing me as much as I am missing you.

I could have wished the boss somewhere when you rang me today, he was a bit on edge as he was giving me a letter, and I purposely asked 'were you speaking from Mornington', so he would know it was a trunk call and he shuffled out, but came back just as the three minutes were up. When you asked me today how was town, I meant to tell you that it was swarming with Yankee soldiers and sailors. They were all over the place, and especially conspicuous on hotel corners. They look a pretty cheeky crowd. Some of them seem rather fine types but these are few and far between, and to hear their nasal twang as one passes by is 'shure cute'. Darling, if they gave me the British, American, or any navy to choose the best man from, I would want that man to be you.

Well, Darling, my arm is getting a trifle crampy, so will bid you goodnight.

All my love, Fay

On 19 February, mainland Australia came under attack for the first time when Japanese forces mounted two raids on Darwin. The two attacks which were planned and led by the commander responsible for the attack on Pearl Harbour ten weeks earlier involved 54 land-based bombers and approximately 188 attack aircrafts which were launched from four Japanese air-craft carriers in the Timor Sea. The attack ceased after about forty minutes and the second attack began an hour later. 243 people were killed, and between 300 and 400 wounded. Twenty military aircraft were destroyed, eight ships at anchor in the harbour were sunk, and most civil and military facilities were destroyed. With Singapore having fallen to the Japanese only days earlier, and concerned at the effect of the bombing on national morale, the government falsely announced that only seventeen people had been killed.

In late February, Fay took her holidays and spent them at Dava Lodge where Jaime and his family had stayed only a few weeks earlier. Meanwhile, he was back at work and missing her as usual.

While at Dava Lodge, Fay couldn't resist speaking to staff about the San Miguel family.

When I spoke to the cleaner yesterday about Leon she seemed to take it for granted that you were a very happy trio and I felt pretty jealous about the whole business. She told me you were in rooms further down the corridor to mine, and I was dying to have a peek. Well, Darling, you may not think that would hurt, but it did and I felt very miserable after it and wished I hadn't said a word to her. If only C would fall in love with another man, it would help a lot.

～

Leon was now twelve years old, and Jaime was making an effort to spend more time with him. Often he would take him to football matches on a Saturday afternoon at Xavier where the boy attended school.

Listening to the wireless one evening, a song came on that made Fay think it was written especially for she and Jaime. Written by Cole Porter, and sung by Fred Astaire for the 1941 film, *You'll Never Get Rich*, the song filled her with sadness about the future of their relationship.

So near and yet so far
My dear I've a feeling you are so near and yet so far
You appear like a radiant star
First so near then again so far

Jaime had some concerns about his job at Dunlop's, which he wrote about in a letter to Fay, on the 25 February as she was still holidaying at Dava Lodge.

Things at Dunlop's are not so good, and there is an air of uneasiness. Everybody seems to be leaving or being asked to look for another job. It is just Dunlop's form to do this to their employees. If things are running smoothly everything is okay, but as soon as things get a little bad, they let you down. So far the mechanical section that I am in has not been affected, but for how long?

Sometimes Jaime's jealousy raised its head when Fay was away, and he often misconstrued a letter or phone call, which he did on 3 March.

3 March 1942

My dear Fay,
I suppose I have cooled off a wee bit since I rang you at lunch, but I still feel damn hot under the collar. When Saturday night came along with its beautiful moon, I went out to gaze at it and think of you and be with you, but I felt you were miles away, not close as usual. I had a dream that you were not my Fay that night, and that the marvellous moon had gone to your head. In the dream, you say you were out alone underneath the dangerous moon with the same person. Then you add fuel to the fire and say that this man is coming down for dinner on Wednesday to see you, and that he seems very keen. Nobody becomes keen on a person without a great deal of encouragement, and Saturday and Sunday evenings would be enough encouragement for

anyone. You even tell me that you know his age and that he comes from East Camberwell. People as a rule do not find out each other's age unless they get along pretty well. But of course, you hate soldiers and uniforms. I must say, Darling, after such a wonderful afternoon and evening on Friday, I am a little disappointed to know that you forget it so easily during the weekend. I know that you will think I am a cad to write you in such a strain, and that I am a jealous old fool, but darling, I can't help it and if you love me and want to love me you will have to accept this rotten part of my nature.

I am afraid I love very deeply, so naturally I am very jealous. I give a lot, and expect a lot in return. Well, Darling, I might be wrong, and I hope so, and a bit hasty in my judgement, but I expect a good explanation about Saturday and Sunday evenings. Until then I shall continue to love you, and hope I am wrong in my fears.

All my love, Jaime

Of course, Jaime was wrong, although occasionally Fay did like to test his jealousy when her frustration of being the 'other woman' overcame her.

As the war continued, other changes would take place, especially concerning Jaime's career.

Night And Day

Jaime picked Fay up from Mornington on Saturday 7 March, and was extremely happy to have her in his arms once more. They had a leisurely drive back to Melbourne, stopping for tea and sandwiches in Frankston. Fay was returning to work on the Monday and expecting a gruelling time: one of the other secretaries was away, and Fay had to cover her job as well as her own.

Around mid-March, Jaime was told by Dunlop's that his job was no longer needed, and he found himself out of work. This was a time of extreme concern for him, and he immediately set about looking for work. Before the end of the month he had landed a position with the United States Army, as Manager and Controller of tyres in Sturt Street, South Melbourne. His job was to organize and set up their Tyre Depot, and the work covered the disposal, procurement, storage and replacement of all tyres and tubes. Fay sent a congratulatory note when she heard the news.

25 March 1942

My Darling,

I intended dropping you this note yesterday to celebrate your very successful day, but here it is Darling and conveying to you all the best of luck in your new venture. I know Darling you will be successful in this new job, because no matter what you tackle, you give it all you've got. You will probably think, Darling, that you are lucky getting in with them, but actually they are very lucky getting you, and I know they will find this out to their advantage very soon. Well, Darling, this is only a good luck note, so will save any further news until this evening.

All my love,

Fay

Easter was approaching and Jaime booked their old bungalow at Woodend for the holiday. Fay was ecstatic, and couldn't wait to return to their original love nest. They drove down on Good Friday the third April, and would return on Monday evening — four perfect days and three whole nights together. Jaime had begun his new job on 30 March, so had only been in it for four days when the Easter break began. They intended to play golf most days, however the weather changed and it rained buckets, and so much of their time was spent making love in their little room. Neither of them, of course, objected to this.

By Monday morning the sun was out, and they enjoyed a pleasant day on the golf course. After an early dinner, they drove back to Melbourne. Although Fay had not told her mother the whole truth about her holiday, Annie was suspicious and when Fay walked in the door she was waiting, angry and impatient.

'I prayed for you at Mass yesterday Fay,' she said hollowly, following Fay into her room. 'I prayed that you had not spent Easter in sin but I was wrong, wasn't I?'

Fay put her case on the bed, then turned to her mother, her face worn. 'I'm tired and I don't wish to discuss this tonight. Please mother, just let it be.'

They heard the click of the front door; Lea had arrived home. She entered the room with a skip in her step, flushed from being out to a dance with some girls from Foy's. Thankfully for Fay, this prompted their mother to leave the room and their conversation was put on hold.

Lea was anxious to hear all about Fay's sojourn, but more excited to confess she'd met a boy who she liked and had experienced her first real kiss. Despite the fact that Lea was an attractive girl with coffee-coloured hair and big brown eyes, she was painfully shy and it had taken a long time for her to feel at ease in a man's company. Tommy Carson was the one who had stolen her heart that night. At twenty-nine years old, a year older than Lea, Tommy was tall with sandy hair, pale blue eyes, and a crooked smile. He was in the Australian Army and would soon be posted overseas. Currently on leave, Tommy had asked Lea out for dinner on Wednesday evening, and she was beside herself with excitement.

'Oh Fay, wait till you meet him!' she gushed. 'He's so handsome and charming. I know you'll like him right away.'

In fact everyone liked him, including Annie. When he bought Lea home on Wednesday night, Annie insisted he join them for supper. She too was charmed with his good manners and humour, and happy that her youngest daughter, had at long last, met a nice man. Over the next two months, Tommy Carson became a regular visitor at their home. It was as if Lea was a changed person; she was much more confident and completely happy. Tommy was based at the Puckapunyal Army Camp in central Victoria, and whenever he was on leave he spent it with Lea. They played tennis, went to the pictures, and had picnics and dinners together. Lea intended to wait for marriage before becoming intimate, and Tommy respected her wishes; he too was a Roman Catholic, and that also pleased Annie.

Sometimes Annie's constant nagging caused Fay to question her relationship with Jaime, and she would discuss this with him. Nevertheless, despite her mother's concerns, she knew in her heart she could not live without him. After a little tiff Fay wrote to him on 30 April.

I knew I had hurt you Darling, and I suffered more knowing it, because all my resolutions and half thought out promises to my Mater vanish into thin air after I have left you and realise how they have hurt you. If you love someone terribly, how is it possible to see them looking unhappy? You have told me very emphatically that you can never and will never recapture any happiness in your home life with the other party. I am convinced of our need for each other, and fail to see any solution to our problems. I love you and can't seem to do anything about it.

~

On 3 May 1942, 40-year-old Violet McLeod was found strangled in Victoria Avenue, Albert Park, Melbourne. She was partly naked and had been badly beaten by her attacker. Two more women, 31-year-old Pauline Thompson and 40-year-old Gladys Hosking were the next victims of what became known as the Brownout Strangler. In all three cases an American soldier had been seen in the area where the bodies were found. 24-year-old Edward Joseph Leonski of the 52nd Signal Battalion was eventually arrested and confessed to the crimes. Leonski was Court Marshalled by an American military court in a hall in Russell Street, Melbourne. He was sentenced to death by hanging. General Douglas MacArthur confirmed the sentence on 4 November 1942. Leonski was hung at Pentridge Prison on 9 November the same year. The murders scared everyone in Melbourne, especially the women.

20 May 1942

Darling,

Just a very short note to thank you for the lovely little gift you handed me yesterday. It reminded me of a certain shopping expedition in Sydney, which I will always remember as one of the happiest shopping days in my life. That certain day left a very lasting impression of sunshine and some very happy hours. Remember our luncheon al fresco afterwards on one of Sydney's skyscraper rooftops? So many wonderful memories, Darling.

On another note, everyone at the office and home are terribly worried

about these awful murders. Lea now catches the tram with a co-worker from
Foy's each evening, and of course, I usually have my Darling to drive me
safely home.

   Well, Sweetheart, I will see you tonight,
   All my love,
   Fay

In mid-July, Tommy Carson was being sent to Papua, New Guinea with
the 7th Division of the AIF Prior to him leaving he proposed to Lea and
she accepted. He presented her with a sapphire ring and she was over
the moon. A small engagement party was held the weekend before his
departure. On Monday 13 July, Lea said a tearful farewell to her much
loved fiancé. At lunch on the same day, Jaime was feeling uneasy.

   'I have a bad feeling about Tommy leaving today,' he said to Fay.

   'Whatever for?'

   'The thirteenth.'

   'Oh, don't be ridiculous, Darling,' she laughed. 'I thought only us
Irish believed in such rubbish. He'll be fine.'

   Jaime forced a smile, though his knee continued to twitch with
nerves. He had met Carson on a number of occasions and thought him
a very nice chap. He was happy that Lea had found love, but couldn't
understand why he felt so off that afternoon

   On the 21 July 1942 the Japanese landed near Gona on the north
coast of Papua. The next two months they drove the Australians and
their Papuan allies back over the mountains towards Port Moresby. This
town was vital to the defence of Australia, if they took Port Moresby
the Japanese planned to begin a bombing offensive against North
Queensland, and had they decided to invade Australia, the invasion
would have been launched from Port Moresby.

   Over the rugged mountains of Papua, New Guinea, along a narrow
track, called the Kokoda Trail, Tommy Carson and his comrades began
their excruciating march through putrid mud and hellish conditions.

On Saturday the 29 August, during the Battle of Isurava, Tommy Carson was shot by a Japanese sniper and killed instantly.

Monday evening, 7 September, Lea received a telegram from the Australian Army informing her of Tommy's death. After reading the news she fainted. Fortunately, both Fay and her mother were home. Lea was inconsolable and never really recovered from the disastrous news. She felt she could never, ever, love another man the way she loved her Tommy.

Everyone was mortified by the news: Lea took a week off work, and Annie had to take her to the doctor as she was so distressed. Now that the Johnston family had been touched by the atrocities of war, they all wondered when the horror would end. After the tragedy, Jaime and Fay didn't write for a few months. They felt too guilty that they still had each other, and Lea was alone again.

~

As Jaime was working in South Melbourne for the American Army, his daily lunches with Fay were now limited to once a week, although he still met Fay after work and they would either go out or he would drive her home, depending on his family situation. It seemed a continuous struggle for them both; the problems with Fay's mother, and Connie's refusal to get a divorce

3 November 1942

Darling,

I just had to write this little note to thank you for the exquisite brooch, the theatre tickets, and the other very special gift you handed to me last Friday evening. I really don't deserve all these nice things, Darling, and I'm sorry for being so priggish lately. It is only because I love you so much that I get so weary and impatient with other people's interference (on both our sides). Physically, it seems to be an endless war we are waging, but if the strength of our love means anything, we should come out on the winning side which I hope is not far off. I want you for keeps, Darling, night and day, which reminds me of a strange coincidence on the wireless this morning. It was whilst I was having my breakfast that it was playing Tomorrow is a Lovely Day and I was thinking to myself what lovely words they were, and how soon or how long we would have to wait for our tomorrows. As it played on, I started thinking about our song, Night and Day, and then to my utter amazement the wireless played the latter directly afterwards. I am not very superstitious (perhaps the tiniest bit) but I felt it was a good omen and hope that it is a message of happier tomorrows. Well, Darling, I must bid you adieu until tonight.

All my love,

Fay

Another year was coming to an end, and the war raged on. Jaime only had the public holidays off over Christmas and New Year, whereas Fay had her usual annual leave, and once again returned to Dava Lodge. She had hoped Lea might accompany her, but she was still in mourning for her fiancé. Fay caught the train to Frankston late Christmas Day, and then a bus to Mornington.

Mornington, 25 December 1942

10.15pm

Darling,

I have just retired to bed, and you will gather I reached Dava safe and sound. How are you, Darling? Did you enjoy your Xmas dinner? My Aunt Anne came round and we spent a very pleasant day with her before I had to leave. She really is a darling, and I think she thoroughly enjoyed the day. We had a very chatty sort of day, and I found out in the course of conversation that she is a trained singer, and used to sing at concerts etc. Although she was rather modest about her accomplishments, I think she must have had rather a fine voice. So much to my surprise there is singing talent in the Johnston family. I told her what a perfectly rotten voice I had (did I hear you say, 'Hear, hear'?) but as I did not prove it to her, she was unaware of its atrocity. So you see, Darling, I may yet give birth to some budding songsters — it is in the blood somewhere, and if I find the right branch on the old family tree, I may be successful yet.

Wasn't it a perfectly lovely Xmas Eve? At least I was grateful for being able to spend it with you. How I wish you were right here with me now, we could continue where we left off last night. Friends of Lea talked her into attending a party, and some chap has got pretty keen on her, but she doesn't like him a bit. She says no one will replace Tommy. I hope she will meet someone and fall in love again. I must go to sleep now, Darling, but will write again tomorrow.

All my love,

Fay

Jaime's new job kept him very busy, however, it didn't stop him from spending time with Leon. Problems at home continued, and he wrote the news to Fay.

C/O USA Army,

Sturt Street Ordnance Depot,

130 Sturt Street, South Melbourne

Wed. 30 December 1942

Fay,

At last I have the opportunity to drop you a line. I have to write to you while in the office, and here I have a great number of interruptions, everybody is buzzing around me. I have just received your lovely letter. Betsy Brown and Dorothy Hunt want to know who the lady is writing to me from Dava Lodge. Sticky beaks, aren't they? Wouldn't they like to know?

Friday, Xmas Day, we had dinner at Mrs O'Reilly's in the Dandenong Ranges. After a drive, we returned home for tea after visiting my mother to wish her a happy Xmas. On Saturday I went to work, and strangely enough was very busy in the morning. At noon Leon came in for his first swimming lesson at the Olympic Pool. He came back with me to the Depot and played around until it was time to go home. On the way home the Pontiac started to play up, and I was hardly able to get her home. Went to the Rivoli Theatre Saturday night and nearly boiled. Sunday morning the fuss started, and lasted more or less all day. I spent most of the day (it was terribly hot in Melbourne) cleaning the gas producer. Just a labour of love, hoping that whatever was wrong with the car would be fixed in time to slip down to see you one day during the week. Sunday night the fuss broke out afresh, C had one of her worst ever nerve storms. Did your ears burn? You were the lady who had blighted our lives etc., etc. It was about 2.30am before I got to sleep.

I am sincerely hoping the car will be ready by Saturday, and then I could drive and arrange to bring you back on Sunday. We might even stop and have a game of golf at Frankston. At any rate, I will make final arrangements on the phone on Saturday. Well, Darling, I just hate Melbourne without you. I love you.

All my love from your HUSBAND.

PS I will probably want to eat you up on the way home, so we might forget the golf.

Jaime and Fay saw the New Year of 1943 apart, so plans were made for a weekend together in Torquay for late February. Jaime rented a flat, as it was close to the beach and not far from the golf course. They drove down late afternoon on Friday 19 February. It was an idyllic holiday, the weather was perfect and they swam, played golf, and enjoyed meals that Fay cooked. She whipped up a perfect savoury omelette, and roasts were her specialty. They both felt as if they were married. Waking up in each other's arms was the joy of the whole weekend. Yet neither of them knew what these two days and nights of pleasure would result in, and the painful decision they would soon have to make.

As Time Goes By

It had now been nearly twelve years since Jaime and Fay first met and fell in love. They still hoped Connie would relent and agree to a divorce, yet as the months passed by, nothing changed.

In March, Fay's menstrual period was late; at first she was unconcerned, blaming her workload and the war. When two weeks went by and it still hadn't come, she made an appointment with her friend Judy's doctor who practised in another suburb. Her worst fears were confirmed; she was pregnant. Although she and Jaime were always careful during intercourse, there had been times when their passion overcame them, and this had been the case during their weekend in Torquay. On Tuesday evening, 23 March, when Fay met Jaime after work, she resolved to tell him.

In other circumstances this news would have given them great joy, yet sadly they could see the complications and scandal that would arise should they keep the child. They made their ultimate decision based on the only sensible answer they could think of. The pain it caused them was overwhelming — the one thing Fay had always prayed for was having a baby with the man she adored, and Jaime felt the same way. They would also be committing another mortal sin in the eyes of the Catholic Church, yet they felt there was no other choice.

A former school friend of Jaime's, a doctor, gave him the phone number and address of a colleague who terminated pregnancies.

4

Darling although only 2 days have elapsed since I saw you I am missing you dreadfully already and am counting the hours for your return. I hope there will be a letter from you when I arrive home tomorrow night as I leave before the Postman in the mornings.

Cheerio Darling, enjoy yourself & save up all your surplus energy for next week because we will both need it. I don't know what excuses I am going to make at home but nothing can stop me from seeing you this side of the Globe.

Hoping you are well.

All my love

Jay

P.S. I am sealing the letter & enclosing some for you to put on my letters.

Although it was illegal, many doctors took the risk and performed them at their surgeries. The only other person who knew about the pregnancy was Judy, and she offered Fay a shoulder to cry on all through the torment. Jaime accompanied Fay to the surgery on the morning of the procedure. Afterwards he would drive her and Judy to Rosebud, where she would recuperate at Judy's boyfriend's beach house.

Fay had taken the day off work, calling in sick, as had both Jaime and Judy. It was a very sombre trio who arrived at the doctor's rooms in Albert Park at 10am on Monday 29 March 1943. Fay could hardly speak for the rest of the day. She wondered how her life had come to this, and what kind of a woman was she to have let it happen. She could not live with herself if anyone ever found out.

As hard as the experience had been, however, it brought Jaime and Fay closer together, and Fay would never forget the joy of that weekend in Torquay regardless of its sad outcome.

Friday, 2 April 1943

Jaime, I haven't said thanks for that lovely weekend,
Those three days of heaven you helped me to spend
With glorious memories of just we two alone
Having breakfast together and trips to Geelong.
The six holes of golf that we shouldn't have played
And the tale by the Greenkeeper who wished we could stay,
I know you will laugh when I hand you this poem
But it hardly describes all the hours spent alone
With someone I love
More than you'll ever know
The only drawback to that lovely weekend was
Those three days of heaven soon came to an end
But before I conclude
It leaves me to spend
The rest of my days loving you to the end.

Fay took extra holidays prior to Easter, and headed to Dava Lodge with Lea on 18 April. Their mother was going to Warragul to spend the break with Harry and Marie, five-year-old Ronald, and the new arrival, Phillip Anthony George Johnston, who was born on 16 January 1942.

Mornington, 19 April 1943

Darling,

How are you? As you will see we arrived safely at Dava, and are well pleased with our rooms. Lea was lucky enough to get the best and brightest, as it overlooks the back portion of the house and she gets rather a good view with the morning sun shining through. I am just opposite her room but my window looks out across to the lounge. I am quite satisfied as there is plenty of fresh air.

We did not go down on the morning train, as it was such a frightful morning, so caught the 3.34 from Caulfield (we were lucky in getting a lift over — just as we were waiting for the bus outside our place, some old Johnny came along in a big car and offered us a lift to the station). By the way, the Mater decided at the last moment to go to Warragul, and she is catching the 8.45 train this morning. She did not like the idea of being alone in the house as Cam is also away. We were much more relieved to know she would be down at Warragul.

The crowd here are pretty punk, there are only about twelve to fifteen people left. Mrs Ross said it is always quiet just before Easter. Darling, how I wish you were down here, or better still, we were at Torquay.

I hope Connie and Leon have both recovered. I suppose you were kept pretty busy as nursemaid over the weekend — I hope you don't catch cold as a result.

Last night they turned out a few games here, and a few girls had some Americans with them, but they looked very so-so and they had to leave by 11.30pm They have issued a rule and regulation that no soldiers are allowed to be on the premises or grounds after 11.30 and no one allowed in bedrooms.

I suppose some of them went too far. I believe one soldier (a Yank) got too much drink in him and started to fight everybody. They had to employ the Military Police to get him out.

I suppose I had better change for lunch. If Lea comes over and finds me still writing (which she is going to find me doing a lot), she will think I am crazy — but I don't care.

Cheerio, my Beloved, I love you a thousand times more than I did last Friday, and that was a heap.

Your loving wife,

Fay

Ever since the abortion, they signed their letters 'husband' or 'wife'. Although Jaime felt angry at Connie for continuing to deny him a divorce, he always came to the rescue when she or Leon were ill. Yet he still had pangs of jealousy whenever Fay was on holiday.

20 April 1943
1.20pm

My dear Fay,

I am hurriedly scrawling this note to you at the YMCA. I have just had lunch here. I don't want to be back late from lunch this week, as when you are in Melbourne I usually am. Thanks for your nice letter this morning. Yes, I did have a hectic time as 'nursemaid' during the weekend, but both parties are better now.

Fancy Dava having such few visitors. I suppose it will be pretty crowded at Easter. Anyhow, I can't imagine you having a dull time for long, because unfortunately for me, even if it's only one man there, it won't be long before he gets his eye on you. So if a few more arrive at Easter, there will be a queue waiting. I trust if there are a few Yanks about that you will watch your step, and not let their charms put you off your guard. I want you to come back to me, just as clean as you went away, and don't forget you are my wife and

I am your husband. I am watching you all the time, and KNOW what you are doing. At the same time, please thoroughly enjoy yourself, and don't let me spoil your fun, or your holiday, (as long as there are no kisses etc.) for the remainder of the time.

I am going to register this letter for safety's sake.

With all my love, from Jaime (your husband)

PS Have just met John Cooke, he is on furlough from New Guinea.

John Cooke had joined the Australian Army during World War I, and did so again in World War II. He saw much action and fortunately survived both wars. After the war Cooke returned to his profession as a solicitor, in his company, Cooke and Cussen, and he remained Jaime's best friend for the rest of their lives.

Back on 7 August 1942, allied forces, predominately American, landed on the islands of Guadalcanal, in the southern Solomon Island. Their objective was to deny the Japanese the supply and communication routes between the United States, Australia, and New Zealand. The allies also intended to use Guadalcanal and Tulagi as bases to support a campaign to eventually capture the major Japanese base at Rabaul on New Britain. The allies overwhelmed the outnumbered Japanese defenders, who had occupied the islands since May 1942, and captured Tulagi and Florida, as well as an airfield that was under construction on Guadalcanal. Codenamed 'Operation Watchtower' by allied forces, powerful US naval forces supported the landings.

Mornington, 20 April 1943
12.45pm

Hello Darling,
Have just arrived back from Mount Martha. We went to see the Presentation of Stripes and Military Medals to the US M Corps for conspicuous

bravery at Guadalcanal. It was most impressive, and they had a marvellous band. It started at ten o'clock so we walked there. Admiral Howson and General Van Cliff (I think that was the name of the latter) presented the stripes and medals to seventeen of the Marine Corps — quite young lads — and it was announced through the microphone the name and deed of each soldier. One in particular, who had a bullet wound in his cheek (we could see the scar), was awarded for going to the rescue of his comrade under heavy gunfire and saving his life, to say the least of quite a few others. A few young men had hair shaven almost clean on the head, and it just stood up in front like a toothbrush.

Well Darling, I have to be at lunch by 1, so I will write again this evening.

All my love, your wife, Fay

In May, Jaime had leave from work, and went to Barwon Heads with two male friends for a golfing holiday. So now Fay was the one left in Melbourne working. It was hard to coincide their holidays together, especially Jaime's job with the U.S. Army and the war in progress.

Through his tennis tournaments, Jaime had become good friends with the renowned Davis Cup tennis player, Harry Hopman. In 1933, Hopman had moved from Sydney to Melbourne after joining the staff of the Melbourne *Herald* as a sportswriter. He captained the winning Australian Open team in September 1939. Australia beat the U.S. 3-2 after Adrian Quist and John Bromwich both won their final singles matches. Harry also enjoyed golf, and often joined Jaime on the links. He was a big gambler though, and often wanted to bet on their golf games. Jaime always refused the wager — he hated gambling.

16 May 1943

Fay,

I would love you to be down here with me, Darling: the golf and the nights together, it would be heaven.

I think the manager kids himself a bit. Today he came and said he was sorry, but he wouldn't be able to take Harry Hopman in on Wednesday, as he was full up. We were very annoyed as he told Harry it was alright. Now we have had to book Harry in at a local boarding house and there is no certainty that he will come down.

I had a disturbed night last night. C had a touch of poisoning and vomited violently. I was up acting as nurse for about an hour, 4am 'til 5am, and then I had to get up early to clean the gas producer. I wonder how C and L got on today, as they were going to Mount Macedon.

17 May 1943

Darling Jaime,

I played tennis yesterday afternoon with Lea up at Spring Road. I felt pretty bored, and we nearly froze to death. I had a pretty good row with the Mater on Saturday night. It started all over Marie, and finished up over you. I will save all the bits and pieces till I see you, but I cleared off to bed before I said too much. Lea went mad at me for what I said, but I just couldn't help it. I don't know how things are going to work out, but I just can't take much more of it.

Fay

Although Fay's brother Harry and wife Marie lived in Warragul, Fay always kept in touch with her sister-in-law, who she loved very much. Even though Marie had produced two grandchildren, Annie still disliked her daughter-in-law, and this upset Fay greatly. Jaime always worried about the pressures Fay was under at home, it distressed him to hear about arguments with her mother. Even though he was away on holidays, reminders that Australia was at war continued.

Barwon Heads, 19 May 1943
Fay, Darling,

I am sorry about the row with your Mater, but keep the chin up, and don't be goaded into saying some thing you might be sorry to have said later.

While driving down to the Barwon township to meet Harry Hopman, we ran in to the local constable. He pulled me up because I had no blackout headlights, and as a punishment, I have to put them on tomorrow and report to the police station. It was rotten luck because they are troublesome things to put on, and we only went down to meet Harry for a few minutes. I wanted to walk, but one of the others said he was tired, and to take the car.

This morning when I woke up, I was dying to put my arms around you, and hold you tight, as at Torquay. I am just dying to see you and make love to you, so look out next week. You know, as much as I've enjoyed this holiday with the boys and looked forward to it, I much prefer a holiday with you. I miss your company, your cooking, and the lovely home comforts at night with your lovely warm body beside me. I also prefer your company at golf, we have got so used to each other on the links that it feels strange without you.

Well, Darling, the boys have just come in looking for me, so I must go.

All my love from your HUSBAND Jaime

On 14 May 1943, the hospital ship AHS *Centaur* was torpedoed by a Japanese submarine off North Stradbroke Island in Queensland, killing 268 persons. After hearing the news, Fay became angry; the death of Tommy Carson and many others who were wounded or killed raised her hackles. She speaks of her hatred for the enemy in a letter to Jaime who was still away on his golf trip.

Melbourne, 18 May 1943

Hello Darling,

Things have calmed down considerably at home and the Mater is quite friendly again, but I had to break the silence first.

A client just called in with the drastic news about the bombing of the hospital ship just off the Queensland coast. The blighters are getting close, I hope they catch the yellow scum (pardon the latter, but they are the scum of the earth).[1] *I think I will join up. It certainly makes one feel like getting in to the army. I can't understand some of the young chaps still walking round town and trying to evade the call up. After this atrocity, you would think they would want to avenge it. Although I think the bombing of the Dams in Germany was not quite 'fair' warfare, I suppose it is just giving them a taste of their own medicine, or giving them an idea, which they will soon carry out as a reprisal.*

Well, Darling, I should not be writing about all this sordid war talk when you are on holidays and trying to forget it for a week, but my patriotism (which doesn't go very deep, perhaps unfortunately) is properly roused. The Centaur bombing is like kicking or shooting a wounded man, but it proves the type of enemy we are up against. I won't write another word about it, Darling, and will finish this letter when I have calmed down.

Till then, I love you,

Fay

Jaime was due home on Sunday evening, 23 May and Fay sent him a letter on the twentieth.

Date: 20 May 1943
Time: 11.30am
Thought: You

Well, my Darling,

Here I am again and feeling much better since receiving your letter last evening. Glad to hear you are enjoying yourself, and have been getting good weather. Bad luck for Harry Hopman that they could not accommodate him after promising. They seem to do and say what they like now in these guest houses, and get away with it. Wouldn't he be disappointed, especially after looking forward to it and probably arranging to have his holiday at a certain time. Anyway, I hope it all works out alright.

Last night I went to the Windsor Picture Theatre with the Mater and saw a marvellous picture (a revival, I think you told me you had seen it) — Swanee River with Don Ameche. I loved every bit of it. I said to the Mater on the way out (as I looked a bit bleary eyed) that I must have Darkey blood in me, it stirred me so, even more than Irish music, and she thought it a great joke. But it was terribly sad, and I think you must have gone to sleep when you saw it because I don't think you sounded very impressed when I asked you about it.

Tomorrow evening, I have an appointment at the hairdressers for a perm, and won't get out until about 9.30, but the Mater knows about this, and also that you are away. I am going to let her think that you will be away next week too, so it may work out better for us. Sorry to hear you had so much trouble on the eve of your departure — I hope that there weren't any scenes. You must have felt pretty tired by the morning when it was time to get up.

Hilda rang me today, and she and Mollie are meeting Judy and me on Sunday afternoon at three o'clock on the corner of Wattletree and Glenferrie Roads. We are going for a drive and then back to her place for tea. You could ring me there after tea if you return in time. Phone number is Hawthorn (W.J.) 4700.

Well, my Darling, I was pleased to hear you have been missing me as much as I have been missing you. But we can make up for lost time next week.

All my love, your wife Fay

∼

Jaime's job with the U.S. Army ceased in July 1943, when owing to a general curtailment in the area of his duties, the work was classed as completed. The job had lasted for sixteen months. In mid-August he took on another position at the South Yarra Tyre Service, in Chapel Street, South Yarra. Jaime found the work tedious, and soon became unhappy and bored.

On 21 August, Australia held a federal election and the incumbent Australian Labor Party, governed by John Curtain, was returned to power. The war had now been raging for five years, and everyone prayed it would soon end.

8 November 1943

Good morning, my Darling,

You hardly expected this in the mail bag this morning, did you? Well I thought it was high time I put it in writing again just how much I love you. I think you were just a little bit jealous today but I love you in any mood, Darling, and I guess I have to take the good ones with the bad ones because you have had to put up with mine for many years now. It is more my patience that wears a trifle thin at times, not my moods or my love. I wish to heaven this infernal war would end and let you get back to your normal work. I hate this present job of yours (not half as much as you do, I suppose).

I hope we can enter that Tournament together — wouldn't it be a thrill if we won the trophy. It is my lucky golf course. Well My Beloved, I will ring you sometime today, (which will be tomorrow). I hope you receive this note intact without any nosey parker comments. We must hurry up and take the balance of those snaps — a good idea would be to take them on the day of the Tourney, both of us holding the Trophy. Remind me to tell you how much I love you the next time we meet.

Fay

By late November, Jaime had started applying for other jobs, and by early December he had landed one at the Hobart Manufacturing Company based at 478 Collins Street. It involved the selling of food equipment, a very different product to what he had been selling before. Nevertheless, he felt anything was better than the conditions at the South Yarra Tyre Service.

Fay and Jaime spent one Friday night at the pictures, and saw the 1942 film, *Casablanca*, starring Humphrey Bogart and Ingrid Bergman. Fay cried her eyes out; even Jaime shed a tear at the final scene. The film's theme song, 'As Time Goes By', written in 1931 by Herman Hupfeld, was sung by Dooley Wilson in the film. It was re-recorded by Rudy Valley, and resulted in a hit record for him in 1943. Fay adored the song, the words of the first verse reminded her of the years spent waiting to be with Jaime permanently.

> *You must remember this*
> *A kiss is still a kiss*
> *A sigh is just a sigh*
> *The fundamental things apply*
> *as time goes by*
>
> *And when two lovers woo*
> *They still say 'I love you'*
> *On that you can rely*
> *No matter what the future brings*
> *as time goes by*

Fay sent a letter to Jaime congratulating him on his new job and also reminiscing about the film.

9 December 1943

Darling,

I hope this will be the lucky last letter addressed to you at the South Yarra Tyre Service. I am terribly glad you are leaving there. I haven't wanted to encourage or discourage you, because I knew you were doing your best to make the most of it. But now that you are leaving, I feel very much happier about it. I am sure this new job will be much more satisfactory. Congratulations, Darling.

I haven't enjoyed 1943 very much and will be glad to welcome in 1944. I hope it brings us more happiness than this year has (especially what we went through earlier in the year). I also hope it will bring an end to the war.

Darling, I still think about the film we saw last Friday, how sad it was. The song 'As Time Goes By' is etched into my head.

Well, Darling, this is only a very brief note to wish you luck in your new venture.

Fay

Christmas of 1943, Fay was back at Dava Lodge in Mornington while Jaime was settling into his new position.

Dava Lodge, 27 December 1943
Monday

Good morning, my Darling,

Here I am once more installed comfortably at the above. I have a lovely room facing Beach Road up near the tennis courts. The crowd is rather stodgy and staid; very few young people, no young girls (with the exception of myself?). It is mostly married couples around about forty-ish, a few lads about nineteen or twenty, and a young girl about eighteen. The rest are made up of forty to sixty. So mix all these ingredients together, and you have the Plum Pudding at Dava, but I haven't found any threepenny bits yet.

Tuesday, 8pm

Yesterday we went to a gymkhana in Mornington. Two chaps at my table drove another girl and myself there: a Mr Austin and a Mr Henderson. The latter has a gorgeous Daimler car with a sliding door on the roof and we did it in great style. He (the owner of the Daimler) reminds me of one of the Ritz Brothers, only more ferocious. I don't like him very much, he has a decided caste in his eye, which makes him look rather evil eyed. But they are quite friendly and good sports.

Last night they had moving pictures in the lounge. Some man here has a

marvellous moving camera; he must belong to the Theatre in town, because
he was showing 'the real stuff' from America. With American actors and
actresses, Joe Brown Jr was in one of the pictures. Well, My Beloved, I must
go and have some breakfast. I still love you, Darling, and wish you were here.

Always yours,

Fay

PS I am getting cigarettes for us both in Mornington. She allows me two
packs a day with the rations, so am keeping yours safe, or should I post them
to you? Let me know, Darling.

Jaime had driven Fay down to Mornington on Sunday 26. His new job
was turning out to be harder than he anticipated and he sometimes
suffered from nerves, especially after a scene with Connie.

28 December 1943

5.30pm

My Darling Fay,

I am just on my way home, so have pulled up in a side street at
Camberwell to drop you this line. I have had a day at work on my own and
I have mixed feelings about it. The job at the moment seems very difficult
because I suppose I feel I know so little about it. But I hope as time goes on,
my knowledge will improve and I shall feel more at ease. You see, if you don't
know much about the articles you are selling, you haven't the confidence you
should have, and that is the stage I am presently going through. Somehow I
have felt nervy today, and when I had to demonstrate to a customer at three
o'clock in the showrooms, I felt I could have done better. However, I have
a good chance of clinching the sale of the Hobart Slicer later on this week,
despite my inward nervousness.

I think the state of nerves was caused by one of those scenes by C. On
Sunday night, after my return from Mornington, everything appeared okay
until while having a cup of tea and during an ordinary conversation, C swung

the discussion round to how I refused to be a proper husband to her etc., and that started it. There were hysterical scenes, threats of suicide etc. etc.

She even rang up to try and get a taxi to clear off at 1am, but there were no taxis available. After much arguing, I finally got to bed about 2.30am Fortunately, Leon slept through it all. Of course, the holiday yesterday was a washout, and only for having to leave Leon on his own, I would have got in the car and driven to Dava, chancing gossip. Quite a lot of home truths were said on both sides. But don't you worry about it Fay, I will tell you more when I see you. I suppose my nerves today were the aftermath.

Well, how are you enjoying yourself? I'd give anything to be down there with you. Gee, I will be glad when this darn war is over. Well, Darling, I had better get home to tea. Think of me occasionally, and when you are making 'conquests', don't forget your hubby still loves you madly. When scenes that I have described above occur with C, I feel more strongly drawn to you than ever. You know I feel better already, after writing this letter, I feel I have got something off my chest. I may not get the same opportunity to write as long a note, so I took it now.

All my love to you, Fay,

Jaime xxxx

This was only the very beginning of suicide threats from Connie; it would become a regular routine, as the years rolled on. Sadly, during these years and for many to come, no one fully understood about depression or mental diseases, and any 'scenes' were described as one suffering from hysteria. Connie continued with the prescribed Lithium.[2] It made her sleepy yet did not curtail her tantrums, and just added to her habit of staying in bed for days at a time.

The Day After Forever

It distressed Fay when Jaime was upset about anything, including his job, so she would often use humour as a weapon. As in this typed note she handed him one lunch time, on her return from Mornington.

> *12 January 1944*
> *Memo Mr San Miguel*
> *Kiama Café, Flinders Street, next door to Hatchers Laundry, close to Queen Street*
> *Very old weighing scales — I think 1923 model.*
> *No bread slicer — waited ten min. for them to cut sandwiches — then lady made extreme apologies for crumbling bread — practically had to eat sandwiches with a spoon when I got back to office.*
> *Sandwiches I think very definitely cut with* blunt *knife.*
> *Quite a nice lady — I think you could sell her a slicer.*
> *PLUGGER Johnston*
> *NOTE: In fact, a few cafes fairly close to this one that you might try.*

As Fay received four weeks leave annually, she usually divided it into two holidays through summer. In mid-February, she returned to Dava Lodge. A few years back she had met a fellow named Sydney Morgan at Dava. He was the youngest son of Val Morgan,[1] who founded the largest cinema advertising company in Victoria, Val Morgan and

Sons Pty Ltd. In 1933, Sydney was appointed managing director of 3KZ Broadcasting, one of his father's companies. His eldest brother, William, held the reigns for 3KZ Advertising. Sydney was a similar age to Jaime, and he usually holidayed with another brother, Stan. Both brothers were charming, handsome, hopeless flirts, and Sydney took a particular shine to Fay; he did his best to woo her one summer holiday. Jaime knew of Sydney, and was jealous at the time.

Dava Lodge
19 February 1944

Good morning, Darling,

My attempts at letter writing have been very unsuccessful, but I have had a fair amount of letters to write. I sent one to the Mater, Lea, Doreen at the office (she wrote to me and I had to answer) and my aunt.

Last night we were invited to a cocktail party at six. It was quite a party and there are some very nice people here. Darling, I know you are going to get terrifically jealous. I have been wondering whether to tell you or not because I don't want you to worry about it; what with the worry of your job, you might go and do something you would regret (like giving notice before thinking well about it).

Syd Morgan and his brother are here for about three weeks. I am sitting at their table with another lass, who is just throwing herself at Syd, and the latter can't be bothered with her but she follows him round like a puppy dog. He has been playing tennis and golf with me, last night we all went to the pictures (six of us), and each night we have gone in to Mornington for supper, and straight home to bed. We all just hop out of the car, and say 'goodnight', generally. The other lass has been trying to get Syd on his own but he just says 'goodnight' and he and Stan wander off to their rooms. They are both going to Cowes today, but may not be back until tomorrow.

Darling, I don't want you to worry, because you have no opposition in that quarter. They are both very charming, Stan is lovely, I think he is nicer than Syd, but they are certainly used to having a good time. I think Syd just laps up the free life; I can't see him settling down. He was telling me all about his trip to New York, and is anxious to go back as soon as the war is over.

Darling, I hope you will forgive me for staying an extra week, but I am sure you do not blame me, and it would be a shame to waste this perfect weather idling my week at home. We can always get weekends, but not the week days.

Well, Darling, I know you will be thinking this letter is all about a 'certain party' but if I didn't tell you all the news, you would be thinking I was holding something back. But it is one of the reasons I haven't written before, and I wanted an opportunity to explain it to you.

I hope you are not worrying too much about your job. I hope Len Henwood's proposition turns out alright, but don't rush in to anything. Well, Darling, you are probably in no mood for me to tell you that I still love you more than anything in this world and when I compare you with all these other people, I realise just how much you really love me, and it only makes me love you more than ever. I will be true to you, Darling, you need have no fear of that. But you won't blame me for enjoying myself, and you know how much I enjoy holidays. I do hope you won't tick me off altogether, and will look forward to hearing from you.

All my love,

Fay

Jaime was finding it very hard to make sales, in one week he had only sold one slicer and a set of scales. After running into his brother-in-law, Patricia's husband, Les Henwood, they stopped for lunch, and Les said he could possibly help Jaime find a more suitable job. The pressures Jaime felt seemed to escalate when he received Fay's letter.

21 February 1944

Fay,

I don't know why I am writing to you, I really did intend not to write to you at all, but I find myself writing to you again. Perhaps it is because I feel a bit better this afternoon, maybe it was after talking to you on the phone, or perhaps the prospect of a re-assuring letter tomorrow makes me feel better. I was terribly disappointed not receiving a note from you by Friday, and when on the phone you made the weak excuse about not having any note paper, it was the last straw. I felt then your other pre-occupations were more important to you than a note to me.

I had hoped that words in your letter (expected Friday) might have had me scurrying down on Friday night, or probably down for the day on Sunday. But no, not a word, I felt pretty bad about that, so much so that I had intended not to write or ring you at all this week.

I don't know why, but I hardly closed my eyes Friday night, not worrying about my job but just thinking of you, and heaven knows I worry about my job enough. During the weekend I missed you so much, I thought I must see you next weekend, and I then (despite my determination not to ring or write you again) made up my mind to ring you and make arrangements to come to Dava for the week. But I felt they may not be able to accommodate me, and I was relying on you, being on the spot, to get me the room.

But just imagine how I felt today when I read your letter. I felt burnt up inside, and I really mean burnt up. No letters last week — why? No Torquay weekend — why? The answer seemed perfectly obvious after the news in your letter today.

I don't blame you for wanting to stay the extra week, but the whole thing pointed to one thing, and the answer seemed to be in your letter today. Why the urgent desire to stay on the extra time? However, I will wait and pass judgement tomorrow; it will probably decide a lot of things. I had a bad week last week. I was sick of my job, I missed you badly; in fact, I was in a bad way. I really am not in a mood to be trifled with and that is why I am determined to get away for the weekend. I had hoped it would be Dava, but it looks like Barwon Heads now.

Fancy, of all people, the Morgans being there. It almost looks like a collusion. Are you sure you didn't know? Then being at their table, it seems almost as if it was pre-arranged. Of all the people that I know, Syd was the last person I thought and hoped you would run in to. Knowing your present state of mind, and knowing my recent moods, I don't think it would take much to snap our long romance. Maybe that time has arrived, maybe it hasn't. I am, I'm afraid, going to take a lot of convincing. You can't tell me you haven't been tempted to weaken, and if you haven't down there, it's the prospect of what will follow when you return to town. You see, Fay, Syd is probably a good catch, and all girls will throw their hats up to him. Even my Fay, whom I trust and respect, has ordinary human weaknesses. So a lot will depend on your story when I see you again.

Perhaps I shouldn't have written to you in my present mood, but I feel so mixed and churned up inside that I probably don't know what I am writing. All I hope is that Syd, who nearly once hurt us, is not going to be the one to do it now.

Well Darling, I must close. Perhaps if I had waited until tomorrow, I wouldn't have written this note, but you know me, I always act on impulse. So if I have done wrong, please forgive me.

Jaime

Although Jaime admired Fay's fierce independence, he hated having no control when she was away. Fay, on the other hand, did enjoy the attention of other men regardless of her love for Jaime. She always tried to be honest with him but deep inside, she rather enjoyed his jealousy. Still, on the Sunday, feeling somewhat guilty, she wrote him another letter.

20 February 1944

Well, my Darling,

I suppose I am a complete deserter and on the black list by now, but I don't deserve to be because I haven't deserted you. I hope you are not worrying too much because you know you can trust me. I know you will start thinking all sorts of crazy things about the party I mentioned who was down here, but that is your least worry. They are nice chaps, and they don't fuss over anyone in particular. The girls here (and there are quite a few) just throw themselves at Syd and make a great fuss over him — he flirts with them all but I think that's as far as it goes. The two brothers stick together and when they have parties in their rooms, they just empty everyone out about eleven.

There is a girl here with her mother and father (Mr and Mrs Benton). They live in Irving Road, Toorak. I heard they are 'Benton's Pastry'. They dress exquisitely and seem to have pots of money, gorgeous car, a marvellous cupboard (the only drink they haven't got is champagne, I think). The girl has been going for Syd, and he seems to be a bit interested. She is terribly plain, but pretty willing, I think. They were going over to Syd's room tonight (about six of them) and Stan asked me, but I said I wanted an early night. The Benton girl looked tickled pink about it, because she knows I have been with them swimming, golfing and tennis, and I think she thinks she is cutting me out.

There was a bit of a dance here last night, but it fizzled out. Everyone seems to go out to spotting parties. There are three American soldiers staying here — they have their girls with them, or at least the girls were here on their arrival. Stan introduced me to the World's Third Ace tonight (Air Commander Harry Cobby).[2] He was here for dinner tonight, and had his secretary with him, a very dashing blonde who I believe will be staying here for a few days. Cobby is down at Mount Martha. He wrote a book, I believe, High Adventure, about his experiences in the last war — he shot down thirty-eight German planes. He is a nice looking chap, and the decorations on his chest would dazzle you. Stan said he topped the list for decorations in the last war.

Well, Darling, I have tried to tell you all about Dava in a nutshell. I haven't kissed anyone or been untrue to you in any shape or form, and I know you will believe me. I have been playing excellent tennis, and yesterday played with two 18-year-olds. They are Melbourne Grammar lads waiting to go into the Navy. One of the lads is the image of Leon — Graham Fuller is his name. The other one, Doug Joyce, his father owns Joyce and Howard Shoe Manufactures (they brought out Hec Marshall Shoe firm). There are some very wealthy gentry staying here. There are about twenty beautiful cars parked around the grounds, and they all seem to have a lot of petrol.

Anyway, Darling, have you been true to me? Perhaps you have been flirting in my absence — I hope you still love me because you are the only one I want to be loved by. Will write you later in the week, and hope to receive a letter from you early this week.

All my love,

Fay

PS I think Syd might know about us — he made one remark which I will tell you on my return — on the other hand, I may be wrong.

The day after Jaime wrote his letter, he rang Fay at Dava Lodge. Fay convinced him that nothing untoward was happening with Syd Morgan, and all was forgiven.

2pm, 22 February 1944

Darling,

You are my lucky break. Just after ringing you today (a few minutes ago), I decided to drop you this hurried scrawl. I thought perhaps first I had better make a call to a chap I could catch at this particular time. Well, what do you know, I walked into the canteen and sold the chap a slicer, my first sale this week. If I hadn't have rung you, I wouldn't have made the call and got the sale.

I feel very happy now since I spoke to you, the world feels much brighter. God, I must love you a hell of a lot. Do you know these two weeks have dragged like months? But now I have something to look forward to, Friday. I can leave town about four and reach Frankston about five o'clock. We could have a swim and spend the evening together. You could say you were visiting friends at Frankston.

Darling, I know I am selfish, but if you could see your way clear to come home Saturday, I would be very happy. It would be almost as good as a weekend for me, I would be so thrilled. How about it, Darling?

All my love, always yours,

Jaime

5.15pm, 22 February 1944

My darling Fay,

How is my disguised writing on the envelope? Did you recognise it, or did it deceive you? I bet it didn't. Well, Darling, I suppose you think I have gone mad writing to you again, after only just posting you a letter at two, but the truth is I can't get home too early after always being late when I see you of an evening. So as I have a little time to fill in, I thought I might just as well fill it in with you.

I have made general enquires about another job today. First I went to the secretary of the CYA and had a word with him. He hasn't anything but he told me the Hobart Company could do nothing if I left them. They actually owe me money. According to the law, they should be paying me 6 pounds 11 per week, plus 3 pounds 10 for using my car. I also went to see Les Henwood's friend at Collingwood Man Power office. I told him, and he agreed that it would be best to stick to my present job until something worthwhile comes up.

Darling, it makes me mad to think that only a few years ago, yes, even as recent as when we went to Sydney together, I had a good job and a good property income, and sitting pretty with quite a good income altogether. Now my property income is not worth a damn, owing to heavy taxation, and I am wandering the streets looking for a job with even a reasonable salary. And yet on paper, I am worth some thousands. It doesn't seem fair, does it?

When I read of all the people you tell me about at Dava, apparently with plenty of money, I feel bitter to think that I, who had quite a bit of it myself a few years ago, have dwindled it away to such an extent. Yes, I should be like Syd Morgan, and have been in my own father's business with a nice cosy job, but unfortunately he became an invalid when he did and that was that. I suppose I must be thankful for what I have, however. And yes, more important than money, I am thankful for your friendship and love.

Well, Darling, now knowing I have nothing to fear, I feel happy, and I am glad you are enjoying yourself. But nevertheless, these two weeks have been awful without you. I think my love for you now must be even more deep-rooted than it ever was.

All my love,

your Jaime

Fay was deeply moved when she received Jaime's two letters. She decided not to stay the extra time at Dava and instead return home with Jaime on the Saturday.

23 February 1944

Darling,

Just received your letters, and believe me, they run very deep. It touched the old heart and made it ache for you. I loved you so much when I read them, Darling, that I had a silent weep. When one loves as deeply as we do, it is something so rare and beautiful that even poets would have difficulty in defining it. But our love for each other is a magnificent poem, and someday I'm going to write you one which will describe to you all the beats of my heart for you, my desire for you, my love for you — our friendship, our love for the field of sport, and our love for each other. The foundation of our love, Darling, is built on all that, and makes for a perfect love. Such as understanding, and trust, and mutual feelings for each other. Now do you believe I love you with all my heart and soul?

Darling, I have dozens of little stories to tell you, some have quite a flavour, and some are quite spicy, but it would take too long to go into detail in a letter. I have been true to you, Darling, and haven't been alone with anyone down here, so you needn't worry. I am sorry you have worried so much — I tried to spare you that, and that was the reason for holding back the letters.

Glad you sold a slicer after ringing me — perhaps I am your lucky star. I am feeling dangerously well, so look out on Friday evening. What about celebrating with some good old port? We could think of quite a few toasts. Well, Darling, I had better go and change into my tennis togs, as it is nearly time for my game. I will see you on Friday.

Fay

The second weekend of March they returned to Torquay, and everything was quite idyllic. By April, Jaime had found another job, working for Payne's Sport and Aircraft Company in Queensbury Street, North Melbourne. He enjoyed it, and his main task was selling sports products and model aircraft equipment, which he revelled in.

Things turned sour in mid-May. Sydney Morgan began phoning Fay at her office. He asked her out many times; at first she refused, but soon his charm weakened her. He was a very wealthy man, and used this in his pursuit of Fay. She knew he would take her to all the very best parties and theatre shows in town, and he also mentioned trips to Europe and America after the war ended. It was extremely tempting. The thought of a normal date, and not having to hide, was considerably appealing. When Jaime found out about it, he was both angry and frightened.

18 May 1944

My dear Fay,

I am enclosing postal note for 12/6 for the Tivoli tickets. I said I would pay you for them, and I always keep my promise. I'm sorry I won't be seeing the show with you on Friday, as I had been looking forward to it all week. But apparently you would prefer to see another show, with almost a perfect stranger, than with the man you profess to love. Now that you have chosen Syd Morgan in preference to me, you can go ahead and have him. I only hope your decision won't rebound, and hit you back hard.

At any rate Fay, before you finally land him, I am giving you this warning that I am personally going to see that he knows what you and I have been to each other for the last twelve years. See how he reacts to that information — that ought to prove his sincerity. Don't worry, I give you full permission to pass on the same information to Connie, whenever you so desire. You may think and say that this action is a low trick, but on thinking it over, I don't think so. You see, Fay, you belong entirely to me, and I belong entirely to you. We are both entitled to hang on to one's possessions by any means in our power, and after all, there is a saying that all is fair in love and war.

You say that I will have to take a chance, the same as you have to take a chance, but that is not true. I have promised to stick by you, no matter what happens. You are pretty certain because you know my feelings towards Connie. I have promised to come and live with you when the way is clear, and to provide for you on my death. But you haven't made any such promises, you simply say, I will just have to take a chance. Fay, a man doesn't ask a girl out as often as Syd asks you unless he is a bit keen. Every time you go out with him, you get more familiar with one another, and Syd certainly would think he was entitled to make advances. He isn't going to continue to take you out without some reward. At this time you would find it difficult to knock him back, and then what would become of all your promises to me?

I did not sleep a wink last night. I think I will accept the one big hurt now rather than a whole lot of little ones, and then the inevitable big hurt later. Perhaps it won't be too painful after the first week or so, because you certainly have changed since your last two vacations at Dava. You have developed a sense of hardness, foreign to you, but oh so like your mother. A certain amount of conceit and shallowness has crept in and your sense of sincerity and loyalty is now lacking. In other words, you have fallen off your pedestal.

I suppose I shall be very lonely on Friday night. I shall probably go up to the Lanyon Café for dinner, and then go to the Gazettes. It will seem strange after all these years. Even lonelier will be the weekends, they will be hard to fill in. But I suppose time is the best cure. Well, before I close, I will again say this; I have loved you and probably always will. But I have been first fiddle for so long, that I am now not going to play second fiddle. I am not prepared to share you now, when I thought we really understood each other, and after all these years, certainly not with Syd Morgan — or for that matter, any man.

Jaime

Fay broke down when she read Jaime's letter. She was in a quandary, how long would she continue to be the 'scarlet woman'? Sometimes what her mother said made sense. Leon was turning fourteen years old in August, and he would be fully aware of his parent's problems. Perhaps if she stayed out of Jaime's life, it would be the best for everyone. After a harrowing fight with her mother, Fay wrote Jaime a distressing letter.

22 May 1944

Dear Jaime,

After the scene which lasted into the small hours of the morning last night, I have come to the conclusion that as far as we are chasing happiness, it goes on eluding us to such an extent that it only seems to bring chaos and disaster in both our homes.

My mother said some things last night and this morning, which even I could not deny. After thinking things over, I think it will be best if we try to give each other up. The way things are at the moment are pretty hopeless and it is a case of my mother's health (and Connie's too) or our happiness. It looks as if there is only one alternative, as you can't build happiness on the wreckage of one's ill health and unhappiness. We will just have to forget about our own feelings when theirs is so desperate.

My mother has threatened me this time, and I know she means it. Poor old Lea gets the brunt of it, and the same with Leon. When it affects other people to this extent, it is time we came to our senses and looked at it from their point of view. I know you will think that past events have prompted me to write this note, and you will be thinking of the party we saw on Friday night, but believe me, if you had seen my mother's condition last night, you would realise just what we would have to put up with if it continues. Both Lea and I didn't get a wink of sleep last night, and if it goes on like this year in and year out like it has been doing, the substitute for our so-called happiness is a poor one.

Personally, I think Connie and the Mater hold the trump cards — no matter whom we sought advice from, I think an independent person would side with them. We will have to forget about ourselves, and make life more bearable for them. I don't know what my plans will be. I am thinking seriously of getting out of Victoria and away from it all. As you know, I have been feeling like this for a long time. The tension at home has been smouldering, and it certainly came to a head last night.

I don't know in what light you will see all this, but if you have any suggestions to make, or any answers to the problem, I would like to know what they are. I am too sick and tired to think too clearly this morning, but upsets like these couldn't go on indefinitely without having drastic results. I don't think it is worth the little happiness we are getting for all the unhappiness it brings in its trail.

Fay

Though as much as they tried to stay apart, it was consistently a losing battle, and Jaime and Fay continued to see each other for another month. Fay promised never to see Syd Morgan again, however her problems at home came to another nasty head in June, and again she tried to break it off.

17 June 1944

Dear Jaime,
When I arrived home last night, my mother was waiting up for me and

the usual storm took place. I am writing you this note to try and tell you just how my reactions are to these scenes. Of course, neither of us got any sleep for the rest of the night, and every word my mother said is absolutely right. I have definitely come to one conclusion, and that is I am not going to see you anymore. For a few years I knew a little happiness in your company, because I suppose I had a remote hope that things could turn out for the best for us. I don't possess the remotest hope now, and when you abandon hope for something you have existed on for twelve long years, things just become impossible.

I am miserable and unhappy; in fact, all of us are, Connie and Leon and my mother and both of us. And as far as I can see, we will never know any happiness until we do the right thing, and that is to stop seeing each other. My mother made some very true statements which even we must admit are true. I think I have acquired enough courage to face the future going my own way. If I can pluck up enough courage I am going to confession this weekend, and I am really going to try and do the right thing in the eyes of the church. If we contemplated doing the things suggested, we would not only be despised and scorned by those we love most, but by everyone we know. I would never be happy knowing we were deliberately wrecking other people's lives.

I don't know what your reaction to this letter will be, and even if you decide to tell C I am not prepared to do anything about it. I can't go on seeing my mother's health impaired, and I don't see how you can stand up to it either seeing your home in the condition it is. If you give up seeing me things might be more bearable for you. You might say it is too late now, but it was even that way when I first met you, so you can't blame me entirely, and as you say I did some good for you by giving you my companionship over the years which I have had no regrets over.

I think the poets or some wise man said, 'Love knoweth no bounds' and 'Love conquereth all things', but perhaps these quotations only materialise to the good people of the earth. In the small hours of this morning, I think it aged me two or three years, and the strain is too much for any one of us, and we can't go on like this indefinitely. I hope you will try and give your home life a bit more attention, now that my disturbing influence will be missing.

If I can't have you honestly or rightly, I do not intend to drag our names through the mire, we would only regret it.

I have given you the best years of my youth, and as I still have a few more years to make life bearable, you should leave me alone. I hope you won't ring or try to see me, because I will not see you. I would rather it stop at this letter.

Yours,

Fay

Jaime had gone to Mass at St Joseph's on the Sunday morning expecting to see Fay, however Lea was there by herself, and handed him the letter Fay had given her to pass on. Jaime read the letter a few times but he still couldn't bear to accept the words. This time, Fay sounded deadly serious, and it sent him into a panic.

8am, 19 June 1944

Dear Fay,

Yesterday I was sorry I did not see you instead of Lea, and after the first flush of reading your letter I told Lea that I intended to see you today to find out what it's all about. After reading your letter again and pondering over its contents, I don't intend to see you today, and I am glad that you were not there yesterday. One thing, however, is that I am very glad I got your note when I did, and not here at work. It would have been too upsetting and too difficult to read in the circumstances. Yesterday I had plenty of time to peruse it, and to think deeply, very deeply indeed. It was a very cold and calculating letter. The many phrases and 'quotations' proved and looked to me as if it had been well thought out.

Just a week ago today, and at this very hour we were making violent love to each other, and you were promising me that no matter what happened, you would stand at my side, the same as I was prepared to stand by you under any conditions. I was also willing to stay by your side two or three years ago when I had my first big crisis, but apparently now that your own crisis has arrived, you haven't got what it takes. Just when I need you most, you have decided to desert me.

Quite a few things occurred at my end during this weekend, even before I knew what was happening at yours. I am beginning to think that C was right when she said on Saturday, 'I am sorry you have chosen Fay, because I don't think she is good enough for you.' As a matter of fact, after the rational conversation we had, I even think that C might be prepared to agree to a divorce. But now I am not so sure that I would be prepared to persuade her.

I blame your mother for all of this, her attitude towards you, an attitude which I think in our exceptional case was unreasonable, as we are both not children. Perhaps I have changed too, I know I have been very nervy since the war started, the heavy taxation, the change of jobs, the distressing scenes at home over a period of years (scenes far more difficult and unpleasant than your recent ones). I think my luck changed when I left Dunlop's, and a great deal of my happiness too.

Fay, despite my bitterness, I shall never forget all those wonderful years spent in your company. Such a marvellous thrill when being in your arms. I say without hesitation, the hours spent in your company were the happiest of my entire life. I am going to miss you, and can't imagine going on in the future without you. As a matter of fact, I am still too dazed to realise it yet.

In a way, I am sorry now that we didn't go ahead and have our baby. The bonds then would have been too great for even your mother to break. Despite your decision, I very much doubt it will bring your mother any improvement in health or happiness. After a while, she will find some new worry to blame for her sleepless nights, and your sacrifice will have been in vain. All neurotic types are the same. Perhaps now that she has triumphed, she will get some satisfaction in knowing she has smashed the nearest thing to true love that I could possibly imagine. It is a pity that having waited so long, that a little more patience could not have been exerted when we were so close to that end we had always sought.

You say you are not prepared to have your name and mine dragged through the mire. Well, unfortunately, that is beyond our control and there lurks a very definite danger. I have only to answer some difficult questions which I may not be able to evade and we would be front page news.

You ask me to leave you alone, you need not worry, as I still have a little pride left, and know when I am not wanted. I am afraid we will have to have one final meeting to exchange a few small possessions we have of one another's. But I suppose that can be arranged later.

I am still very puzzled over your drastic change overnight. Your decision must have been made under very severe threats and great duress. One minute we are very happy together at the pictures, and the next morning I am severely dumped without warning. I am sad you haven't given me a final 'adieu' in person. Was it that you were afraid?

Jaime

For three long months they stayed away from each other. No letters, phone calls, luncheons, or Friday nights. The pain they both felt was crushing. Jaime belted tennis and golf balls in his frustration, whereas Fay spent many a night at the pictures with Lea, crying over a sad film. One picture they saw was *Going My Way*, starring Bing Crosby and Barry Fitzgerald. A song Crosby sang in the film rekindled all of Fay's memories of her love for Jaime. It was called 'The Day After Forever'.

All day tomorrow,
I'll be whispering your name
And the day after forever
I know I'll do the same

May time or winter
I won't let you out of sight,
And the day after forever,
We'll talk about tonight.

Your laughter is a melody
That I'll remember long,
It plays along my heartstrings
It's my favourite song.

All through a lifetime
I'll be loving you and then
On the day after forever
I'll just begin again.

Fay was turning thirty-five in October and Jaime would be forty-six in July. Their love affair had spanned twelve years, and Fay wondered whether she should have remained with him all this time. His mention of their baby in his last letter had resurrected every agony that she had experienced at the time and for many months following.

You Belong To My Heart

On a Friday afternoon, 29 September, Jaime could bear it no more and telephoned Fay at her office. Hearing his familiar voice over the phone melted her heart, and when he suggested meeting for a drink after work, she readily agreed.

She met him in the foyer of the Menzies Hotel, and the moment their eyes met, both of them knew they would never be parted again. Much was discussed that night, and Fay told Jaime he was right about her mother. Annie continued to argue over one thing or another. She disliked any friends Lea bought home, and her malice towards Marie was always a talking point. Jaime said his home life was as disruptive as it had ever been, and he assured Fay nothing could alter it. He was also concerned about the effect it was having on Leon.

They enjoyed a leisurely meal at a nearby restaurant, and then Jaime drove Fay home. He held her in his arms and kissed her.

'My darling Fay,' he said. 'Fate bought us together all those years ago, and as far as I'm concerned, it is destiny that we should be together always, no matter what.'

The moment Fay walked in the door, Lea knew straight away she was back with Jaime. She had witnessed the many tears and the heartache her sister had experienced over the past few months, and knew the only remedy was a reunion. Lea was still grieving for Tommy, and felt life was too short when you were really in love.

'Fay, you and Jaime are made for one another,' Lea said, holding her sister close. 'Hang on to your dream, one day it will all come true.'

~

Christmas came, then New Year's Eve, and Jaime and Fay welcomed in 1945 together. They now accepted their situation was in God's hands, and whatever would be, would be. On 11 February, Fay returned to Dava Lodge for a fortnight. As a regular guest, she was well looked after by the staff. Jaime remained working in Melbourne, missing her, although he occasionally drove down for a day. An old friend of Fay's, Mollie Wright, was staying for a week with two girlfriends. Lea and their mother had gone to Clifton Springs.

Monday morning I played tennis, and went for a drive to Mornington in the afternoon with Mollie Wright and three other girls. One of them has a little baby Austin (car). We had some afternoon tea, and had heard that a Fortune Teller was in the township, but you had to make an appointment with her. She is going to see us all on Thursday night. She gives you supper, and makes a small charge, I suppose about 2/-. 'Wanda' is her name, but she looks a fraud. I suppose we will get a good laugh out of it. Mollie and I were in hysterics having afternoon tea. She reminded me of some very funny experiences we had at Allambec in Healesville when we were about eighteen, very raw and inexperienced. I had forgotten all the little incidents when we thought we were fashionable Flappers. It all seems such a long time ago.

I received a letter from Lea yesterday. She says Mother loves the place, and is looking and feeling remarkably well. They had roast duck on the menu, and cream with their sweets. She said a barbecue was given on the cliff top on Monday night. They roasted a suckling pig, and everyone sat round the fire and sang songs.

On Wednesday night they had a dance here, which was really a great success. The orchestra was full of pep, and made the dance go with a great swing. Half a dozen air force lads duly arrived, and they were the pick of the forces — really charming men. One lad in particular danced with me. He is leading a spitfire squadron and will have 350 men to look after when he goes North (to the Philippines) next month. They are only down here for six weeks at the Mount Martha Instruction School. He had a lovely speaking voice (very English, really) although he is an Australian. He would knock Errol Flynn into a cocked hat for his smile and personality. But don't worry, Darling, he is no opposition to you, and certainly not interested in your better half, but he was a very nice chap all the same. I can just imagine Leon looking like him when he is twenty-eight (same speaking voice), so you will have to try and cultivate Leon's accent. But I wouldn't change a head of your hair, Darling, you are just 'you'. Perfection as far as I am concerned.

On Sunday 18 February, Jaime met Fay at Frankston and they spent the day together. On his return home another argument with Connie took place.

My darling Fay,

I am sitting on a bench in the park in North Melbourne in the beautiful sun, wishing I was at Mornington with you. I feel much better now, after that lovely day with you at Frankston; it certainly was wonderful to see you again. Did you get back safely to Dava? I left after you and was home at seven. But gosh, what a welcome. C was in one of her moods, I could have gone mad with annoyance. Did your ears burn? Because your name was mentioned quite a bit, coupled with the Sydney trip. However, I will tell you when I see you again. I gave Leon that hug from you.

Tuesday, 20 February 1945

Hello Darling,

Here I am again with my little luncheon letter to you. Did you get the tennis balls I sent you? And did you manage to send me the cigarettes? By the way, how did you feel when you got back to Dava, Sunday, not too shot I hope, after the vino? I felt good — oh on the way back to Camberwell until I got home. Things have improved slightly, although still boring. Leon is the only salvation. After our lovely day Sunday, I feel more contented about your love for me, not that I really ever doubted it.

Now that Leon was getting older, Fay sometimes accompanied he and Jaime to the pictures on a Saturday afternoon. She was extremely fond of the young lad, and he in turn liked her much to Connie's horror. Fay still had a weep when she thought of her pregnancy termination, yet still had hopes that one day she and Jaime would bear a child.

On 7 May 1945, all German forces surrendered, and on 2 September, Japan gave up their fight. World War II was at long last over. The whole country celebrated, and Fay and Jaime took it as a good omen that their wish for the future would soon be granted.

∾

Every time Jaime tried to discuss a divorce with Connie, she would become hysterical. Threats were made to expose his affair with Fay in a variety of newspapers; she even swore she would phone Xavier College and tarnish Jaime's good name. Every now and then she would threaten the very worst and talked of throwing herself in front of a train, so Jaime thought it best to back off the topic of divorce. Leon was, after all, his main concern.

In late January of 1946, Jaime took Connie, Leon, and a school friend, Eric, for a week's holiday to Queenscliff, a small town on the Bellarine Peninsula in southern Victoria. He had booked accommodation at a guesthouse, Osprey House, in Hesse Street. On viewing the rundown property from the outside, Jaime was nearly tempted to go elsewhere, however on entering the building, he soon changed his mind.

Osprey House, Queenscliff
29 January 1946, 12.30pm

My darling Fay,

This is the first opportunity I have had to write to you. First of all, Darling, I love you and miss you terribly, and am wishing all the time you were with me. This spot is a lovely place, and with you it would be heaven.

We left Sunday at noon, and eventually arrived at 2.15pm We drove down the main street and couldn't see Osprey. Eventually we were directed to a funny-looking place on the main street. Our hearts sank; it looked so awful, in fact, that if I had not paid a deposit, we would not even have gone in. However, after some hesitation we bowled in and were agreeably surprised. Small place but spotlessly clean, excellent meals, nice tennis court, and only a minute to the beach — you never can tell a book by its cover.

The weather Sunday was beautiful. The boys and I had a swim, then tea, and an early night. Monday morning had two sets of tennis with Leon and Eric, and some other guests, and played excellently. In the afternoon we had a swim, and then had a look at a Bathing Beauty Competition for the local hospital. There were only six candidates, and believe me, Darling, you could have fallen over and beat them easily.

This is the first time the boys haven't been with me. Connie has tried to keep up with the boys and myself, but couldn't take it, and got sick yesterday afternoon. She has been in bed all of today so far. I think the heat yesterday was too much for her.

Well, Beautiful, I will try and write again.

All my love, Darling,

J.

The summer of 1946 produced a number of heat waves, with temperatures rising over 37°C. Fay was feeling the swelter stuck in Melbourne, while everyone was away. Nevertheless, she made the most of things by enjoying outings with girlfriends.

28 January 1946

Hello Darling,

Here I am and nearly a grease spot — what a hot day! First of all, how are you, and did you have a good trip down? You had a perfectly lovely day for travelling. I'm dying to hear all your news. How is the accommodation? I hope the table is good.

Today Vera rang me bright and early, and suggested I catch the 10.20 train from Malvern to Mordialloc, where she could then meet me at Ormond. Hot and all as it was, she suggested having nine holes of golf and then a swim. We walked to the course from the station and got there about 11.15, and as lunch was at noon, decided to wait. I might add we had a couple of iced beers whilst waiting for lunch, and felt that we had deserved them. After lunch we played twelve holes and were just about exhausted. I played a good game but Vera is a champion. She's been playing since she was a child. We met her sister (also a champion) at Brighton where she has a flat with her husband, and then we all went for a swim. It was not too pleasant, as there were too many people there and the water was not too clean. Vera wanted me to go to the pictures with her and her boyfriend, but I was a trifle tired, so said if she didn't mind, I would go home.

Well, I am propped up in bed writing this as I retired early. Every now and then, I have to wipe the sweat off my fevered brow as it is still pretty warm.

Tuesday morning.

I have just been talking to Judy, and she seems to have had a super weekend with John — mostly out in the boat. I am lunching with her, so will probably hear all the news then. I do so wish we had a holiday hideaway like them.

I am dashing out to the Camberwell Junction after work this evening to pick up a skirt at Mabel Clay's. Perhaps I should wander along there to Stodart Street and see if you have been robbed. I could throw Darkie a bone and have a chat to him, but I suppose you got accommodation for him elsewhere.

Lea rang me last night from the Springs; they seem to be enjoying themselves. She has also got the Mater and her in for the third week, which is the week I commence my holidays, so we won't have the worry of the Mater being left on her own at home.

Well, my Beloved Bandito De Spaniardo, I had to stand in a queue about ten yards long to get your ration tickets from the Motor Registration.

Always yours,

Fay

Although Fay never told Jaime, she did go to 18 Stodart Street to have a peek. She was curious about his home, and the flat he lived in on top of the garage. It was a strange feeling seeing the street he so often walked. On reaching the house, Fay first noticed how impeccably clean the tennis court was. She pictured Jaime meticulously mowing the grass court. The home, a deco Italianate style of cream brick, also had a magnificent, well-kept garden. Fay knew Jaime had a regular gardener to take care of the large grounds; as he would laughingly say, 'I don't have a green thumb at all!' The flat, above the garage, at the end of a long gravel drive was a small version of the house. When Fay noticed a neighbour watching her she left. It would be a huge upheaval for Jaime to leave this beautiful home, she sadly reflected, as she boarded a tram home.

Queenscliff

31 January 1946, 3.20pm

Darling Fay,

I posted you a card earlier today, but as I am alone again for a short time, thought I would drop you this note in case I don't get another chance. We have just come from watching the aircraft carriers going through the heads. Leon and Eric have gone for a swim, and C is lying down, so thought I would drop you this note. Will go for a swim too, as soon as I post this.

Today has been most unpleasant with the hot, north wind, but up until now the weather has been perfect. Well, Darling, I will continue to see if you have sent me any more letters, but as it is now so near the end of the week, and as I told you not to bother, I shall not expect anymore here. Darling, I wish you were here; it would be perfect with you. Am dying to see you again.

J xxx

PS Book for the Savoy Theatre next week, I believe it's good.

Things were hard for 15-year-old Leon; he knew his parents' marriage wasn't 'normal'. He had heard the arguments for many years, and by now tended to go elsewhere if a row exploded. Still, he loved the summer holidays spent with both his parents, and the fact he could bring a friend along. It seemed to prevent his mother from acting up.

Jaime was back in Melbourne for work on 5 February, and Fay was due to start her holiday a week or so later. She wrote to Jaime welcoming him back to Melbourne.

1 February 1946

Well, my Darling,

Welcome back to the Big Smoke — I guess you will suffer from Mondayitis pretty badly today. Hope Reggie doesn't push you round too much and find too many heavy jobs for you to do.

You must have read my thoughts about booking for the show on Wednesday next, as I had already booked two seats for the Savoy: A Song to Remember starring Merle Oberon. I have also heard it is a good show — Chopin's music all through. But I chose this program mostly because someone told me there is a very good picture on, How to Play Golf with the Irons, so I thought that would interest both of us. I have to pick up the seats before 6.30 on Wednesday.

I suppose you are as brown as a penny, and will be making my pale tan look about two shades paler when you don the swim-suit. Well, my Darling,

I will post this on the way home, and as it is now a few minutes to 5, I will have to make it briefer than I thought — but I want to be sure you get it on Monday morning.

Yours forever and ever,

Fay

Prior to leaving Queenscliff, Jaime sent a post card to Fay. Although the war was over, petrol and cigarette rationing still applied.

Queenscliff

2 February 1946, 10.30pm

My darling Fay,

You might wonder how it is I am writing to you at this time of night, but we went to the local pictures tonight, and I was so bored I walked out. So here I am writing to you. Thanks a lot for everything: the petrol tickets, your letters, and then the cigarettes. You're a darling, and I love you very much.

We come home tomorrow, and though I have enjoyed it here, I shall be almost glad, because it means seeing you. Yes, Darling, I have missed you terribly, and have thought of you morning and night. I played in the local Golf Tournament this afternoon and won it — not bad, eh? Fay, will you try and have your lunch between 12 and 1pm on Monday so I can see you?

All my love,

JSM

Fay and Jaime had a week to see each other before Fay was due to begin her summer holiday at Dava Lodge. Her friend, Mollie Wright was rooming with her. Jaime hated her holidays, he knew how much she loved him, nonetheless always had a tinge of jealousy when she was out of his range. Over Christmas he had given her an eternity ring, on a band of white gold, with tiny sapphires and diamonds. He said this would be *their* ring, and a sign of eternal love for one another.

10 February 1946, 8pm

My darling Fay,

I bet you will get a surprise to receive this note so soon (I hope it will be Monday morning). Darling, whatever time did you leave on Sunday? I rang you at 1.45 to say goodbye, I was going to pretend I was May Wilson (and try and put on a female voice) but I could not raise anybody at U.Y. 6373. Did you get away early? I was terribly disappointed that I missed hearing your voice.

How did you get on on Saturday? I couldn't remember a great deal after I left you. Did I give you our ring to keep its eye on you? Well, Darling, have a good holiday, but be careful when swimming. Also be good, and I do hope the Morgan brothers are not there! Hoping to hear from you soon.

All my love, Jaime

PS When you write, do not use a Dava envelope; it would be best, I think.

Dava Lodge, Mornington
11 February 1946

Hello Darling,

What a lovely surprise when I got your letter this morning. Sorry I was not there to receive the phone call. Our lift rang and said he would call about eleven, so we arrived down in time for lunch. The Mater must have been up the street or at the Aunt's.

Well Darling, I guess you are wondering what's what at Dava. To be perfectly honest I am rather bored with it all. Yes, the Morgans are here (for a month) and the Bentons, and you would think they owned the jolly place. They have their own little gang for their drinking orgies — but I am certainly not interested in them. I am friendly with them, but their wisecracking etc. pales a bit.

I believe there is to be a dance on Friday night. Alex Thompson has been trying to get an orchestra and he has asked me to give him a hand with the supper. As Lea has tired of Clifton Springs, so have I tired of Dava — Mollie feels the same about it — she is not coming here again. They keep a lovely table, as good as the Springs at Xmas. But when you haven't got the person you love with you, it is dull.

Well, Darling, you did give me the ring, and I have it safe with me. The vino certainly became more potent as the night wore on, but I was so busy, and so was the Mater, that it went unnoticed.

I went for a walk along the road last night with the Bentons and Morgans and a few others, but was in bed by 9.30. Ronnie Benton is chasing Syd as usual, and he seems to like it but he keeps her guessing, as he likes to be a free agent, and he and Stan wander off to the local pub and you don't see them, only at meal time. I think the reason he was so much quieter the last holiday he was here, was because he was just getting over a big operation, and was not allowed much drink. But he is sure making up for it now!

You really needn't get worried about them being here. I would rather have one hour in your company, than a lifetime with Syd. I am looking forward to our weekend with a vengeance; they are worth all these holidays alone. I must give Judy a ring and see if I can manage an invitation for Saturday. Even if we don't go down there, we could have some golf in Frankston.

Well, Darling, I love and miss you terrifically and wish you were not here but at Torquay for the rest of the fortnight, where I know we would be perfectly happy, and have done with all this pretence and hot-air talk that goes on at these holiday places. It is all a stage, and the people the actors — nothing very sincere about any of them.

I think I'll go and have a hit of tennis now, there seem to be a few on the court.

Fay

11 February 1946, 5.30pm

My darling Fay,

Last Monday I was jumping out of my skin, I felt so well, but today I am 2/- a pound, I feel so ill. I must have caught a chill yesterday playing golf in the rain. I would have stayed in bed, only that bloody so-and-so in the office would kick up such a fuss, he carried on even today when I actually came in. But believe me, I won't be in tomorrow if I feel as bad as this. At any rate, if I don't come in, Miss Kane is going to hang on to any letters from you.

According to the stars, this is a bad month for the sign of Leo, so I hope it's not the forerunner of more bad omens. I never did like February. Well, Darling, the weather has not smiled on you yet, but it will as it always does for you. I am dying to hear from you. I had my fortune told today, very interesting!

All my love,

Jaime

Jaime was writing to Fay daily, especially when he heard the Morgans were at Dava, and his insecurities and jealousy got the better of him.

12 February 1946, 6pm

Darling,

I struggled going into work today for two reasons, one because the blighter Reggie goes so silly if I am not there, and the other is because I expected a letter from you. I had intended if the Morgans were at Dava, not to bother about you for the next two weeks, but as your letter this morning was so nice and reassuring, I shall try to forget it. However, just the same I am sorry they are there, because it will possibly start something again, and believe me, I don't feel up to it anymore.

Well, Darling, thanks for your letter, it gave me a thrill and am pleased you feel the same way about our holiday together, as I do, and that Torquay would be ideal. I have always felt that way about it.

All my love,

Jaime

Fay's boredom was growing at Dava Lodge. The same old crowd, year after year. She thanked her lucky stars her half-hearted romance with Syd Morgan had been so brief and innocent. He was a ladies man who loved a good time, particularly if it was fuelled by plenty of alcohol. Not seeing Jaime each day made it all the worse and she looked forward to the short time he spent with her when he joined her for a day at Mornington.

We had a sing-song last night — a few of the men played their ukuleles, but not being able to sing (as you know), I just listened and went off to bed about ten. There are no young girls here, with the exception of Shirley. She is twenty-two and with an aunt — quite a bright lass, but there are no young chaps for her and she thinks it a dull place. I think all the young girls that have been here in the past never come back, and tell their friends not to come here. It certainly is no place for young people who like a dance at night and plenty of fun. I know I would never come back here if I didn't play golf.

Jaime was planning to come down on Saturday to spend the day with her, on the Thursday before she sent him a note.

Dava Lodge

14 February 1946

Darling,

I rang Judy this morning and had a chat to her. They are having a few down for the weekend, and I said we may blow in. She said she would love to see us — but I think if they are having a few there, I don't think we'll bother. What about ringing me tomorrow night, around 7pm? I can make arrangements to see you on Saturday, and we can spend the day together, any time that suits you. I'll find out the times the buses leave here, and meet you in Frankston or Mornington — or outside Dava if you like. But I think it would save a few explanations if I kept out of sight down here — not that I give two hoots, but I think it would be better that way for both of us. If you find you cannot make it, don't worry, but I would love to hear your voice on the phone tomorrow night.

All my love, Darling,

Fay

Their affair was now into its fourteenth year, and still it had to be kept under cover. It was frustrating for both of them, the continual secrecy and avoidance of being seen as a couple — even with friends of Judy and John, who were somewhat in the same boat. However, John had separated from his wife, and was now waiting for his divorce to be finalised. Fay also found it hard to take when Jaime had guests for lunch and tennis with his wife and son. She wished *she* were the hostess; at least Jaime would have her to play and enjoy a tennis game with.

17 February 1946, 8.30am

My darling Fay,

I am up early as you can see, to get the court ready, it looks as if it will be fine after all. Am writing this early so that I can get a chance to post it later, before all the visitors arrive.

Well, Darling, I left you at Dava at 10.20 last night, and was at Camberwell at 11.05. It only took me forty-five minutes to do the trip, and I didn't exceed 45 miles per hour at any time. So you see, Darling, if the petrol was available I wouldn't mind popping down every now and then to see you, it seems so easy. I hated leaving you last night, and wished I was staying at Dava with you.

Darling, thanks for a marvellous afternoon and evening, I loved every minute of the time, and I love and adore you. I am glad you are having another week now, as I know that you love me. I will write again tomorrow.

All my love,

J.S.M.

Fay had hoped their holiday at Torquay would be the weekend after she arrived home; however, Connie had made arrangements for Leon that required Jaime in town, so Fay decided to spend another week at the guesthouse. It was certainly better than dealing with her mother in Melbourne. Jaime, as promised, wrote again the following day.

18 February 1946, 5.45pm

Fay, Darling,

Am on my way to catch the train, as I left the car at home today. I rang Lea today, and had quite a long chat. Am meeting her for lunch on Wednesday. Well, Darling, little Reggie and his wife and the others came yesterday, and strange as it may seem, he behaved himself very well. The rain conveniently kept away till after the tennis. We had some marvellous tennis, as I had Lionel Brodie (fifth ranking player in Australia) and Bob Schlesinger (ex-Davis Cup man) up to make a gents four. I played with Bob and we won 9-11, 10-8, 9-7, a total of fifty-four games in all. Yours truly played very well, but it was very strenuous .It seems strange that players of their calibre were far more generous of their praise for the house and their afternoon's game, than little Reggie and his wifey, who never said a word about the court, house, or anything. But then, of course, we expect that of him. As soon as the tennis began, C went to bed, so Leon and his friend looked after the guest onlookers. Am looking forward to next week when you return, so watch out!

All my love,

J.S.M.

With Jaime's job working for Paynes Sports and Aircraft Company, he felt he had to be sociable with Reggie, a nephew of the owners, and also his boss. A short, thin man, with a long pale nose, Reggie was as unpleasant inside as out, and took great pleasure in bossing everyone around, including his painfully shy, wispy wife.

Jaime had intended to drive down and spend Friday evening with Fay, having dinner, and seeing a picture at Frankston. But plans were aborted as a dance was being held at Dava on the Friday night, and Fay was put on the organizing committee, much to Jaime's annoyance.

Darling, blow them having another dance on Friday, because that puts an end to my plans for slipping down Friday night. Why don't they have it on Saturday? Well I lunched with Lea today, and thoroughly enjoyed it. It was the next best thing to being with you. She told me all the tit bits of her holiday at Clifton Springs, and she seems to have taken a great fancy to Jack, whose sister she became friendly with first. She also got me some cigarettes, for which I was truly grateful. Perhaps this Jack may mend her heartache for Tommy.

Although Lea had enjoyed her holiday at Clifton Springs, having her mother in tow made it difficult. She had become friendly with a girl named Beth who was staying there with her brother, Jack. Lea and Jack played tennis together, and shared supper on a number of occasions, yet as soon as Annie got wind of the romance, she feigned feeling ill, and Lea spent the remainder of her holiday at her mother's beck and call. Consequently, the romance came to an abrupt end.

Fay was making the most of her last week on holiday, and continued to write whenever she had the chance.

Dava Lodge
21 February 1946

Good morning, Darling,

Sorry I didn't give you a letter this morning, but I had to write to the Aunt (who hasn't been at all well) plus Harry and Marie, Lea and the Mater. Mollie teases me that all I seem to do is write.

Today is just perfect, the best we have had, so I am just spending the whole of the afternoon on the beach. One of the chaps down here, Harry Ramsay, of Kiwi fame, has a moving picture camera, and took us all on the beach this afternoon in Technicolor. I hope they turn out alright — they should look good.

I am glad Lea was able to get you some cigarettes, and that she is looking well. I do hope she hears from Jack, but am afraid the Mater has frightened him off. I wondered why they didn't hold the dance on Saturday night, but it appears they can't get an orchestra that night. Anyway Darling, it will be a busy night for me, as I have to help with sandwiches etc. and they end at twelve o'clock.

Syd Morgan has been making a fuss now of Dorothy (Gwenda's friend) and has more or less dumped Ronnie Benton. For mixing his drink and his women, he is about the worst type I know of for this sort of thing. But he seems to like it that way, and gets away with it. Apart from sitting at the same table with him, I haven't been in his company very much, only for a few games of tennis and a few swims with the crowd. I don't think there is one sensible word spoken at mealtimes, they just fool all the time — they are a mad lot.

22 February 1946

I am being driven home on Sunday after lunch by Laurie Cook, the chap Lea knows. He has a daughter who is twenty-three, so don't worry, Darling. I feel terribly envious of the wives here with their husbands. They have such a secure look about them.

They had a meeting (Committee only) tonight, to make arrangements for the dance tomorrow night. They are charging 2/6 per head, and all guests provide their own liquor which they are finding pretty difficult to buy by the bottle.

Well, my Darling, as I have more letters to write, I shall say goodnight. I love you and miss you and cannot wait to see you again.

All my love,

Fay

The dance at Dava was a success, although the only joy Fay felt was hearing the orchestra play the 1945 hit song, 'You Belong to My Heart', sung by Bing Crosby, with the Xavier Cugat Orchestra, English lyrics written by Ray Gilbert.

> *You belong to my heart*
> *Now and forever*
> *And our love had its start*
> *Not long ago*

> *We were gathering stars*
> *While a million guitars played our love song*
> *When I said 'I love you,' every beat of my heart said it too*

> *'Twas a moment like this*
> *Do you remember?*
> *And your eyes threw a kiss*
> *When they met mine*

> *Now we own all the stars*
> *And a million guitars are still playing*
> *Darling, you are the song*
> *And you'll always belong to my heart.*

One Has My Name (The Other Has My Heart)

The weekend at Torquay didn't eventuate until the first week of April. Fay's Aunt Anne, her father's sister, died after an illness, aged eighty-three years. All of the Johnstons were extremely upset, especially Fay, who had been close to her aunt. As Anne had never married, and her siblings all deceased, her estate, including money, furniture and bric-a-brac was left to her sister-in-law, Annie, and to Fay, Lea, and Harry.

A week before their trip, Jaime wrote to Fay. He had booked their usual flat in Torquay; they both felt like a married couple on these occasions, especially as Fay usually cooked the meals.

31 March 1946
9.30am

Good morning, Darling,

Surprised to get this note, I suppose, but I just wanted to write and thank you for a lovely evening on Friday and a more beautiful afternoon yesterday. Yes, and I say this now when I am cold sober, too!

Darling for years, your hair, your face, and that lovely body of yours has bewitched me, but now your eyes have begun to work on me too. Whatever you have done to them I don't know, but they now have a shine all of their own. Yes, they are beautiful.

It seems to me that the older you get, the lovelier you are, and I am just wondering what further pleasant surprises you have in store for me. This time next week I hope to be getting ready for a game of golf, but not before I taste a delicious omelette compliments of my Darling.

Yes, Darling, I am looking forward to our weekend with all my being. Just to be with you, gaze at you, talk to you, and make love to you. I can't wait. Reggie comes back tomorrow and it will feel rotten after two weeks of being able to do what I liked, lunch when I liked, and nick out occasionally. All good things come to an end, except my love for you, and that just burns me up.

Well, Beautiful, I must finish now. Don't forget to remind me to get that electric jug, and make arrangements to hire the wireless next week. Will look forward to hearing from you Monday morning.

In the meantime, all my love to my darling Sweetheart from her Jaime
Xxxxx

They set off for Torquay on Friday evening, 5 April and were returning on the Sunday night. Now whenever they picked the key up, the landlord referred to them as 'Mr and Mrs Miguel'. Jaime felt that shortening the name was far safer. Fay adored being referred to as his wife, and dreamed of the day it would be a reality. Still, they had two nights and three days to be solely together, and as always they made the most of it.

～

Jaime rarely saw his siblings anymore. Everyone was aware of his 'situation', and apart from occasional contact with Tony, Jaime never spoke to them. His mother, now in her eighty-third year, was ailing, and Ines, who remained a spinster, looked after her at Montalegre. His youngest sister, Patricia, continued to enjoy a very social life. She was often mentioned in the social pages and her and husband Leslie Henwood regularly travelled over seas. However, their marriage was beginning to falter.

The Argus, Wed. 9 October 1946
I Heard and Saw (Gossip Column)

HANKY HUNT

When I heard that Mrs Leslie Felix Henwood had turned on a hanky party for bride-to-be, Judith Lilley, I immediately saw in my mind's eye thirty frantic females dashing hither and thither from store to store trying to do justice to Judy.

Judy is to be married to Dr Thomas Paul Rowan at Xavier Chapel on 28 October at 10am and Mrs Henwood's party for her at Tre-Pol-Pen, Balwyn, was the last word in entertaining. Guests gasped when they saw the array of spring flowers in the reception rooms, but when they went to the dining room for afternoon tea they could hardly eat for admiring the festive-looking table.

From a scarlet centre rose the most glamorous French doll — the Henwoods bought it from Paris — and from doll to each plate were ribbons, each of which tied one of the hard-to-get hankies.

By the way, don't you love the sound of Tre-Pol-Pen? It's Cornish.

~

By the end of 1946, Jaime had left Paynes and the obnoxious Reggie, and taken a sales position at Commercial Importers and Exporters Pty. Ltd in Queen Street.

1946 faded into the summer of 1947, which Jaime and Fay welcomed in with the same optimism that perhaps this year Jaime would become a free man. Fay booked in at Clifton Springs Hotel this time round. Her holidays at Dava Lodge had come to an end after so many years. On Saturday 15 February, Fay began her annual fortnight-long holiday. Jaime's co-worker Mr Ferguson and his sister were travelling to Clifton Springs the same day as Fay. Miss Ferguson was also holidaying at the hotel, so Jaime suggested they come in his car, along with Fay. He would drive them all down, and then return to Melbourne in the evening with Miss Ferguson's brother.

> *18 February 1947*
> *12.30pm*
>
> *My darling Fay,*
> *Up to the present moment, I have not received any letter from you, but I suppose that will come tomorrow. We (Miss Ferguson's brother and I) had a good trip up to town, and I was well in bed before Connie and Leon got back from the pictures on Saturday night.*
> *The car ran very well, but the generator was not charging, and on Monday when I took it in, they discovered it had burnt out, so she is in dock now and won't be out until this evening. Connie rang yesterday and wanted a lift home (she'd been shopping in the city). When I got home, the fireworks started in earnest, as she evidently thought I was meeting you instead. I didn't enlighten her, so she actually came a bit of a thud. However, during the storm, she stated that I didn't want a divorce as I was scared she might oblige. So, I challenged her to try it on and see, and she retorted not to be too sure, as one of these days, I might get a subpoena. Leon, I thought, appeared quite in sympathy with me.*
> *I am working hard but missing you a great deal.*
> *All my love to you,*
> *Jaime*

Before Jaime took his car in for service, he had taken his golf buggy out and left it under the porch. When Connie returned home from shopping, she had rifled through it, and found one of Fay's love letters in a side pocket, and kept it as evidence of his affair. She had also discovered the phone number for Tooronga Road and threatened to telephone Fay's mother. The letter, especially, enraged her, and led to more outbursts.

25 February 1947

My Darling,

Thanks for your letter this morning, I did appreciate it. By Jove, you certainly pick the weather; it's been marvellous, not too hot, or too cold. I hope it keeps up for this weekend. Yes, Beautiful, I will be down for the weekend. As far as I know now it will be Friday night (unless the office calls me in Saturday morning). I shall let Lea know in good time. What a pity your Mater isn't going to Warragul for the weekend. Then if Connie rang, no one would be home.

Connie was in one of her vicious moods last night, and believe me, they are nasty! When she spoke about you, I told her I thought more of your little finger than twenty of her. She spoke of divorce, but said I would have to make it worth her while. She said I was more interested in money than you. I replied by challenging her to go ahead. I even offered her more evidence to make sure. By Jove, she went to town then. I told her she would be treated fairly, but I wasn't going to let her have all my assets and snap her fingers at me and you, which she would like to do. During the heat I told her I was going to go away for the weekend, to get away from it all. She said, 'I know you will be going away with Fay,' and so it went on and on. I was trying to attend to the samples for work in the dining room while that woman harped and harped. I had to put up with it, as I wanted the use of the table. But I saw red when at about ten o'clock, Leon walks in and she tried to get him into the argument, which he flatly refused to do. At any rate, she will lose patience before me, and when she does, we will get what we want.

However, Darling, I must not bore you with my problems, although I suppose it has to do with you too, so it would interest you.

Thanks again for your letter this morning, it was like a breath of fresh air.

All my love,

Jaime

Jaime was thankful he had put a padlock on the flat door; otherwise, Connie may have found the case under his bed containing Fay's letters spanning fifteen years. The constant heated arguments of his parents was taking its toll on 16-year-old Leon, who had developed asthma, and a number of allergies. On weekends he preferred to stay at his friend, Eric's house, one of harmony.

The quarrels at Stodart Street continued over the next few days and Jaime thought of taking Leon with him to Clifton Springs. He mentioned it to Leon, who was anxious to go — the problem was Connie.

26 February 1947

My darling Fay,

Last night, I went through even a more torrid time than Monday. I think at times C must become demented, she certainly acts and speaks like it, and I won't forget it in a hurry. One very good thing came out of it, and that is I will be down on Friday night for certain. So I will get in touch with Lea and let her know. So if you have any fond farewells to say to any of the men down there, you had better do it Thursday night!

Would you get a great shock if I bought Leon with me? He certainly would love the tennis, table tennis, and swimming. And I know he likes you. I would not bring him down unless he promised not to be biased about you. But I suppose C will be the stumbling block. Well, Darling, are you missing and thinking of me a wee bit? I am working hard so will have to finish.

All my love, Jaime

As predicted, Connie put her foot down and prohibited Leon from going away with his father. Although disappointed, Jaime knew he'd be able to spend more time with Fay; every minute in her company was precious.

∼

On 22 July 1947, Fay's brother, Harry and his wife, Marie, welcomed their third born child, a daughter, Jennifer Fay, into the world. Fay was tickled pink with the compliment. Still living in Warragul, Marie and Harry made plans to move to Narrandera, in southern New South Wales later in the year. With the money he'd inherited from Aunt Anne, he was able to put a deposit on a house, built on a large block of land.

At the beginning of September, Jaime began another job at Hedley's Sporting Goods Pty Ltd, based at 291 Toorak Road, South Yarra. He felt more confident selling goods he was familiar with. It also meant he would be travelling frequently, and although it was time away from Fay, it was also a break from the vitriolic atmosphere at home. In late September, Jaime had a sales trip to Colac, a small city in the Western District of Victoria. He took Leon along, letting him drive to gain practice. Jaime had been teaching him all year, and although he could not obtain a licence till he was eighteen, Jaime wanted him accomplished beforehand.

Victoria Hotel, Colac
29 September 1947

My darling Fay.

Just a short note to tell you I am well, and still love you, and am thinking of you. I have had a very busy day, and am still at Colac. Will probably make for Camperdown tomorrow night or early Wednesday morning.

We had a good trip, and I let Leon drive all the way. We did exactly 100 miles for the trip. Left Camberwell at 2.15 and got here at five o'clock. Had a fairly successful day, although the battery ran down, and we lost a bit of time through this. We are just going off to the pictures to see The Razors Edge at the local show.

All my love,

Jaime

Leon thoroughly enjoyed road trips with his father, especially during his school holidays. Playing the odd game of golf with Jaime was always a challenge as Leon also loved sports, especially swimming and tennis. This also gave them time away from the tension at home.

~

Jaime suggested to Fay that they drive to Adelaide for a fortnight's holiday in late December, as fortunately, their vacation began at the same time. So on Boxing Day they set off from Malvern at 10am, both extremely excited. After spending a romantic night at Border Town, a small South Australian township near the Victorian border, they drove through Tintinara and Tailem's Bend, where they passed through millions of grasshoppers, until they reached Bridgewater. At 5.30pm they arrived at their lodgings at the Hotel Brighton. They had a scrumptious dinner and cruised around Brighton and Glenelg, before retiring for an early night. Sunday was extremely hot, so they swam at Glenelg beach in the morning and evening. Monday was spent at the Interstate Tennis, where they watched Jaime's friend's wife, Mrs Harry Hopman defeat Adelaide woman, Mrs Theil. Tuesday was spent on the golf course. New Years' Eve they shopped during the day, and saw the old year out in Glenelg, where the Mayor came out onto the balcony of the Town Hall and delivered a speech.

As they kissed at midnight, Jaime promised that this would be the year he would become a free man, and although Fay wished it with all her heart, she wondered whether it would ever come true. They had a late supper and champagne at the Top Hat Café, before heading back to their room, where they fell into each other's arms.

The first day of 1948 was more than either of them bargained for. Jaime had told Leon which hotel they were staying at, in case of an emergency. Connie harangued him into divulging the name and then booked a flight to Adelaide, bringing along her anguished son. They arrived at the Hotel Brighton at 11am, just as Jaime and Fay were about to go out. It was an uncomfortable confrontation and Fay felt sorry for Leon who seemed embarrassed and forlorn. Jaime took both Connie and Leon to nearby Seacliff, where he had a long discussion with them both, begging Connie to grant him a divorce. Even Leon agreed this was the only answer, yet Connie remained stubborn. They returned to Melbourne on a 6.30pm flight, leaving Jaime and Fay bewildered.

After dinner at the Café Torrens River, Fay put a penny in the slot machine; it showed 'uncontrollable' for Jaime, and 'lovable' for her. A waste of money, she noted. Still, their holiday was memorable, plenty of golf, thrills and spills at the motor races, and a trip to the National Gallery, Museum and Zoo. On Sunday 4 they went to St. Francis Xavier Cathedral, founded in 1856, and in the evening visited the Aquarian on the pier, where they hungrily tucked into fish and chips for supper. Tuesday 6 was spent shopping in town, and Fay purchased nylon stockings for Lea and a pair of gloves for her mother.

On the seventh, they left Adelaide en route back to Melbourne. Driving between Meningie and McGrath's Flat, they witnessed a fleet of pelicans, both agreeing it was a beautiful sight. They passed through Salt Creek, and then had 53 miles of desert, until they reached Kingston, nearly 185 miles from Adelaide, where they stayed over night. Leaving at 10 in the morning, hundreds of white butterflies greeted them in Millicent. Stopping for lunch at Mount Gambier, they dined at the Cave Garden Café, and then went up to the top of Mount Gambier, where they viewed the magnificent scenery through a telescope at the tower. Trouble with the car forced them to stay overnight in Mount Gambier, while a local garage fixed the self-starter.

After a light breakfast, they headed off, lunching in Portland on corn beef and pickle relish sandwiches and fresh strawberries and cream. As no accommodation was available at Port Campbell they drove on to Laver's Hill, thirty miles inland from Port Campbell, where they spent another passionate night.

On Saturday 10 January they stopped at Anglesea for a swim in the surf and had lunch at The 4 Kings, before a leisurely drive back to Malvern. It had been a thoroughly romantic and enjoyable holiday, apart from Connie's surprise interruption.

∼

By early 1948 Harry and Marie were comfortably settled into their new home at Narrandera. Fay had already spent a weekend with them in early December of 1947 along with her mother. In late February, she took the train again to spend a week with her brother, sister-in-law, nephews, and baby niece. Prior to the trip, Fay had bought a pure-bred Border Collie puppy from a licensed breeder, as a present for 10-year-old Ronald, and 6-year-old Phillip. The two little boys were thrilled to bits with their new pet, who they christened Rover.

Back in Melbourne, Jaime was coming to terms with how fast the years had gone. It was Leon's last year of school; he was turning eighteen in August, and already had a girlfriend, Margaret, who Connie disapproved of.

Monday, 1 March 1948

Darling,

I suppose I shall have to break it down in this letter, in case the Johnston Family (mother, brother, sister-in-law, or nephews) get hold of it, or will you keep it under lock and key?

Have just left the factory, been helping George and Tom test some racquets. Well, how did you get on during the long trip on the train? Did the taxi arrive alright, and did the dog see the trip out? I suppose there was great excitement in Narrandera; did the brass band turn out okay?

Well, Darl, I did not win the golf on Saturday, but played very well. Took Leon to the motor races on Saturday night, and told him at the last minute he could take Margaret, as C did not come home for tea. I knew she would be wild when she heard it. Leon was tickled pink, and the three of us, Leon,

Margaret, and myself had a good night. Fortunately, there were no accidents. C was very annoyed when she heard we took Margaret, as she reckoned I was trying to get around Leon.

Yesterday, although it rained early, we had some tennis and the new Hedley racquet I tried out was beautiful, I don't think I have played better for years. These Hedley's are pretty good!

Well, my dear, I had better finish, it's now 6.30. Have missed you quite a bit, and am looking forward to seeing you on your return. Give my regards to everyone in Narrandera. Am enclosing a couple of stamps for Ronald.

All my love, in haste,

Jaime

During Fay's last stay at Narrandera, some of Jaime's letters to her, and ones she'd written to him disappeared, and she suspected Harry had taken them to show their mother.

3 March 1948

Well, Darling, I think this is about the first letter I have written from here, since the others were confiscated. I am not quite sure, but I hope this deserves a better fate. Maybe dear Harry had them in safe keeping for her. Too bad if his wife found them. It would put them on the spot!

During Fay's sojourn in NSW Jaime wrote to her every day, regardless of the security problem. He had plenty of news about Connie.

2 March 1948

When I got home last night, C was out for dinner, so Leon and I had the night to ourselves, for which I was glad, I didn't even hear her come in. This morning she was up early again, and I said to Leon, 'What's your mother doing up so early?' and he said she was going out early today. So I said to

Leon, 'Is the American Fleet in again?' and he laughed heartily at the remark. So I don't know if C will be home or not tonight again, I hope she isn't home.

3 March

I am going to try and get to bed early tonight, for the lack of sleep last night. Perhaps C won't be home, and that will be all the better. By the way, I found out why C has been getting away early of a morning. She has taken a temporary job at some women's hostel, helping the matron. She said she was short of cash, and had to get some money somewhere. She gets 10/- for the afternoon, and 10/- for the morning. Of course, I don't know how long this will last. If I know C, it won't be for long.

C/O The Public Schools' Club of Victoria,
390 Little Collins Street, Melbourne
4 March 1948, 8pm

My darling Fay,
I am writing this at the Club Rooms. Last night C was home, and after dinner she asked me in no uncertain terms to pay an account for a coat she had got some time ago. This started an argument, so I told her to pay for it herself, and to go hopping. She said, 'Where's your ... is she on holidays?' and a few more abusive terms, so I went up to my little flat over the garage and stayed there. This morning she started again, so I decided not to go home tonight to be abused. Since the weekend, C has been very quiet, but I knew her viciousness would come out again sooner or later. She can't help herself. I only hope that she didn't decide to stay out too, as Leon would be left on his own, of course. If it's just the two of us, we enjoy each other's company. She is the only one that puts the mozz on it.

Strange as it may seem, the week has gone very quickly, though I have missed you so much. You see, my present job keeps me very busy, and I like it and enjoy it, different to when I was at Reggie's, and those other wartime jobs.

It's now about 8.45pm, so I will finish up and have an hour at the Gazettes, before making for Camberwell. If I was certain that C wasn't going to be home tomorrow night, I would ask Leon to meet me in town, and have dinner with me. Then again, she might think that you were away, and that you had just dumped me. But on second thoughts, what do we care what Poison Ivy thinks!

On Saturday, I will play golf in the afternoon, then slip into town and have dinner, then probably an hour at the Gazettes, then meet your train. Leon is going to another dance at Powerhouse, near the Albert Park Lake, so I will probably arrange to pick him up at twelve o'clock, if that is okay with you. I suppose the Mater would not like me to be still hanging around after that time. Do you think she will mind me driving you home, and then coming in for an hour? She'll have to put up with it anyway. Of course, this will be my last epistle to you before you return. Unless you decide to desert me and stay another week. Then I will get hold of your lovely bottom and smack it hard (then probably kiss it and make it better).

Well, Darling, au revoir till Saturday night, all my love,
Jaime

Fay was as prolific as Jaime at letter writing, even though her hands were often full, entertaining Ronald and Phillip. Harry seemed to have accepted Fay's relationship with Jaime, and teased her about the daily arrival of a letter. She no longer worried he would interfere. She thought maybe Marie had a stern word in his ear.

4 March 1948

Well, Darling, the kids have arrived home from school so I won't get much peace from now on. Yesterday Phillip took the pup over to a neighbour's place, and arrived back in tears. Their cat had got to the pup and scratched him quite a bit, and poor Phillip was carrying him and howling his eyes out. The pup's nose was bleeding, and round his mouth. But he soon rubbed it off

in the grass (and after rendering a little first aid from the medicine chest),
much to Phillip's joy. They are now playing cricket out in the backyard, pup
and all.

Have just come back from a walk down the street with Phillip. He said
he had a headache this morning and did not want to go to school. I did
not mind, as I knew he was only kidding — in fact, we all did. But one day
wouldn't hurt for a six-year-old!

There are quite a lot of aborigines here, and this morning a few of the
girls from the convent walked past, and one of the girls was a half-caste,[1] so
I guess there have been a few inter-marrying. Little Phil just asked me who I
was writing to, and I told him, and he said to give you hugs and kisses (ten he
says). Will do this when I see you!

Am missing you dreadfully, Darling, and will definitely be home on
Saturday.

5 March 1948

Have just got into bed. I feel worn out, more tired than if I had played 36
holes of golf! Our fishing was not very successful, as we had the wrong kind of
bait, and they were not biting. When we got home, we got a tin of salmon and
told the family we had caught them in a tin, much to Phillip's amusement! We
also had a swim, and did some sunbathing. When we got home I had a game
of cricket with the kids, so I am just about worn out. Ron and Phil went off
on their bicycles to school this morning, it seemed funny to see little Phil on
his small bicycle, going for his life down the road.

~

After Fay and Jaime's holiday in Adelaide, Annie realised she could
no longer stand in her daughter's way. The affair was now into its
seventeenth year, and she secretly liked Jaime, especially the fact he
came from 'old money'.

Leon was fed up with his family problems, and asked whether he could board at Xavier for his final year. Jaime happily agreed, but Connie complained she would be constantly on her own, and flatly refused.

Jaime enjoyed his job at Hedley's as much as he had at Dunlop's, and even the travelling did not faze him. In mid-March he was back on the road and wrote to Fay from Albury.

Soden's Hotel, Albury
17 March 1948

My darling Fay,

Sorry I have not written sooner, but I have been very busy. Up to date, I have booked about 300 pounds of business. I have thought of you quite a lot, and have missed you very much, as passing through all these towns reminds me so much of our Xmas trip. Am wishing all the time you were with me.

By the way, I hope C hasn't been worrying you while I have been away. She was in a very hostile mood on Sunday and Monday morning, and threatened to tear up any letters I wrote to Leon if she got them before he got home. So I am dropping him a note to Xavier College tonight after I have finished this epistle to you.

Did you get my telegram from Beechworth? I bet you were surprised! I didn't think I would be going through that town, but I discovered it was only about 4 or 6 miles further through Beechworth than direct to Albury. In addition, I wanted to look over the place where my Darling's mother came from. Well, Darl, Beechworth is not a bad town, quite big and situated in a very pretty spot. Tell your Mater I liked her town very much.

Well, Darling, I have to get my samples ready for tomorrow, so all my love.
Jaime

Throughout 1948, Jaime was constantly on the road, and always wished Fay could be with him. In early August, he wrote to her from Camperdown, a rural town in south-western Victoria, 121 miles from Melbourne.

Old Leura Hotel, Camperdown
3 August 1948

My darling Fay,

Well, here I am at Camperdown. Gee, with my double bed to myself I was wishing you were here with me to keep me warm. What a waste and a shame, it's a lovely bed!

At Colac I met another traveller who had a girl with him, and tonight they turned up at this hotel. I noticed at dinner she had a ring on her engagement finger. About 8.30pm, after sitting in the lounge for about twenty minutes, they trotted off upstairs, and goodness knows where they went, and who cared! I probably was the only one who noticed them, and I was quite envious of their good fortune. At a place like this you would not know what rooms they had, and even where they were. So next trip, I want you by my side.

Has Connie been round to see you to cause you trouble? I would not put it past her, especially as we had a hectic parting on Monday morning. Leon said she got up to say goodbye peacefully, but we finished up yelling at one another, as she could not help being caustic in her remark, to which I retaliated with gusto. At any rate, you ought to know by now what to say if she does trouble you.

I don't know if I like my moustache. It's growing so long now that I'm conscious of it all the time and it's getting in my soup. However, I will keep it until I return, and if you like it, I suppose I will put up with it. What one does for love!

Well, Darling, I must get some sleep, as these trips are hard work. All my best love and am dying to see you soon again.

Your very own,

Jaime

Connie didn't visit Fay's home, although there were quite a number of hang-up calls, which exasperated the Johnstons. Jaime had made up his mind that he would move out of Stodart Street later in the year. The constant battles had caused his blood pressure to rise, and his doctor strongly advised a change in his living environment.

Despite Jaime having dark hair, his moustache grew a bright ginger red, and when Fay eventually saw it, she was horrified. She'd expected it to be black or dark brown, like the screen idol, Robert Taylor.

8 August 1948

How is the moustache going? Will give it the once over on your return, and if we don't like it, off it comes! I have bought myself a new hat and hope you like it. We will have to celebrate your birthday when you return, seeing you were on the road on the twenty-third. We will have to make up next week for this week, so hope you are feeling dangerously well and very much in love, because I am, so watch out!

In late August, Jaime had an eight-day business trip to Tasmania. He took Leon, who was on school term holidays. They flew to Bernie in a very small plane; the flight was rather bumpy, and caused Leon to be air-sick. Fay, on the other hand, was about to go on her first plane ride. She was flying to Narrandera, instead of taking the train. Jaime was, by now, the top salesman at Hedley's, selling hundreds of pounds worth of sporting goods each week.

Launceston
25 August 1948

My darling Fay,

I hope you get this before you leave for Narrandera on your plane trip, but this has been my first opportunity to write, as this trip has been a mad rush. Landed at Bernie early yesterday morning, after a rough trip, the old Taroona certainly tosses around. Poor Leon was sick, but I managed to weather the storm. Did Bernie and got some very good orders there, got away about ¼ to 5, and made Devonport about 20 to 6. Too late to see anyone then, but saw the largest dealer at eight o'clock was with him till after ten, showing him samples etc. and got a decent order from him. Leon has been invaluable, lugging the samples around for me. The scenery from town to town is beautiful, and the people charming. Will be thinking of you Friday, and hope you have a nice trip. Wish you were here with me, all my love, Jaime

On the same day, Fay also wrote to Jaime, addressing the letter C/O the Hobart Post Office, where Jaime had arranged for any mail to be sent. She was very much looking forward to her debut flight.

25 August 1948

Darling,

I have been thinking of you each day and wondering how you are getting on. Hope you have plenty of orders and big business. The old fortune teller told me last evening, that a friend of mine with the initial 'J' or 'G' (she thought it was 'J') would be very successful in business — in fact, would branch out on his own. But apart from this little titbit, she was an old fraud. Although we all had a good laugh at her expense (ours too!), and Dorothy prepared a very nice supper.

I got Josie to pick up my ticket today at TAA and I have to be at the Swanston Street office by 6.10, and the plane leaves the drome at 7.50am so I'll have to get up in the middle of the night. I am now off to lunch, Darling, so will say 'adieu'. I love you just as much as ever I did — or even more so, and am missing you terrifically.

Love,

Fay

In Hobart, Jaime and Leon stayed at the swanky Wrest Point Hotel, which he was suitably impressed with.

Wrest Point Hotel, Hobart
27 August 1948

My darling Fay,

Well, here I am in Hobart, and this is the first real opportunity I have had of being 'alone with you'. I have been thinking of you every day, particularly today, the day of your big adventure in the air. I got your three letters, Darling, for which many thanks. We were lucky to get in here at Wrest Point, it's in a lovely spot, and it is very luxurious. We each have our own room. We still have plenty of calls today, and so far the weather has been marvellous. Looking forward to hearing all about your flight, and sending all my love,

Jaime

Fay's first plane ride wasn't as pleasant as she had hoped. It was a turbulent journey, and she became air-sick. Fortunately her return trip was smooth, and her weekend at Narrandera enjoyable.

In mid-September Jaime was in Ballarat selling his wares. He had hoped Fay could join him for a weekend, as her mother was at Narrandera. Unfortunately Fay had to work on the Saturday, and could not arrange for another secretary to take her place, as one was interstate and the other a bridesmaid. A good friend of Fay's, Gwenda Piece, was travelling to Europe and America and would be away for a year. She had suggested Fay join her, but Fay preferred to wait and experience the adventure with Jaime.

16 September 1948

I am going to miss you over the weekend, but it will be spent very quietly at home. I am not sure yet whether the Mater will be returning on Saturday or not, but according to her last letter she is coming back on Saturday's train and one of us will be expected to meet it. I think I will insist on Lea going along, seeing as I saw her off.

I had lunch with Gwenda today and she is getting all ready for her trip to England. She is having a party in early October, which she wants me to go along and bring a boyfriend, so you will have to put that down on your list. She said to me, 'What about coming over, if I write you that I am liking it?'

I said that after my plane experience of air-sickness, I would hate to think what I would be like on a voyage of some duration, but I would be willing to risk this with a certain party. How did you guess? I think it is high time your firm got the idea of sending you overseas with your 'private secretary'. But seeing as you have sailed the seven seas a number of times, I guess you are not in a hurry to sail them again.

I still see you in my dreams, in the lunch-hours, after five, and just before I get wrapped up in the arms of Morpheus — and wonder why it isn't Jaime. But that glorious uncertainty of waking up the next morning and wondering what is in store gives one the courage to face up to what's around the corner.

Jaime and Fay felt more relaxed about their relationship, and referred to each other as 'boyfriend' and 'girlfriend' when they attended parties or get-togethers. In late 1947, Patricia, Jaime's youngest sister, had announced that her marriage to Leslie Henwood was over, and for a while moved back to Montalegre with her mother and sister, Ines. Rebecca San Miguel had been ill for quite some time, her heart was weak, and she suffered dementia, so Ines continued to nurse her at home. By August of 1948, Patricia had begun seeing a chap named Ed Edgerton,[2] and by 1949 had moved in with him.

While Fay's mother was in Narrandera, Rover, the Border Collie, was extremely sick, and just before she returned to Melbourne, the 6-month-old puppy died. He had contracted distemper from another dog in the area. Ronald and Phillip were devastated, especially little Phil, who had become very attached to his four-legged friend.

At a football match while in Ballarat, Jaime ran into his old flame, Ally, now divorced from Angus. This caused Fay to feel jealous and insecure. She knew the story of how Ally had broken his heart, and panicked in case his feelings for her had returned. However, she had nothing to worry about; Jaime had forgotten about his first love long ago, when he met Fay.

21 September 1948

My darling Jaime,

Received your long and very welcome letter and letter-card this morning, and feel a bit more normal now. Darling, don't ever leave me again for such a long time. The days have seemed endless, and I have missed you more than I thought it possible. I have yearned for you, Darling, and the weekend seems such a long way off.

I thought you might be at the football match on Saturday, and I don't know why, but I knew someone else would be there. I seem to be psychic like you in this respect. Saturday and Sunday were such perfect days and nights, especially Sunday night — it was just one of those soft, velvety, moonlit nights made for lovers, and I just longed to be with you — the only taste I had of it was when I took a letter up to the post (to Ronald and Phillip, expressing my sadness at Rover's passing). I tried to stem the pangs of jealousy when I thought you just might be with someone else, but I knew that you would be true to me.

This city is enough to get on one's nerves, and sometimes I think, 'I've had it,' and wished we had a place like Judy and John to go to of a weekend. I think we will have to keep our eyes open, and see if we can find one — they should be getting a bit more plentiful now. By the way, I don't think you will have much chance of getting a place at Torquay at this time of year, but it is worth a try.

Judy was saying that John is thinking of retiring — just looking in a few days a week on the job, but he is in the happy position of being able to do that and his income keeps rolling in. She was saying that he is selling the Jaguar, and buying a brand new Alvis. He is waiting to see some of the new models out at the Show, and Judy said they are a lovely job — no trouble to them!

Well, Darling, look out next weekend! I am likely to be suffering from a very severe attack of Spring fever and as it is supposed to be very contagious, you might be affected as a result of your alliance with me, but perhaps you are quite willing to take the risk?

Darling, just received your phone call. I will be on the 6.30 train for Geelong on Friday evening, I am so pleased you were able to obtain our flat at Torquay for the weekend, and glad to hear old Taylor is still there. Am looking forward to seeing you — it has seemed ages. I'm yours for keeps, my Darling.

All my love,

Fay

In October, Jaime took his doctor's advice and finally moved out of his flat above the garage in Stodart Street. He rented a room at 28 Arnold Street[3] South Yarra, which was close to his work base on Toorak Road. Apart from his blood pressure problem, he had developed cramps in his stomach, which the doctor diagnosed as nerve pains. He was disappointed that one of the house rules was no female visitors; still, he was happy to be out of the turmoil and chaos, which had been his living existence for so many years. Connie was livid that he was leaving, and screamed at him, 'How dare you leave while Leon is doing his matriculation!'

~

On Tuesday, 14 December 1948, Rebecca 'Birdie' San Miguel died at her home, Montalegre. She was eighty-five years old. Three days later on the 17 December, her older sister, Rebecca Grace Albon, aged eighty-seven years, also passed away. Geyseyne, the youngest (adopted) sister had died a few months before, aged seventy-three. She had married a Mr McKellar and bore no children. By 1931, at fifty-six years old, she was living with her two spinster sisters, Grace and Annie, in Black Rock, Melbourne. Jaime had not been close to Aunt Grace, Geyseyne, or Annie, although he had a close relationship with their sister, Maud. Jaime had visited his mother throughout her illness, but her death still came as a shock. In Rebecca San Miguel's estate Ines received half of the value of Montalegre, and Francisca an investment property, Reba. The value of the furniture and the other half of Montalegre were divided between all the siblings. A large number of shares in Australian Paper and Pulp Manufacturing were divided with Ines receiving the most, followed by Francisca. Lionel inherited a car, while Tony, as requested in Antonio's will, received the highest amount of cash, being the eldest son. Jaime and Patricia collected the lowest amount, which left Jaime bitter.

The Argus, Wednesday, 15 December 1948

SAN MIGUEL. On December 14 at her residence, Montalegre, Rebecca, dearly loved wife of Antonio San Miguel (deceased) and loving mother of Antonio, Francisca (Mrs Howson) Ines, Lionel, Jaime and Patricia (Mrs Henwood), aged eighty-five years. Requiescat in peace (private internment).

On hearing about Jaime's mother's death, it bought back sad memories for Fay of her father's passing nearly eleven years ago.

16 December 1948

Darling,

Once again may I express my sympathy. I was thinking of you on Wednesday and this morning, and knew how you would be feeling. The loss of a parent comes to us all sometime in our lives, but when it does come it is a very big loss, and leaves one feeling very bewildered and sad. Only time is a healer. I can hardly believe though, that on New Year's Day next, it will be eleven years since my dad passed away.

Well, Darling, I hope you are keeping well yourself, and I will be looking forward to seeing you.

With love and sympathy,
Fay

PS Judy rang and asked me to convey to you her sympathy. She saw it
in the paper.

It was a time of change, Jaime told Fay at dinner one evening in late 1948. Peoples' attitudes had altered, and he felt that they should consider moving in together. Leon had finished school and would be starting a job as Supply Manager for Reg Ansett, of Ansett Airlines in February of 1949. He was already a member of the Citizens Military Force, which he had joined immediately after leaving school. His time as a cadet at Xavier College had given him a taste of army life, and although it was only a part time activity, it kept him away from home problems with his mother.

Fay was still concerned about how her mother would react, and changed the subject whenever Jaime discussed it. She still secretly hoped Connie would grant him a divorce, yet Jaime now knew better.

Top left Ally, circa 1918.

Top right Jaime San Miguel, Captain of Xavier College, 1916.

Bottom Ally and Jaime outside *St Abbs*, 1918. Courtesy of Hayley Callander

Top

Alma May Lumsden (Connie) on her wedding day, 29 May 1926.
Courtesy of Greg San Miguel.

Bottom left

Patricia San Miguel on her wedding day to Leslie Henwood, 1926. The wedding party is standing in front of *Montalegre*. Francisca, left, and Ines, right, were bridesmaids. Rebecca, mother of the bride, is far right and Jaime, far left, is a groomsman.
Courtesy of Chris Allen and Annette Blight.

Bottom right

Patricia San Miguel on her wedding day, 1926.
Courtesy of Chris Allen.

Top left
The author's maternal great,
great grandfather, William
Hill, in the 1800s.
Courtesy of Ron Johnston.

Top right
The author's maternal great,
great grandmother, Ann Hill
(nee Patterson),
in the 1800s.
Courtesy of Ron Johnston.

Bottom
Annie O'Halloran (Fay's
Mother) in her youth, circa
1898.
Courtesy of Ron Johnston

Top Left
The Johnston family, 1916. Left is Annie Johnston and husband, William, with Lea and Harry. In front is Fay.
Courtesy of Ron Johnston.

Top Right
George Johnston and his wife Ann (nee Hill) and children, circa 1866, taken before William Patterson Johnston was born.
Courtesy of Ron Johnston

Bottom
Agepito and Josefa Ferran in Alella, circa 1920s

Top

Harry and Fay, 1912.

Courtesy of Ron Johnston.

Bottom left

Fay with two friends at the Naval and Military Ball, 1933.

Bottom right

Lea and Fay, early 1920s.

Courtesy of Ron Johnston.

Top
Fay beside Jaime's Pontiac, 1937.

Middle
Fay with Frank Birt at his farm, 1933.

Bottom
Beach holiday at Lorne, 1938. Sitting on the sand is Connie, standing are Fay, Jaime and Leon.

Bottom left
Jaime and Fay in Lorne, 1938.

Bottom right
Jaime at Wattle Park, 1918. Photo taken by Ally.

Top
Jaime with his son, Leon, circa 1933.

Middle
Rebecca (Birdie) San Miguel, left, holding dog in Alella, Barcelona, when she travelled with Patricia and Ines in 1929. Patricia is on her right and Josefa Ferran is next to Patricia, with relatives and their children.
Courtesy of Silvia Vidal Marti.

Bottom
At Wattle Park, circa 1930s. On the left is Rebecca San Miguel. Standing are Leslie Henwood (Patricia's husband), Francisca and her son, Lionel Howson. In front are Patricia and her daughter, Judy, and Charles Howson (Francisca's husband). Note that all the adults are smoking.
Courtesy of Jeanette San Miguel.

Top
An early photo of *St. Abbs*, in the 1800s.
Courtesy of Juris and Ilona Briedis.

Bottom
Hartland, Elmie Street, Hawthorn, where the San Miguels lived from 1903 to 1906.

Top
Fay and Jaime, circa 1941.

Bottom Left
Annie Johnston with daughters Lea and Fay, 1942.

Bottom right
Lea and Fay Johnston, 1944.

Top left
Left to right is Stan Morgan, Fay,
Sydney Morgan and friend. Dava
Lodge in Mornington, 1945.

Top right
Fay with baby Dolores, 1950.

Bottom
Fay and Jaime, circa 1941.

Top left
Harry and Marie Johnston with Ron and Phil, 1942.
Courtesy of Ron Johnston.

Top right
Beryl Mitchell (Harry Johnston's daughter) aged fifteen years, 1944.
Courtesy of Lynden Thiessen.

Bottom
123 Tooronga Road in Malvern, home of the Johnston family.
Courtesy of Ron Johnston.

Top
Lea, Annie and Fay Johnston with
Ron and Phil, circa 1944.
Courtesy of Ron Johnston.

Middle:
Fay with Ron and Phil at Tooronga Road, 1944.
Courtesy of Ron Johnston.

Bottom:
Fay Johnston, circa 1938.
Courtesy of Ron Johnston.

Top
Harry Johnston at Postal
Exchange, 1938.
Courtesy of Ron Johnston.

Bottom
Fay and Lea Johnston with Ron
and Phil, 1945.
Courtesy of Ron Johnston.

Top left
Jaime with Fay's best
friends, Judy Reid, left,
and May Wilson, right,
circa 1945.

Top right
Jaime and Fay, 1945.

Bottom
Judy Reid and May Wilson at
John Telford-Smith's beach
residence in Rosebud, where Fay
recuperated, circa 1945.

Top
Fay hosting a dinner party,
1957

Bottom
Fay and Jaime with the
author, circa 1957.

Top
The author in Alella
with her Spanish
relatives, July 1973.

Middle
Walking with relatives
in Alella, July 1973.

Bottom
The author with
Josefa Ferran, 1973,
holding the San
Miguel family portrait
that hangs in the
Ferran home.

Some Enchanted Evening

In February of 1949, Jaime closed all of his accounts at a number of department stores, including Manton's, Foy's, Buckley and Nunn,[1] Georges, and the Mutual Store. He informed them that he was no longer responsible for the accounts under his wife's name.

> *8 February 1949*
>
> *Dear Mr San Miguel,*
> *This letter is an acknowledgment of yours dated February 4.*
> *We note that you will not be responsible for any debts charged in your name, or against your wife, and have issued necessary instructions to ensure that no further purchases should be charged.*
> *Yours faithfully,*
> *Manton & Son Limited*
> *C.C. Brooks — Credit Manager*

Throughout 1949, Jaime was regularly on the road. He would spend at least ten days travelling through country townships, taking orders for Hedley's Sporting Goods, and then return for a week before heading off again. Whenever possible, he would take Fay away for a weekend. Sometimes things didn't always go as planned.

Ballarat
Monday, 26 September 1949

My Dear Fay,

I was very disappointed when you did not arrive on the 8.25 on Friday. I got a call over the loud speakers and the station master gave me your message. He said you were not well enough to travel. I hope nothing serious is wrong. I had a feeling you would not turn up, and I had no chance to ring you, for had I waited at any post office to ring you, the delay would have prevented me from getting to Ballarat. I am going to try and get back next Wednesday, and am taking Thursday off, so hope to see you then.

All my love,
Jaime

Melbourne
26 September 1949

Darling,

I was terribly sorry about the weekend. My feelings were at their worst at 8.25pm when I knew you would be waiting for me at the station. I had been laid up (with cold) on Thursday and part of Friday, and on Friday evening I was sitting in front of the fire, looking at the darned clock and hating every minute of it. To make matters worse, shortly after 8.30 the wireless started to play Night and Day, and I almost felt as if you had had a hand in this just to make me miss you more. And did the weekend drag — I felt like catching a train on Saturday morning, but had no idea where you were staying and the Mater would have thought I had taken leave of my senses if I had suggested I was going away. Well, Darling, I hope you didn't have as miserable a weekend as I did. I thought of you on Sat. and Sun. night, and how I wished I could have been with you.

Well, Darling, I will look forward to Wednesday with a vengeance and hope I can make up for a lost weekend.

All my love,
Fay

In early October of 1949, Jaime's favourite aunt, Maud, had become gravely ill. At nineteen years old, Maud had married Edwin Purches on the same day that her sister, Rebecca, married Antonio San Miguel in 1888. With Edwin she had a daughter, Winifred Grace Purches, but by 1901, she began her second marriage to Arthur Cash, and they had three boys together. Although she had been living in Drouin, a town in West Gippsland, fifty-six miles east of Melbourne, Jaime would call in if he was in the area on a business trip. Maud's husband had died earlier in the year, and it seemed as if Maud would also not see the end of 1949.

October 5 1949

My darling Fay,

Just a short note to wish you a very happy birthday on your special day. I am looking forward to tomorrow night very much, as apart from the show, dinner, and company, I hope to see your new suit. I think you ought to look very glamorous by the description you have given me. So, I hope the weather keeps fine and there is no rain. I also hope my poor old Aunt Maud recovers and does not throw a hammer in the wheel, but I have heard nothing yet.

Well, lots of love and I hope you have chosen something nice, even to the price of a new hat, as my present.

All my love,

Jaime

Fortunately, Fay's birthday was as happy as Jaime had hoped, as his Aunt Maud lasted for another two weeks.

Fay had decided to leave her job at Frank Brennan and Co. by the end of 1949. She had been there for eleven years. A secretarial position was available in late January of 1950 working at the Federal Members Rooms for a number of politicians. The pay was extremely tempting, so she accepted the position, after an interview in early December.

Due to the high number of sales Jaime had achieved throughout 1949, Hedley's rewarded him with a massive bonus at Christmas, and gave him an extended holiday in February of 1950. At the end of the year sales finale, Hedley's described Jaime's selling abilities in their newsletter.

JAIME SAN MIGUEL

Dogged persistence, constant planned effort, always reliable, nearly always gets his man — possibly related to Sherlock Homes.

Jaime decided to go on a golfing holiday and booked accommodation at St. Andrew's Golf House at Flinders, located on the Mornington Peninsula at the furthermost point of Western Port Bay, and nearly forty-seven miles from Melbourne. He would remain there for two weeks, and Fay would join him for the second. On the 10 February 1950 he arrived at his destination. Golfing friends of Jaime's were also staying there. Bart and his wife, Myrt, and a woman named Ivy, who Fay also knew.

12 February 1950

My darling Fay,

I am exceedingly well, and the weather has been beautiful since I arrived on Sunday. I am at my top golf form. Myrt and I squared a match with Bart and Ivy.. Yesterday afternoon we went to Point Leo, and had some surf and sunbaking. I was in the water for a solid hour surfing, and felt marvellous after it. Frank and Stan are here, and Admiral Collins and his wife are at our table (which, by the way, is very good). Am looking forward to your arrival.

All my best love,

Jaime

During Jaime's absence, Fay wrote nearly every day. Jaime, on the other hand, only managed the one postcard, as he was spending every day on the links.

13 February 1950

Darling,

Being the thirteenth, I should be superstitious and not send you a letter, but not being superstitious, here it is. I took the Mater out yesterday — we went over to her sisters in Brunswick, and stayed there for tea, so if you rang at all you would have found me conspicuous by my absence.

My boss rang today to say he wouldn't be in at all. Between 12 and 1pm I went up to the Switchboard and took over. About 12.15 ex-Minister Calwell[2] rang and asked to be put through to Miss Johnston. I told him, 'Speaking,' and he wondered if I would do an afternoon's work for him. I told him I was doing the s'board work, also helping Senator Sheehan (as his girl is now on her honeymoon) and I couldn't do anything for him. He said he would try elsewhere but I don't think he will be very successful — they are all a wake-up to him. I wonder what he would say if some of the members rang up and asked for a loan of his secretary. We all know just what he would say!

I hope you are enjoying yourself and playing good golf. Hope the table is good, and that the question of being on time for meals is a thing of the past. Well, Darling, I guess you won't have much more time to waste on we poor slaves in the city. So I will let you get on with your holidaying. Kind regards to Myrt and Bart — also Ivy — hope the latter is cleaning them all up at Solo.

Tons of love,

Fay

PS Any beautiful blondes, brunettes, or redheads to stand you up and bowl you over?

St Valentine's Day, Melbourne
14 February 1950

Darling,

Have been fairly busy today, one way and another. Even attended a wedding — quite a good omen seeing as it is St. Valentine's Day which is supposed to bring luck to lovers.

Frank Donnelly rang and asked me if I would meet him up at the Statist's Office to witness the Marriage Certificate of a client who was getting hitched. You will remember the guy we put through a divorce for, and who is building Frank's house in the country? Well, it was his big moment today at precisely 3.30. As for the wedding, they were as nervous as a couple of young kittens. I suppose you would almost say that Frank was best man and I was the bridesmaid. Frank handed over the wedding ring and we thereupon signed the Registrar as witnesses. Of course, they wanted me to come and have a drink with them to celebrate, but I knew what that would mean ... the rest of the afternoon! So I asked them to excuse me as I was really wanted urgently back at the office.

Fancy Rear-Admiral Collins[3] and his 'Admiralass' being at your table. I think you knew that his brother Stan Collins has an office opposite Brennan's — we all got a shock one day when we heard he was his brother. Stan is such a modest little guy, you would never think he had such a famous brother! He must have had a charmed life to have escaped from boarding the SS Sydney when she was sunk. I have read quite a lot about his life. His mother is, I think, well into her nineties. They hail from Sydney, of course.

How is the golf form? Playing like a German Band? I believe it is the usual custom to send a poem to your lover on St Valentine's Day so here it is:

Can hardly wait 'til Friday next
To love you, dear, you know the rest

Haven't time to think of rhyme
So fare thee well my Darling Jaim.

All my love,
Fay

The week Fay joined Jaime at St. Andrew's Golf House at Flinders was perfect in every way. The sun shone and beamed down on them as they played golf daily, often with Bart and his wife Myrt, who were both sympathetic to Jaime's 'situation'. Some mornings they drove to Point Leo and frolicked in the surf. The meals at the Golf Club were of superior standard, as was the accommodation. There was a wireless in their room, which they listened to regularly, often when they made love. One evening, the 1949 song recorded by Bing Crosby, 'Some Enchanted Evening', written by Rodgers and Hammerstein for the musical *South Pacific*, came over the airwaves. It would be a song they never forgot.

Some enchanted evening
When you find your true love
When you feel her call you
Across a crowded room

Then fly to her side,
And make her your own
Or all through your life you
May dream all alone

∾

Fay was concerned. It was mid-March and her menstrual period was well overdue. In October she would be turning 41 … if she was pregnant, should she have the baby? Would she even be able to carry a child at her age? What would her mother say? How would Jaime react?

It was a position they had been through before, and she couldn't bear to contemplate another termination. At Flinders, she had agreed to move in with Jaime. After meeting Fay and hearing their romantic story, his landlady had agreed to allow her to move in until they found a flat of their own. But if she was pregnant, it could be a different story.

Jaime was away on a three-week business trip, and prior to his departure Fay told him of her concerns. He insisted she immediately visit a doctor. At this stage they both hoped it was a false alarm, yet deep inside they wondered if it was their destiny, the ultimate culmination of their love.

Colac, Monday night
20 March 1950

My darling Fay,
Have been wondering how you got on at 10am this morning. Thought quite a lot about you and our future during my trip down here. Am anxious to get the news, hope things will turn out better than we expected. Will try and ring you on Wednesday, or even perhaps tomorrow from Warrnambool. Accommodation is hard here as I have to share a room. My roommate has just arrived back and no doubt wants to sleep, so will send you all my love,
Jaime

Jens Hotel, Mount Gambier
24 March 1950

My darling Fay,
As you can see by the above address, I am at Mount Gambier. Arrived here last evening, and am leaving for Adelaide after breakfast tomorrow morning. Had a small problem with the self-starter, these little break downs really do not detract from the good performance of the Vanguard as she really runs beautifully. Do you remember on my last visit here (with you),

we had to stay the night because the Pontiac self-starter broke down? *Strange coincidence, isn't it?*

Well, Darling, I feel I have been away for months. The first few days I found it very hard to concentrate, as my thoughts were full of recent events. I have tried to forget our troubles, but every now and then I start up with a jolt when I realise what is before us. What a pity we were so indiscreet, it's not the present but the future we have to face up to. Anyhow, are you all right? I hope you are well and not too worried, as I suppose worry won't help.

Strangely (or not) the old tummy pains are coming back again, and I am also getting a nerve itch as well. I wonder if things will right themselves, and if everything will eventually come out right. In any case, on whatever course of action you decide, I will concur. Don't worry about the pounds, shillings and pence that will have to be found. Am dying to hear from you, how you are, and what is taking place. You can write to me in Adelaide at the address I gave you for our agent in Grenfell Street.

Well, Darl, have you been to South Yarra at all? That seems like a dream from this distance. Had we not been in this spot of bother, I would be feeling on top of the world under the changed conditions of being away from Camberwell. If I am anywhere near Horsham at the time, I think I will have a few days with Leon at Easter. He is staying with a young friend and I may not get the opportunity again.

I do hope I have not been too down in the mouth, I probably feel lonely. I still love you and hope you are well and not worrying too much. But you really have been marvellous. Will write again from Adelaide.

All my love,

Jaime

As Fay anticipated, the doctor confirmed she was pregnant. Jaime had rung her to receive the news, and although perturbed at the reaction an illegitimate child may cause, left the decision up to Fay. He assured her he would stand by her side regardless of her decision.

Melbourne
27 March 1950

Darling,

I couldn't get in early enough this morning to read your long-anticipated letter. I realised how busy you would be, and the phone call helped last Wednesday, but this week has seemed as long as a year without you. I have missed you terrifically and am longing to be with you again.

As you know, I went to the doctor on that particular Monday, and did not spend more than ten minutes with him. He seems to be a very busy man, and told me all the dos and don'ts. I could not say very much on the phone to you as the Mater was hovering about and could hear every word I said. I think you realised this. But getting back to the doctor, I told him I was worried about the whole business, and thought it inadvisable to go on with it, but he didn't take long to assure me that everything would be all right. What could I say or do? He wants to see me in another month (17 April) with another specimen of that contained in the bottle.

I have been leading a very quiet life since you left. Home every night — I haven't any desire to go anywhere. Yesterday was my worst day; I had a pretty bad attack of dysentery and was sick all day. That nauseating feeling has been pretty bad lately; I guess I am letting it worry me a bit. Lea said the Mater said to her yesterday, 'I think Fay is not very well — she has been very quiet of late.'

Lea has been marvellous, and keeps telling me not to worry unduly. I wish I could believe her.

I haven't seen Judy since you left, only spoken to her on the phone. They went to Rosebud for the weekend. I answered a few ads for houses down the line, and put stamped addressed envelopes in them to her address, asking her did she mind before I posted them. She said she didn't and would let me know if there were any replies today.

Well, Darling, the car certainly gave you a bit of trouble — I didn't think a new car could play up so badly, after having it such a short time, but she gets plenty of wear and tear, so I guess it is not to be wondered at. I haven't been round to the house yet. It is awkward without the trams for getting home to Malvern; goodness knows how long they will strike. I am going to get Lea to come with me on the way home from work one evening this week.

As you say, it does seem like a fantastic dream (or nightmare?). When you reflect back, what a lot of water under the bridge after Flinders. May has just popped in to ask me to have a cup of tea but the very thought of tea or food nauseates me these days. I hope you can manage to spend the Easter with Leon. Don't worry about me — I won't be going away, but will spend the weekend quietly at home.

Well, Darling, the less said about certain events, the better. It is no use worrying too much at this stage. There will be time enough to worry later on. I guess at the back of our minds all along, we knew it could be a possibility, so now that it might be a probability, we will have to have enough courage to face up to it. I really am a bit of a coward when it comes to taking the other course of action. I just can't bring myself to that line of thought at all. I have thought myself sick over it all, and I think I can only let nature take its course and hope it will turn out alright in the long run. If you transgress the laws of nature, I think you pay a bigger price for it in your lifetime, and I guess it is true that two wrongs don't make a right. I have looked at it from every angle, and I really can't see further than just carrying on and hoping for the best. Every day I have travelled along that road with you to Adelaide, and wished I had been with you. Well, Darling, I must get this away by the morning Air Mail and trust you get it before Thursday. Look after yourself, and I am counting the days until I see you again.

All my love,

Fay

Fay confided in her sister, Lea, and friends Judy and May. Although it was a shock, they all agreed it was an inevitable outcome, and rallied around to support Fay who was still somewhat worried and apprehensive. The thought of how she would tell her mother haunted her each day. Judy had married John Telford-Smith in July of 1946,[4] and Fay envied the fact that her best friend had a legal wedding band on her finger, something she had always prayed for. However, John didn't want children. He had two adult sons and had told Judy his time as a father was over, so in one way, Fay felt blessed.

4 April 1950

I rang Myrt yesterday morning, I thought she might be sick, and sure enough she has been. She has been having a pretty rough spin with her periods — they are with her all the time and of course weakening her terribly. She said she was attending a very good man, a specialist at the top of Collins Street. I had a funny feeling it might be the same chap as the one I saw, so I asked her his name, and sure enough it is his partner — they share the same rooms. She is going to see him on Wednesday morning. It would have been funny if she walked in whilst I was sitting there, and the nurse came out and called me in. I said to Judy how easy it would be to bump into someone I knew, but she thought it was a remote possibility — not so remote, after all!

Things have been very quiet at the office (thank goodness). The boss has been mostly in Canberra, but is back now until after Easter. Remind me to tell you about a letter I left on my desk last week. I think Miss Rogers (Devlin's secretary) read it but I couldn't be worried. It was a copy of a letter I had written for a flat, and she would draw conclusions that I was married. I think she told Mr Sharkey, but I will tell you more when I see you. Maybe it was just as well — it will prepare them for what is to come!

The Mater has been exceptionally well and full of beans lately — I don't know how I am going to break the news to her. By the way, I will try and make it for Monday night. As you say, I need only take one of my brief bags. It is just that the trams are still on strike, and I will have to try and catch a cab from South Yarra Station, but on the other hand, they may have started by then — but from all accounts they are out on strike indefinitely.

The old lady at South Yarra was exceptionally nice to me when I went round last Friday evening. I had quite a chat to her and her daughter — they were both out in the kitchen having their tea together. She will expect us when she sees us — I said it would most likely be after Easter, and she said that would be alright. Lea thought the place quite nice and very clean. I had taken her down to Seaford to see a place which was advertised, and it was at the back of a dirty old shop. You would have to see it to believe that anyone could dare to advertise it as a flatette. It was appalling, two pounds fifty a week — not worth 15/- a week! Lea couldn't get over it, so South Yarra looked like a palace compared with the former.

I have just been speaking to Judy on the phone. I answered five ads on Saturday, and she got one letter in this morning's mail. By the way, I am using her address whilst we are not at South Yarra. The person writing said, 'Sorry you are not the lucky one, as the flat has been let.' I'm sure something will come up, so let's keep our fingers crossed. I am looking forward terribly to seeing you — it has seemed more like three years than three weeks. Look after yourself, and be sure and have a good holiday over Easter. Forget all your worries and enjoy yourself — one hundred years from now, who will be worrying? The future generation, I guess. So let's count our blessings.

All my love,

Fay

Fay missed Jaime during his long interstate and country trip, and although she was pleased he intended to spend time with Leon, she anxiously waited for his return. He rang her whenever possible and wrote to her regularly, which did give her some comfort.

Horsham

2 April 1950

My Darling Fay,

Have just come straight back to the hotel after ringing you tonight. It's a rotten job ringing from these country towns, as you have to wait such a long time, and then it's not very satisfactory as you seem to be left in mid-air. I got *accommodation here at the Royal Hotel on Friday night, and have been here ever since. As soon as I arrived here I tried to get accommodation for Easter, but everywhere I got the same reply, 'Full up'. I had given up all thoughts of staying here until I met one of the Committee, Mr Bob Waters, whom I know, and he said he was putting up Leon and his friend at his own home. I told him I thought of staying, but could not get accommodation, and he said not to worry, as he could get me a bed in his private home. With a bit of luck he might be able to arrange for the three of us to stay together. That is Leon, myself, and his friend, Kevin Cosgrove. So that settled it, as I had already written Leon and told him I would try and arrange to stay over the Easter.*

I am glad you told the landlady we would not be back until after Easter, as otherwise she might think we had done a bunk! As Horsham is 200 miles away, and I don't think we will be leaving till late on Monday evening or afternoon, it will probably be pretty late when I arrive in Melbourne. So you had better tell Mrs Gabriel to leave the door unlocked so that I can get in. I would get a lovely surprise if I found you there already in bed awaiting my arrival, but I suppose that is too good to be true. If by any chance you decided on that course, you could leave your luggage at home and we could pick it up on Tuesday night. You could delay getting to Arnold Street as late as possible on Monday, then you would be on your own only for a short time, and you could get a few hours sleep before I arrived. Still, that's up to you. I will probably drop Leon near his home, and come straight home to Arnold Street.

I am definitely going to take Easter Tuesday off to make up for all the overtime and extra work I have done for Hedley's on this trip, and in addition, as I said before I need time to clean the Vanguard as she gets terribly dirty on these long jaunts.

Well, Darling, I am heartily sick of rushing from one town to another, and I feel I have been away for years. If it had not been that I wrote to Leon and told him that I would spend Easter with him, I would hurry back on Thursday, but under the present circumstances I did not want to disappoint him. At any rate, if you leave your office job, you can come yourself on my next trip.

Darling, how are you? I was hoping by now you would be feeling better. I suppose when I get back to town again the full realisation of things will hit me again, though on my lonely car journeys my thoughts have been working overtime. Still, one thing this has done, it has drawn us closer together than ever, and isn't that what we have wanted for years, even though it has been in a bit of an unorthodox manner?

What's going to happen if we don't get a house down the line? Fancy you telling Lea about South Yarra. We might have to stay there till we get a place. Darling, I am dying to see you, and I hope you are not feeling too bad when we get together, as I have a few weeks to catch up on, and I want you to be feeling as well as possible. I suppose I will feel a bit scared of you now, I shall feel you have the Don't Touch sign hanging up.

Well that's about all the news I have, I hope you have a good Easter. When I get blue, I look at your photo and read your letter.

Lots of love and blessings,

Jaime

PS 'Some Enchanted Evening' came over the wireless last night. Yes, my darling Fay, it was some enchanted evening when we conceived our baby son/daughter.

In late April, Fay finally told her mother about her pregnancy. Annie was at first horrified and badgered Fay about the embarrassment it would cause their family. 'And where are you going to live?' she asked shrilly. 'You can't be seen around this suburb!'

Eventually Annie calmed down; she could see it was upsetting Fay, whose morning sickness continued on a daily basis.

After Easter, when Jaime returned to Melbourne, they decided not to move in together until a permanent flat or house was available. As Jaime was constantly on the road, he felt in Fay's condition it would be best if she remained with her family. Nevertheless, she would stay with him whenever he was back in town.

At long last Fay received a reply that a one bedroom flat was available in Upwey, twenty miles east of Melbourne in the Dandenong Ranges. It was much further than they had anticipated living, however, the flat was clean and in a picturesque environment. It was also away from prying eyes. At the same time, she gave in her notice at work. She was only just starting to show, and knew that if she left it any longer, it would be the talk of the office.

~

In May and August of 1950, Ronald Johnston, Fay's nephew, was admitted to the Royal Children's Hospital for two major operations. Back in Narrandera in 1949, he had been in hospital with bronchitis, and was pumped with penicillin to try to remove the shadow that was found on his lung from an X-ray. He recovered from the bronchitis but the shadow remained, so he was sent back to Melbourne for further tests. The medical staff detected a cyst between the heart and the lung, and it required two operations to remove it. In both May and August Harry accompanied his eldest son to Melbourne and they stayed at Tooronga Road. Fay kept well away in May, hiding out in Arnold Street, and by August she was settled in at Upwey.

Leon San Miguel enjoyed his job as supply manager for the Australian aviation pioneer, Reginald Ansett. He was twenty years old and becoming quite independent. In 1947, Ansett had acquired Hayman Island, located off the coast of Central Queensland. Leon's job had him regularly visiting the island, which opened in 1950, and soon gained the reputation as Australia's foremost leisure and honeymoon destination. It attracted widespread international recognition. Jaime offered to help Leon purchase his first car in July of 1950. He was immensely proud of his son, and also hoped Leon would understand when he finally told him that he would soon have a baby half-brother or sister.

Hotel Richmond, Adelaide
August 15 1950

My darling Fay,
Just a hurried note before going to sleep. Arrived safely and am staying at above hotel in Rundle Street in the city. Will be leaving here Thursday night, arriving Friday morning, if all is well. By the way, poor Leon had an unfortunate car accident when he was on that Rally with Bill. It appears they had taken the wrong turning and they were on a single bush track, when a young fool of a competitor, who had also taken the wrong track, had turned and was retracing his steps and making up for lost time. He came round a slight bend and could not stop when Leon appeared around the corner. They were both lucky (Leon and Bill) that they were not hurt. But it's a shame the new little bus should be damaged so soon, due to the carelessness of an irresponsible youth. I suppose I will soon have to tell Leon about our situation. I have a strange feeling C already suspects — have they had anymore phone calls at your mother's?

Business has been only fair up to date, Adelaide is not apparently a Hedley's town. Hope you are keeping well and it is not too cold in the hills. I can't wait to get home to my darling and sample your cooking and kisses.
All my love,
Jaime

Jaime had arranged for a top Melbourne obstetrician to attend to Fay during her confinement. Dr Churches had rooms at the Paris end of Collins Street and was highly respected amongst his peers. While in Upwey, Fay saw a local doctor in nearby Belgrave, a Dr Robinson. In September, Churches noted her blood pressure was elevated and sent a letter to Robinson to alert him.

2 Collins Street, Melbourne
25 September 1950

Dear Dr Robinson,

I wonder if you would be good enough to keep an eye on one of my medical patients for the next few weeks, Mrs. Miguel. It is her first pregnancy in seven years. Her blood pressure was 165/105 on first visit, and lowest reading I have ever obtained was 148/100, which it is today. However, two days ago she had a symbolic of 174 and I was getting rather worried. It was probably a false alarm, but I feel it would be wise at this stage of pregnancy (due 27/10/50) to check it weekly. If it rises over any two weeks, I would not hesitate to put her into hospital.

Yours sincerely,
K. Churches

Dr Churches had arranged for Fay to be admitted to St. Georges Hospital in Kew when the time came. In August, she and Judy visited the hospital so Fay could fill out some paperwork. In the waiting room, she suddenly panicked.

'Judy, what should I call myself? I can't be Miss Johnston!'

Judy suggested she use 'Mrs Smith' as an alias, though in the end it was decided 'Mrs Miguel' would be used.

Jaime felt that they should move closer to town, and St Georges Hospital. So by the 20 October he had rented a house for them at 1 Francis Street, Blackburn. It was much larger than their small flat at Upwey. Although a relatively new suburb, Blackburn still had plenty of vacant land and dense shrubbery in abundance.

In late October 1950, Leon was invited for a weekend at a beach house in Wyre River, near Lorne. He was unaware that he would soon be a half-brother. It was decided that he would be told after the birth.

Mary Jeanette Fullarton, known as 'Jeanette' was staying at her parent's beach house with a nursing girlfriend who had invited a friend called Brian. She asked him to also invite a male friend, and Brian asked Leon. It was love at first sight for Leon and Jeanette. They were both born on the exact same day, the 15 August 1930, so in a way were 'twins'. They were married in 1953 and had five children. Leon died on the 24 May 1984 of prostate cancer. He was fifty-three years old.[5]

John Cooke, Jaime's best friend and solicitor, recommended that Fay legally change her name to Fay San Miguel, so he drew up the appropriate papers to be lodged at the Registry of Births, Deaths, and Marriages. Despite Connie knowing of the impending birth, she continued to deny Jaime a divorce. On the 24 October 1950, Florence Annie Johnston now legitimately signed herself as Fay San Miguel.

Tuesday morning, the 31 October 1950, Jaime drove Fay to St Georges Hospital, where she was admitted to await the birth of her child. After two nervous hours in the waiting room, Jaime was informed that the birth was hours away, so he drove to Hedley's office where the nurse promised to telephone. After work, Jaime returned to the hospital and at 4am on Wednesday the 1st November 1950, Fay and Jaime San Miguel welcomed the birth of a 6lb 14oz healthy, beautiful, baby girl. They were both ecstatic. At first the names tossed up were, 'Carmen' and 'Mercedes', but when Jaime suggested, 'Dolores', it was a done deal. Jaime rang Lea, Judy, and May with the wonderful news.

Telegram:

> *Mrs J.S. Miguel,*
> *Care Maternity Ward, St. Georges Hospital, Kew*
> *1/11/50*
> *Congratulations good health and good luck to you both, love Mum and* Lea.

Telegram:

> Mrs F. S. Miguel
>
> 1/11/50
>
> *Congratulations dear lots of luck and happiness to you both glad it's a girl love Judy.*

Telegram:

> Mrs F. Miguel
>
> 2/11/50
>
> *Fondest love to you and baby daughter May.*

Telegram:

> Mrs F.S.Miguel
>
> 2/11/50
>
> *Congratulations Fay and every good wish to you and your little piccaninny John Telford Smith.*

Fay would remain in hospital for another ten days, a customary practice. When she wasn't suckling her newborn, she put pen to paper.

> *St. Georges Hospital*
>
> *10 November 1950*

> *Darling,*
>
> *I had to beg, borrow, or steal some notepaper as the kiosk didn't sell it and I got one of the nurses to get me some, which she did from the office. And now to refer to that written unread letter I wrote you last week. I'm afraid it is a little difficult to produce a facsimile of it, but I did start off by saying, I had written several letters that day to not very important people telling them the news, and that it was high time I wrote to the most important one of all and sent my congratulations and thanks for having presented me with*

a 'belated birthday gift' in the shape and form of the most adorable little girl, Dolores Fay. Darling, you'll just love her. She was worth every minute of the anxious hours, weeks, and months we had together and I feel now, after all these years, we have reached the culmination of our love. I just feel as if I could burst with happiness when they bring her to me, and she is so much more lovable because of you.

Darling, I don't know how I would have lived through those months if I hadn't had your patient reassurance that things would work out somehow, and you were really wonderful through it all. I know there were times when we both felt pretty depressed and miserable, and it would have been much easier for you to take the least line of resistance than it would for me, but you stood by me against terrific odds, and I hope now you will feel a little easier and happier now that some of the strain has been lifted. We still have a few obstacles ahead but I guess we can face up to them after what we have been through. When you are confined to bed for days on end, one has plenty of time for retrospection and reliving some past events.

It seemed inevitable after eighteen years that some change was forecast, and I guess I started the changeover when I left Frank Brennan at the end of last year. How much water has flowed under the bridge since then. But I'm counting our blessings now and hope the future holds some pleasant surprises for us. Dolores is one of them.

Darling, I am longing to get home to look after you. How I used to look forward to you coming home at Upwey. Each day seemed as long as a wet week, but I feel now that the sunshine is beginning to peep through, and my days will be happier ones in our new residence. I also am looking forward to putting my arms round you at 3am (to say the least of you doing the same) and snuggling into each other. Won't Dolores be jealous? She will be when she is old enough. Will tomorrow morning at 11am never come? Today is just dragging on and on.

All my love, Darling,

Fay

Back in Narrandera, NSW, on a November day, there had been a spring shower when 12-year-old Ronald Johnston walked the long path to the mailbox, situated near the front gate. He had recently begun correspondence with a number of penfriends, and often made the effort to collect the mail in eager anticipation that there would be a letter for him. When he checked the wooden mailbox, he discovered only one heavy envelope, which was damp, and disappointingly, not from one of his penfriends. On further inspection, he discovered that the envelope was no longer sealed and addressed to his mother. The curious 12-year-old then removed the contents and discovered it comprised numerous pages of correspondence with many different dates. He began to read some of the pages and was amazed to discover his lovely Aunty Fay had given birth to a daughter. He realised that Fay must have been confined to bed in a hospital and spent days prior to the birth in writing her thoughts to her sister-in-law.

He hurriedly folded the pages back and returned them to the envelope. Then guiltily returned to the house and handed the envelope to his mother, who questioned him about it being unsealed. He innocently told her that it was the way he had found it and suggested that the postman was probably the reason for its wet appearance. Fortunately, he wasn't asked as to whether he had read any of the letters. Ronald was now privy to the biggest secret of his young life, but dared not share this illicit information with his little brother Phillip.

It was not until six months later in 1951 that his parents, Harry and Marie Johnston, sat Ron and Phil down and informed them solemnly that Aunty Fay now had a daughter. There were no smiles of happiness at what should have been a joyous announcement, as Dolores was their first and only cousin. The announcement instead reflected the mores of the age. Dolores was an illegitimate child and shame and embarrassment dominated the reaction to the birth.

Fay and Jaime happily settled into family life in Blackburn with their baby daughter, Dolores. One afternoon, as Fay returned to the house with the baby in a pram, a carton of eggs fell and smashed onto the ground. All of a sudden, a Tiger snake slithered towards the broken eggs, splattered near the pram. As it reared its head towards the pram, Fay gave a scream and the neighbours opposite appeared at their front gate. The man's wife ran inside to get her husband's shotgun. Keeping his eye on the predator, he asked his wife if the gun was loaded. As she didn't know, he took his eye off the snake for a second and it quickly disappeared into the shrubs. Not long after this encounter, they moved to a flat at 51 Studley Avenue, Kew, where they remained until Jaime purchased the property at 24 Fellows Street, Kew, in 1958.

True Love

It was now well after midnight. I finished the last sip of my tepid tea and carefully put the cup down on the coffee table.

'And so you see Dolores, your Father and I never married. In other words, you are viewed as an illegitimate child.'

I looked into my mother's worried eyes and grinned.

'Oh Mum, far out!' I laughed, giving her a hug. 'This is amazing. I'm a love child!'

'You're not upset?' she asked, looking slightly perplexed. 'I thought you would be ashamed of us.' She fiddled with her teaspoon as she met my gaze.

I had grown up in the swinging sixties with the discovery of the contraceptive pill, and had lived with my boyfriend Paul for nearly three years in London. To find out I was the product of such an incredibly passionate love story just blew me away!

'Ashamed? Of course I'm not,' I said, giving her hand a squeeze. 'I'm honoured to be the product of such deep love. This is the most romantic story I've ever heard! I'm so pleased you told me. Oh Mum I *love* you, and I'll miss Dad so much.'

Mum took me in her arms. 'Yes, I will miss him too — my Darling, my wonderful Jaime.'

≈

It was Saturday afternoon, 10 April 1999. 89-year-old Fay San Miguel sat down with her magnifying glass and began a letter to her sister-in-law, Marie. Her eyesight was worse than ever, and it was hard work writing anything these days. Her brother Harry had died nearly a year before on September 8 1998 and sister Lea[1] had passed away aged only sixty, two months after Jaime in 1974. Fay often had her granddaughter, 10-year-old Charlotte, Dolores's youngest daughter staying with her, and she referred to Charlotte as her 'second pair of eyes'.

10 April 1999

Dear Marie,

News is scarce in this neck of the woods. Charlotte stayed with me Thursday night, but Andy picked her up yesterday afternoon and had her for the weekend. We only went shopping yesterday and on our way out, Charlotte saw this big black spider on the hall door. It was the biggest spider I have ever seen in my eighty-nine years. I took off my shoe and killed it, crushing it against the door. It wasn't a Huntsman or Tarantula. It had long legs and arms and wasn't a Daddy Long Legs either. Dolores said I should have put a glass over it and trapped it and taken it to have it tested, but with my impaired vision, I wasn't capable of that. I just hope it has no parents or brothers and sisters. I think they come in from the garden — but I am imagining spiders everywhere now and had nightmares last night — end of nasty story.

Charlotte is still on school holidays and doesn't go back until Monday week (19 April). She and Hayley spent Easter at Portsea with Andy, and Dolores went to Sorrento and Charlotte spent the Sunday with her. I was left on my 'Pat Malone'. Just had a few friends to afternoon tea on Good Friday.

I am sick of the Meals on Wheels, and I am going to try and fend for myself. Seeing as I don't like poultry and fish, their menu is not to my liking, and it limits me to a great extent. I have tried to acquire a taste but I guess it is too late at this time of my life. Well, I am afraid that is all the news — will probably hear from Phil tomorrow, Sunday, as he usually rings and drops in. Hope you enjoyed the Easter break — the weather was the only perfect thing about it. I find Xmas and Easter rather quiet, am too old to appreciate holidays anymore.

Love to all,

Fay

Fay struggled to address the envelope correctly, hoping it would be legible for the postman. She would post the letter tomorrow; it was too late in the day now. Cooking was a struggle these days, so Fay made some toast, topped with sliced banana for dinner and slipped into bed around 7pm

It was chilly when Fay awoke around 6am on Sunday morning. She opened the blinds and switched on the lounge room light as it was still dark outside. After a light breakfast — more toast — she slipped a cassette tape into the player and sat down to listen to the recording of 'True Love' written by Cole Porter for the 1956 musical film, *High Society* and sung by Bing Crosby and Grace Kelly.

> *While I give to you and you give to me*
> *True love, true love*
> *So on and on it will always be*
> *True love, true love*
> *For you and I have a guardian angel*
> *On high, with nothing to do*
> *But to give to you and to give to me*
> *Love forever true*

The song reminded her of Jaime and the love they had shared for forty-two years. It had now been twenty-five years since her Darling had gone and she still missed him every day. Fay had a shower and dressed, then made a cup of coffee and went into her spare room. She opened the cupboard[2] and pulled from behind a piece of wood, two large bags of letters.

I should tell Dolores where I have hidden these she thought to herself as she sat down on the couch. It was nearly impossible for her to read them with her failing eyesight, yet just holding them made her feel closer to Jaime. Her thoughts went back to Woodend, and the first time she had made love to him on a spring evening in September of 1932. Another memory entered her head, the last time they had been intimate, a month before his final stroke. Close to tears, she packed up the letters and returned them to their hiding spot.

Fay turned on the radio to get the time — it was 8.30am She switched it off and returned to the lounge room. As she sat down her hand started to tingle, and then it felt numb. Suddenly her head began to pound; it was agonizing, as if she'd been hit with a giant hammer. She stood up as the shooting pain flowed from her head and down her neck, and throughout her body. She closed her eyes as a roaring sound over took her aching head. When she opened her eyes she was totally blind — and she realised she was having a stroke. At that moment she fell over and slipped into unconsciousness.

She woke to hear the phone ringing, yet could not move at all. Fay knew it would be Phil and prayed he would call in, it was impossible for her to calculate the time, and how long she'd been lying there. Later on the phone rang again, but still no one came. Fay called out for help; however, the sound of her own voice was a guttural grunt, something she did not recognise. Sometimes she felt the warmth of the sun on her limp body and figured it was still daylight, at other times, she was cold, very cold. The hours rolled by and she slipped in and out of consciousness.

~

On Tuesday evening the 13 April, 1999, Phil Johnston rang his cousin, Dolores. He'd been trying since Sunday to contact his Aunty Fay, but to no avail. Dolores suggested that maybe Fay had the television on and hadn't heard the phone, and said she would ring the upstairs neighbour if she couldn't raise her mother.

Fay heard the doorbell and the sound of her neighbour, Jean, calling for her. She tried to answer but could only make an inaudible rasp. Next she heard the echo of Jean's heels on the concrete steps, and realised she had gone. Would anyone ever come for her? She was feeling cold again when suddenly Fay heard a key in the lock and the door being opened. Strangely and sadly this was music to her ears. The sound of her daughter and granddaughter's distressed voices caused her to explain what had happened, however, once again she realised her words had no meaning. Not long afterwards, the paramedics arrived as well as her eldest granddaughter, Hayley. Everyone was crying and Fay felt helpless. She wanted to hug them all, yet knew her body was paralysed.

The ambulance took Fay to Epworth Hospital, where she remained in intensive care for a week. Another week was spent in a room before she was transported in another ambulance to what she soon learnt was a hospice. Every day, Dolores visited her with Charlotte, while Hayley came on occasions but found it difficult to not cry throughout her visits. Phil came every Sunday, and many of her friends paid a visit. Not being able to talk to them all was frustrating, and her hope was dwindling. On one of Dolores' visits, Fay expressed the wish to die. The sobbing of her only daughter meant she had understood what she had said. All Fay could think of was how this limbo was a living hell.

～

On a warm spring day, Monday the 18 October 1999, six months after Fay had taken her first stroke, and two weeks after her nintieth birthday, she began to feel better; a peaceful tranquillity set in. The blackness disappeared and radiant colours appeared before her. Suddenly, she saw a long tunnel with a beaming white light, and waiting there with his arms outstretched was her 'Darling', Jaime. He was young and handsome, just like the first time she had laid eyes on him. He was beckoning her to join him. Her body felt strong and youthful as she made her way down to the light, and incredible happiness overtook her as she ran into the arms of the love of her life.

Endnotes

Chapter 2 An Enterprising Young Spaniard

1. Cipriano and Francisca San Miguel's firstborn daughter, Carmen, was stillborn in 1841. They also christened their second daughter Carmel, who was born two years later. Salvadora Casilda Teresa, born in 1854, and Jose Jaime Benito, born in 1856, both died in infancy.

2. The Franco-Prussion war (19/07/1870-10/05/1871), was a conflict between France and Prussia that signalled the rise of German military power and imperialism. It was provoked by Otto von Bismark (the Prussian chancellor) as part of his plan to create a unified German Empire.

3. Martin Arenas was declared bankrupt in Sydney in 1894. He was married with three children, although the youngest, Arthur, died aged two in 1892. In September of 1902 the family moved to Melbourne and in 1908 Arenas became the licensee of the Kennedy's Family Hotel in Elizabeth Street, remembered as a 'gloomy hotel'. It is highly likely Antonio would have financially helped Martin out. On April 4 1892, a John Powell was arrested for larceny of some dress clothes belonging to James Gray and W. Nicholson, taken from The Sydney Coffee Palace in 1891. The accused stated the clothing had been given to him by Charles Marlett and Martin Arenas at the Coffee Palace. The clothing answered the description given by the Sydney police and John Powell was remanded in Sydney. The Sydney Coffee Palace Hotel at 393 George Street, Sydney has gone; however, next to the current building is Temperance Lane. Number 395 is still the original building and is now a clothing store.

4. James Albon Jr. returned to England around 1878, and in 1880 married Sarah Ann Mead. They had four children — James, Jessie, Stanley and Olive — and immigrated to Australia, arriving on board the *Orotavia* on 19 July 1890.

5. Jane (Jenny) Albon married John Moss, a widower, in 1878. She was twenty-three years old and he was sixty. Her baby son, John Albon Moss was born in 1879. In 1880, she died aged twenty-five, cause of death unknown; however, it's possible she may have died during childbirth and lost the baby. Her son was only a year old when she passed away, and her husband married for the third time not long after her death. His new wife, Charlotte, raised the baby boy. John Albon Moss died in 1918 at thirty-nine — it is possible he died in World War I.

6. Uncle Tom was Rebecca Albon's brother, and he owned a boot shop. Martha was Tom's wife.

7. Jenny refers to her sister-in-law Jenny Moss and her father-in-law, Mr Moss.

8. On 24 February 1982, Burns Philp and Company Limited bought Mauri Brothers and Thomson. Burns Philp was delisted in 2006 with its business assets acquired by a number of companies. It remains in the private ownership of a New Zealander.

9. 1 Victoria Street, Mont Albert, became 3 Beatty Street in 1917. The original house still stands.

10. Antonio and Birdie were both generous in their donations to charity. Harrison, San Miguel Pty Ltd also made regular monetary gifts. Birdie worked for a number of charitable organizations.

11. Milson's Point, the land that Antonio San Miguel owned was sold to the NSW Government when the Sydney Harbour Bridge was being constructed in the 1920s. Birdie received a large amount of money from the sale.

12. In early July of 2012, I went searching for Hartland, as Elmie Street is within walking distance from my home. I had no idea of the number or house. After walking up and down the street hoping to find the name, I noticed a woman weeding in her front garden. I told her my story and she said that although her home was the right period it was not the one. She took me to another house and that too was another name. Just as I'd given up hope she suggested we try a house across the road. She knew the owner, Ann Simpson and her husband, and when Ann opened the door she introduced me. I briefly told her my story, and said, 'I am looking for Hartland.' Ann grabbed my hand, and replied, 'Welcome to Hartland, come inside!' It was an overwhelming experience walking through the magnificent home my family had dwelled in all those years ago. I also learnt the Simpsons were selling the property, and on the 25 August 2012, Hartland was sold for $3.2 million.

13. After much research, I have found no record of T.S. Harrison leaving Harrison, San Miguel, apart from him not being listed in the 1905 partnership. Although he is mentioned in the 1908 sale advertisement for the selling of the Harrison, San Miguel Co. in Perth. It is also possible T.S Harrison was related to James Harrison (1816-1893), the Scottish born Australian printer, journalist, politian and pioneer in the field of mechanical refrigeration. In 1913, the Harrison, San Miguel Adelaide branch installed machinery which consisted of a powerful refrigeration plant, capable of treating 200 hogheads of beer per week. Interestingly, the company continued under the name, Harrison, San Miguel up until the 1950s.

Chapter 3 Life Goes On

1. St Abbs at 33 York Street, Mont Albert, still stands although on much smaller grounds. The cork tree that Antonio San Miguel planted was eventually ruined by possums and cut down by the current owners in the mid 1990s. Finding St Abbs was also a detective game. My research assistant, Jo Simmons and I went to York Street in May of 2012. I had been shown St Abbs as a little girl, but had only a vague memory of the property. We had no luck and returned a week later, as after more research we had found the street number. Jo convinced me to ring the doorbell, and after much trepidation, we did just that! After introducing myself to the owner, she knew the history of the home (and the San Miguels) and invited us back for a tour. This too was a remarkable experience.

2. Mr John Lothian came out from Scotland in 1890 as a publisher's representative for English and Scottish books. By about 1900 he had set up his own firm, *Lothian Book Publishing Co.* He purchased the property in 1898 and named the house after St. Abbs Head, on the east coast of Scotland near Edinburgh. In 1924, the original 3.5 acre property came up for sale again, and Thomas Carlyle Lothian, now the director of *Lothian Publishers,* bought back the family home. Thomas, his wife Effie, his three sons and two daughters, were to live at St Abbs for fifty years. The publishing company still exists today, having been run by John's son Thomas after his retirement. His great-grandson Peter is now the director of Lothians.

3. Surrey Hills and Mont Albert in Melbourne are both twelve kilometres east of Melbourne's Central Business District. They are virtually the same suburb, so in the electoral rolls, St Abbs and other properties the San Miguels lived in are either listed as Mont Albert or Surrey Hills.

4. In January of 1908 an advertisement was placed in the Perth Sunday Times: *An excellent opportunity to a money-making and established business is now before the public. A goldfields brewery, showing profits averaging £2500 per year is for sale on easy terms. Full particulars from Mr. F.A. Henriques of King St or Mr Harrison of Murray Street.* On 15 February 1909, the business was sold to Joseph Duffell of Perth, who for the past four years had controlled the management of Harrison, San Miguel in Perth.

5. Now buried in the San Miguel crypt at Box Hill Cemetery is Antonio and Rebecca (Birdie) San Miguel, Lionel San Miguel, and Jaime San Miguel. I will be buried next to my father when the time comes. Close by in the Church of England section are the graves of James Albon Senior and his daughter Grace Albon. The Surrey Hills Historical Society takes tourists on a tour of the cemetery and one of the highlights is the San Miguel crypt and the nearby graves of the Parer family.

6. In the late 1920s, The Coca-Cola Company was well established in the US. Coca-Cola did not come to Australia until 1937, when a Perth company became the distributor.

Chapter 5 The Four Seasons Of 1932

1. Phar Lap died at a ranch in San Francisco, California on 5 April 1932. Australians received the news at 10.30am the following morning.

2. In February of 1986, Beryl McDonald (who had changed her name to Mary Ellen, and after her marriage was Mary Ellen Webb) was successful in finding out that her natural father, Harry Johnston, was alive and residing in Wollongong, N.S.W. Harry confided in his eldest son, Ron, and it was he who drove Harry to the station in April to catch a train to Melbourne. Mary Ellen, now fifty-seven years old and Harry aged eighty, met at the Windsor Hotel where they talked for many hours. When Harry came home he confided in his wife Marie, she was shocked and became extremely upset and said she wanted nothing to do with the woman. It was decided that their children would not be told. Although Harry was flattered with the attention of his 'new' daughter and was happy to consider having closer family ties, Marie was adamant that she should be kept at a distance. Nevertheless, Harry kept in touch with Mary Ellen through letters. It was not until May of 1994 that Mary Ellen met her Aunt Fay and in turn met Phillip and Jenni. However, Ron remained loyal to his mother, Marie, and has never met his half-sister. I also met Mary Ellen in 1994 as my Mother was very welcoming to her and we kept in contact. After my Mother's death in 1999, I lost contact. Since researching this book, I have reconnected with her. Ron has also connected with her through letters and phone calls.

3. *Strange Interlude*, originally a play by Eugene O'Neil, is a complicated love story, whereby the film's married heroine falls in love with another man and bears his child, letting her husband believe the child is his.

4. Manton's department store (236 Bourke Street, Melbourne) is now a Target store.

5. Dava Lodge is now a nursing home for the aged

6. Unless both parties agreed to a divorce, it could not be legally granted. Therefore Jaime's hands were tied.

Chapter 6 Stormy Weather

1. In 1968, the Australia Hotel in Castlereagh Street, Sydney was purchased by the huge MLC Insurance and Finance Group who, amid mounting concern, announced their intention of refurbishing and maintaining one of the city's landmarks. However, the following year they announced its impending closure and later demolished it to erect a modern $20 million, 35-storey office block/skyscraper in its place, the MLC Centre. MLC was purchased in 2000 by the National Australia Bank.

2. The Victoria Hotel in Little Collins Street, Melbourne opened on 1 November 1880. Originally known as the Victoria Coffee Palace, it was a Temperance Hotel. The hotel still stands and is a favourite for country visitors to stay just like in the 1930s.

3. The Capitol Theatre in Swanston Street, Melbourne opposite the Melbourne Town Hall opened in May 1924. It was designed by architect Walter Burley Griffin and his wife, Marion Mahoney Griffin. In 1999 it was purchased by RMIT University and is currently used for both university lectures and cultural events such as film and comedy festivals.

Chapter 7 A Marriage Proposal

1. Menzies Hotel was built in 1867 and demolished in 1969 to make way for BHP Plaza. During its heyday, guests included Noel Coward, H.G. Wells, Anna Pavlova, Dame Nellie Melba, Charles Kingsford Smith, and Mark Twain.

Chapter 8 Our Love Was Meant To Be

1. When Marie Cameron Blackwell married Harry Johnston in 1935, the name Blackwell should not have appeared on the marriage certificate because this was the name of Marie's defacto father, George Blackwell. Marie's father was Thomas Cameron who was born in Ballymena, Northern Ireland in 1883. Thomas went to South Africa where he met Gertrude Lovett who was born in Port Elizabeth in 1886. The two lovers eloped to Kimberley (a gold mining town), where they were married in 1908 and then sailed to New Zealand. Marie Gertrude Cameron was born in Auckland on 7 September 1909. The couple and their baby returned to South Africa where the marriage failed. After the marriage break-up, Gertrude then took up with another colonial, George Herbert Blackwell. George came from a large protestant family in Beechworth, Victoria, and went to South Africa, hoping to make his fortune through gold or diamonds. There were family folklore stories that he bought some diamonds back to Australia, however, they were never found. After ten years in South Africa, George Blackwell bought Gertrude and 4-year-old Marie to Australia where they settled in Coogee, Sydney. Gertrude decided to return to South Africa and left behind George and 6-year-old Marie. Being left alone with a defacto father would cause serious concerns in the present day. Sadly, Marie never saw her mother again. When she left school, Marie at no time had paid employment but kept house for her stepfather. When George Blackwell retired from the railways, aged sixty-five, he came to Warragul to live with the Johnston family, and remained with them until his death in Wollongong, NSW in 1956. Marie and Harry's children, Ron, Phil and Jenni all believed George Blackwell was their maternal grandfather until the secret was revealed many years later.

2. Although Harry and Marie were not Catholics, they chose to marry in a Catholic church. However, it was performed in a side chapel, as being non-Catholics, the ceremony could not be performed in front of the altar.

3. Foy and Gibson (also known as Foys) was one of Australia's earliest department store chains. A large range of goods were manufactured and sold by the company including clothing, manchester, leather goods, soft furnishings, furniture, hardware and food. The first store was established as a drapery in Smith Street, Collingwood by Mark Foy. In March 1883 ownership of the business was transferred to his son Francis Foy in partnership with William Gibson. The Bourke Street, Melbourne store was sold to Woolworths in 1967.

4. From December 1935 to February 1936, there was a long shipping strike against an unsatisfactory award and poor working conditions. The strike failed and the union was left divided and crippled.

5. The Coogee Bay Hotel, in Coogee, Sydney was originally the first school in the area, and was converted to become the current hotel in 1873.

6. The building Lionel San Miguel built at 111-125 A'Beckett Street, Melbourne is now a Harley Davidson showroom. It is listed as a heritage building. Lionel died of a heart attack in 1959; he was in his sixty-third year, and only sixty-two at the time of his death.

Chapter 9 Thanks For The Memory

1. Marie and Harry's first child, Ronald Paterson Johnston was born in Warragul, sixty-five miles east-southeast of Melbourne, on the 23 April. He was given his middle name after his grandfather, William Patterson Johnston, however, a typo on his birth certificate left out one of the t's.

2. The Cumberland at Lorne, Victoria still stands and is now a 4-star resort hotel. Erskine House, built in the 1860s, is also a resort.

3. The Honourable Frank Brennan was responsible for the appointment of Sir Isaac Isaacs as Governor of Victoria. Brennan was also the father of prominent author, the late Niall Brennan, a biographer of Archbishop Daniel Mannix and notorious businessman, John Wren.

4. 'Thanks for the Memory' was composed by Ralph Rainger and lyrics were by Leo Robin. It was introduced in the film, *The Big Broadcast of 1938*, and was performed by Shep Fields and His Orchestra with vocals by Bob Hope and Shirley Ross.

Chapter 10 Only Forever

1. Keating's Hotel in Woodend was built in 1897. It is now named Holgate Brewhouse and Keating's Hotel.

2. Café d'Italia later became known as The Latin, a very renowned and popular Italian restaurant in Melbourne.

3. The Palais on the esplanade in St. Kilda originally opened in 1914. It later became known as The Palais de Danse and Palais Pictures and hosted many balls and dances. In 1927 architect Henry E. White built a large more grand theatre, and it is considered one of the finest examples of Art Deco architecture in Australia. The former cinema is now functioning exclusively as a concert venue and is named the Palais Theatre.

4. The Niagara Restaurant in Gundagai is still a restaurant to this day.

5. In 1800 the site of the Wentworth Hotel in Lang Street became part of a developing area of the new colony of Sydney called Church Hill. In 1824 three substantial, two-storey terrace houses were built in Lang Street. The last terrace, No. 3 Church Hill

became the future Wentworth Hotel. In 1950 Qantas Empire Airways negotiated a controlling interest in the hotel. In 1961 approval was granted for Qantas to build a new 400-room hotel next to Qantas House in Chifley Square. The new Wentworth Hotel was completed in 1966 and was the first five star hotel in Sydney. It is now known as Sofitel Sydney Wentworth, 61-101 Phillip Street, Sydney. The original site of the Wentworth is now the Suncorp building.

6. The Regent Theatre at 487-503 George Street was Hoyts' showcase 'picture palace' in Sydney, designed by the architect, Cedric Ballantyne. It opened 9 March 1928 and was demolished in 1988.

7. The New Tivoli Theatre in Sydney opened in 1911 as the Adelphi Theatre, and in 1915 was renamed The Grand Opera House. From 1929 it became a major outlet in Sydney for a variety of theatre, and featured many vaudeville acts. In 1932, it was known as the New Tivoli Theatre. It was demolished in 1969, and the site is now occupied by Central Square, a tower of offices between Hay and Campbell Streets.

8. The Clifton Gardens Hotel in Mosman, Sydney, on the lower north shore was built around 1871, and demolished in 1967.

9. The Paragon at Katoomba in the Blue Mountains, sixty-eight miles west of Sydney was established early in the twentieth century. It remains to this day.

10. The Cahill's Restaurants in the inner city area of Sydney were well known to those seeking a well-presented, inexpensive lunch or pre-theatre dinner served in pleasant surroundings. The chain of restaurants were a feature of the city from the 1930s well into the 1960s, and were operated by brother and sister, Reg and Theresa Cahill. All of the original restaurants are now gone.

11. 'Only Forever' was written by James V. Monarco and Johnny Burke for the 1940 film, *Rhythm on the River.*

12. The house, Green Ivies, at 63 Woodhouse Grove, Box Hill still remains and is untouched by renovation. It is on a much smaller block, as it was sub-divided over the years. Most of the original out-houses remain, as does the tennis court.

13. Gazettes were a one-hour feature at a variety of theatres showing mainly news broadcasts and a couple of cartoons.

14. Robert Menzies' party narrowly won the 1940 election. It produced a hung parliament with the support of independent MPs in the House. On 27 August 1941, Menzies resigned as Prime Minister and leader of the United Australian Party. Arthur Fadden, a member of the Country Party was invited to become PM Menzies spent eight years in opposition during which time he founded the Liberal Party of Australia. He again became P.M. at the 1949 election, and then dominated Australian politics until his retirement in 1966.

Chapter 11 So Near And Yet So Far

1. Jaime's suspicion that Betty Cathcart had 'spilt the beans' caused him to ignore his workmate and friend, Alec, for a number of years. Alec couldn't understand what had happened, and it was only after he confronted Jaime at a golf course, and both learnt the truth about the real offender, that they all became friends once more. All four socialised regularly with one another right up till Jaime's death in 1974.

2. Sheppard's Hotel, 62-74 Argo Street, South Yarra became The New Argo in the 1970s. Later it was shortened to The Argo, 64 Argo Street. In 2012, the hotel was up for sale and many local residents worried it would be sold to developers and a proposed four-storey residential building would be erected on the site. After petitions and court cases the hotel still remains under the name of The Argo.

Chapter 13 As Time Goes By

1. Fay's reference to the 'yellow scum', a term considered undeniably racist today, was widely used during World War II when referring to the Japanese enemy.

2. In the 1950s Connie was put on the powerful drug, Largactil, which was usually prescribed to inmates of mental asylums. From all accounts she was only on this medication for a very short time. In the late 1950s and early 1960s, Connie worked tirelessly for a large number of charities. During Jaime's illness she and Leon visited him at Fellows Street on a number of occasions. Connie died on 8 June, 1985, a year after her son, Leon.

Chapter 14 The Day After Forever

1. Val Morgan Cinema Advertising went on to become the largest advertising firm in Australia. In 1987, when the enterprise was under the direction of the founder's grandson, Valentine Charles Morgan, the family sold its interest in the firm, which in 2005 continued to provide cinema advertisements in Australia and overseas.

2. Air Commander Arthur Henry (Harry) Cobby, CBE, DSO, DFC and Two Bars, GM (1894-1955), was an Australian military aviator. He was the leading fighter ace of the Australian Flying Corps during World War I, with 29 victories in spite of the fact that he saw active service for less than a year. At the outbreak of World War II in 1939, Cobby held senior posts including Director of Recruiting and Air Force Commanding North-Eastern Area. In 1943, he was awarded the George Medal for rescuing fellow survivors of an aircraft crash. He was appointed Air Officer Commanding No 10 Operational Group the following year, but was relieved of his post in the wake of the Morotia Mutiny of April 1945. Retiring from the Air Force in 1946, Cobby served with the Department of Civil Aviation until his death on Armistice Day in 1955.

Chapter 16 One Has My Name (The Other Has My Heart)

1. Apologies if the term 'half-caste' offends anyone; this was a common term in the 1940s describing a child of a mixed marriage.

2. Ed Edgerton and Patricia took many trips overseas after their marriage. Family rumours said the holidays were paid for by Patricia, as was the expensive Jaguar car Ed drove.

3. 28 Arnold Street, South Yarra, was the former cottage of Baron Sir Ferdinand von Mueller, a famous German-Australian Botanist. From 1857 to 1873 he was the director of the Royal Botanic Gardens in Melbourne. The house is now a block of flats.

Chapter 17 Some Enchanted Evening

1. Buckley and Nunn opened its doors in 1851 as a drapery store. It occupied a succession of buildings in Bourke Street, Melbourne, until it was taken over by David Jones in 1982.

2. Arthur Angus Calwell (1896-1973) was a member of the Australian House of Representatives for thirty-two years. He was Immigration Minister in the government of Ben Chifley from 1945 to 1949, so at the time he rang Fay he was an ex-Minister.

3.   Vice Admiral Sir John Augustine Collins was a Royal Australian Navy officer who
      served in World War I and II, and who eventually rose to become a Vice Admiral
      and Chief of Staff of the RAN. During World War II, he commanded the cruiser
      HMAS *Sydney* in the Mediterranean campaign. He led the Australian Naval Squadron
      in the Pacific theatre and was wounded in the first recorded Kamikaze attack in 1944.
      Collins was appointed Chief of Naval Staff in 1948 and held the position till 1955. He
      was knighted as a Knight Commander of the Order of the British Empire (KBE) in the
      1951 New Year Honours.

4.   On their driving honeymoon, John and Judy Telford-Smith were involved in a fatal
      head-on crash on July 26 1946 in Lismore, 170 kilometres west of Melbourne. They
      struck a roadster driven by William Ceaton Williams. A passenger in the dickie seat,
      Mrs Louisa Cumpstay, thirty-two, was killed instantly. Both John and Judy were taken
      to hospital and released soon after without serious injuries. Williams was charged with
      manslaughter, however, he was acquitted in November of 1946. Judy died on the 1
      August 1986, aged seventy-four, after a long illness. Fay was devastated.

5.   The Age, *25 May 1984. Occidental chief dies.*

      *The man who took Occidental Life Insurance Co. from obscurity to a leading position
      in the 'term life insurance' industry, Mr. Lee San Miguel, died in Sydney last night after
      a long illness. He was fifty-three. Mr. San Miguel, originally from Melbourne, entered
      the insurance industry in 1958 as agent for Legal and General. Within three years
      he was agency supervisor in Victoria, a position he retained until joining Unity Life
      in 1964. He joined Occidental in January 1975 as marketing director. In less than a
      year he was managing director and remained chief executive until his death. When the
      Whitlam government came to power and took away tax deductions for life insurance
      premiums he made term life cover acceptable to Australians. Now Occidental has in
      force business of $5.5 billion. Mr. San Miguel leaves a wife Jeanette and five children.*

      Although I met Leon in my early teens and knew he was my half-brother, I was
      told he was from my father's first marriage and therefore I wouldn't see him very
      much. During my time in Sydney in 1971 I saw Leon and his family on occasions.
      After my father's death in 1974 I had more contact with Leon by phone, or when he
      came to Melbourne. A week prior to his death he rang me to 'say goodbye'. It was a
      heartbreaking conversation.

Chapter 18 True Love

1.   Lea Johnston passed away from bowel cancer on the 30 May 1974 at Freemasons
      Hospital in Melbourne; she was sixty years old. In 1969 Lea met George McIntyre at
      her local Bowling Club and in 1973 they were engaged and about to marry. However,
      Lea decided to cancel the wedding when she was diagnosed with a terminal illness.
      George was at her side up until her death, as was Fay, Harry and Marie. George's son,
      Stephen McIntyre is an acclaimed Australian and international pianist.

2.   After my mother's death, I searched her flat for the love letters. It took quite a few
      days before I discovered the two large bags hidden in the cupboard. Due to my grief I
      did not read them properly until I began this book, thirteen years later.